# TOM MARTIN

# THE
# INVISIBLE
# SALE

How to Build
a Digitally Powered
**Marketing and Sales
System** to Better
Prospect, Qualify,
and Close Leads

## que®

800 East 96th Street,
Indianapolis, Indiana 46240 USA

# The Invisible Sale: How to Build a Digitally Powered Marketing and Sales System to Better Prospect, Qualify, and Close Leads

ISBN-13: 978-0-7897-5135-5
ISBN-10: 0-7897-5135-6

Library of Congress Control Number: 2013939273

Printed in the United States of America

First Printing: October 2013

## Trademarks

All terms mentioned in this book that are known to be trademarks or service marks have been appropriately capitalized. Pearson Education cannot attest to the accuracy of this information. Use of a term in this book should not be regarded as affecting the validity of any trademark or service mark.

## Warning and Disclaimer

Every effort has been made to make this book as complete and as accurate as possible, but no warranty or fitness is implied. The information provided is on an "as is" basis. The author and the publisher shall have neither liability nor responsibility to any person or entity with respect to any loss or damages arising from the information contained in this book.

## Bulk Sales

Pearson Education offers excellent discounts on this book when ordered in quantity for bulk purchases or special sales. For more information, please contact

**U.S. Corporate and Government Sales**
1-800-382-3419
corpsales@pearsontechgroup.com

For sales outside of the U.S., please contact

**International Sales**
international@pearsoned.com

# CONTENTS AT A GLANCE

# TABLE OF CONTENTS

# About the Author

**Tom Martin** has spent more than half of his career selling advertising agencies' professional services. His innovative business development programs have generated tens of millions of dollars in new client billings, including an impressive 35% growth rate over four years for Peter Mayer Advertising of New Orleans. As founder of Converse Digital, he has built a debt-free digital agency with a 25% year-over-year growth rate, without a single cold call or competitive pitch presentation. His painless approach to new business prospecting has resulted in a successful speaking career, an ongoing writing position with *Advertising Age* as a contributor to the "Small Agency Diary," and numerous guest-posting roles with influential digital- and social media-focused blogs.

Tom lives in New Orleans with his wife and four children.

# Dedication

*For Missy...*
*It's eleven eleven, make a wish.*

# Acknowledgments

Writing *The Invisible Sale* represents a bucket list item for me. I'm not sure why, but I've always wanted to write a book. And now that I've achieved that, I need to thank everyone who made it possible.

I should start at the beginning with a special thank you to my friend Tim Hayden, who first got me serious about writing a book and introduced me to the wonderfully supportive Katherine Bull, my Acquisitions Editor. And to Katherine for believing in the original ebook idea and encouraging me to develop it further into what is now, *The Invisible Sale*. If it wasn't for Tim pushing me to believe I had a voice worthy of listeners and Katherine helping nourish a germ of an idea into a fully developed book proposal, I would still be chasing my bucket list item.

Even with Tim and Katherine's prodding, this book wouldn't have been possible without the unwavering support of my beautiful wife Missy. Your plate was already so full with your career and our kids, and I honestly don't know how you managed to find more room on it. But thank you for giving even more so that I could have the time to pursue a dream. And to my kids, Madison, Davis, Hayes, and Maes: I hope I didn't miss too many functions, baseball games, or nights with y'all. I really appreciate all y'all have done to help your mom this year.

They say it takes a village, and to write this book it did. To our friends, my family, and Missy's family: thank you all so much for your support and willingness to help out with whatever we needed so that book and client deadlines could be met.

Along with support and love, a lot of great people were kind enough to lend me their time, expertise, and intellectual capital to make this book great. My publisher, Pearson, pulled together an incredible team. A big thank you to Howard Maestri, my peer reviewer, for keeping the geek speak in check and offering up outstanding suggestions that made the book more useful and easy to understand. And to my editors, Krista Hansing and Amber Avines, you made *The Invisible Sale* a better book and me a better writer. I am eternally grateful for both. And finally, to my production editor, Lori Lyons, who kept the trains on time and somehow managed to bring this entire project to the finish line, thank you. I hope y'all are as proud of the final product as I am.

A big thank you to Jenn Wojcik for serving as my unofficial sounding board. Having your feedback and insight during those early days of writing really gave me the confidence and clarity to keep going. I can't thank you enough for all the time and advice you gave this project. And to Chris Treadaway, without whom Funnel Optimized would not exist as a concept. A special thanks to Matt Ridings, Mack Collier, and Jay Baer, whose camaraderie and advice have been invaluable this year. And to everyone who agreed to be interviewed for the book: C.C. Chapman, Ann Handley, Steve Woodruff, Sue Spaight, Bob Knorpp, Todd Schnick, Dave Serino, Brian Matson, Mary McFarlin, Kevin Espinosa, Chris Yates, Beth Harte, and last but not least, Brian Green, thank you for making my job as an author so much easier. I learned so much from each of you and am forever in your debt.

And finally, to my team here in New Orleans, Matt Berman and Caroline Kappelman, thank you for all you did to help support, create, and market the book.

# We Want to Hear from You!

As the reader of this book, *you* are our most important critic and commentator. We value your opinion and want to know what we're doing right, what we could do better, what areas you'd like to see us publish in, and any other words of wisdom you're willing to pass our way.

We welcome your comments. You can email or write to let us know what you did or didn't like about this book—as well as what we can do to make our books better.

*Please note that we cannot help you with technical problems related to the topic of this book.*

When you write, please be sure to include this book's title and author as well as your name and email address. We will carefully review your comments and share them with the author and editors who worked on the book.

Email:   feedback@quepublishing.com

Mail:    Que Publishing
         ATTN: Reader Feedback
         800 East 96th Street
         Indianapolis, IN 46240 USA

# Reader Services

Visit our website and register this book at quepublishing.com/register for convenient access to any updates, downloads, or errata that might be available for this book.

# Introduction

*How much do you love cold calling?*

*If you love it and think it's the ultimate selling tool or the best way to find and qualify leads, then you can stop reading now. This isn't the book for you.*

*If, however, you feel that cold calling on unqualified prospects is the sales process equivalent of World War II carpet bombing, an anachronism of the past and both painful and highly inefficient, then this book is definitely for you.*

*In the pages ahead, I introduce you to the invisible sale, where digitally empowered buyers are self-educating and making key purchase decisions before your company even knows they're in the market.*

Next, I lay out a simple, repeatable process that replaces that carpet bombing with laser-guided missiles. And just like real laser-guided missiles, you'll use data provided by your leads as they move through an invisible sales funnel. With this data, you'll precisely target your marketing activities, key sales messages, and approach to deliver *just in time* sales calls to highly qualified leads. As a result, you'll see shorter sales cycles and higher close rates.

How much more effective would your company's sales efforts be if every time the sales force picked up the phone to call a prospect, the reps already knew exactly what the prospect's primary challenges were? Not on the second or third or fourth call, but the very first time?

How much more efficient would your sales efforts be if activation calls replaced qualifying calls? Those efforts could focus on moving the prospect one or more steps closer to an actual purchase. Would you work less and sell more?

And what if I told you that, by the time you finish this book, you will have learned a systematic approach that allows your prospects to digitally self-qualify themselves and share that information with you and your sales team in real time? This system can even be programmed to alert you and your team to the precise moment an unqualified lead becomes a confirmed prospect—all in real time.

Best of all, that hot prospect alert will contain a complete dossier of every piece of information the prospect has consumed from your website, email marketing, social media, and sales calls (if any have been made)—right there at your fingertips.

Would that be something you'd want to learn how to implement? If not, you're done here, and you can put the book down.

But if you're ready to learn how to build the ultimate marketing and sales process that delivers the sales nirvana just described, read on.

The first thing you need to understand, though, is that this book isn't about some high-level, pie-in-the-sky sales process that requires a team of consultants to launch and manage. No, this book is designed to be *your* guidebook. It's designed to provide you with the knowledge, guidance, tools, and tips to help you go from *living inside the database* to painlessly prospecting for new customers. Each and every section is designed to give you usable insights and detailed steps to guide you along the path of implementation to finding and winning the invisible sale.

To make the process easier for you, I've broken the book into four sections. Each section is a blueprint with the primary steps you need to complete for a successful implementation of that phase.

In **Section 1, "Selling the Premise,"** I give you the outline, highlight key points, and, literally, offer the PowerPoint presentation for selling this idea to your company or sales team. That's right, at the end of the section, you'll find a link to download an unformatted PowerPoint document with all the key points I use to sell my clients and their internal stakeholders on the absolute need to implement a data-based system.

I want you to see the power of this approach right away. In **Chapter 1, "The Tweet That Changed My World,"** I share the story of how a single Tweet (message on Twitter) from a man I had never spoken with led to a lucrative speaking engagement in Malaysia.

You'll want to pay close attention to **Chapter 2, "Living Inside the Database."** I give you the arguments to help convince your boss, company, or sales team that the world has changed and the sales process needs to change accordingly. I review relevant Business-to-Business (B2B) sales research, real-world examples, and common sense logic that together will help you build a persuasive argument for augmenting your traditional sales approach with a modern, digitally centric data-based system.

In **Chapter 3, "The Self-Educating Buyer,"** I focus on the single biggest challenge in B2B sales today: the self-educating buyer who leverages the availability of information via the Internet to reduce reliance on your sales team. This one development is placing the technologically challenged company or sales team at a huge disadvantage. If you're not thinking about this self-education effect on your sales, you're likely missing a huge opportunity. I frame it for you via a review of the latest research on B2B buying trends.

Finally, in **Chapter 4, "The Little Camera Store That Could,"** I take you through an incredible case study: how Adorama, a single camera store in New York City, has effectively augmented its traditional advertising-driven, customer prospecting with a digitally centric, data-based approach. You'll see what this move has done for the company's sales, competitive positioning, brand awareness, and manufacturer relationships. I've long been a huge fan of the company's AdoramaTV, and I'm extremely excited that they agreed to give such a detailed look at how they've used originally produced content to grow their business.

From there, we head into **Section 2, "Developing Your Platform."** After you've successfully convinced your team to adopt a data-based approach, you need to begin building out the framework. This section is designed to give you the step-by-step guidance you need to build a framework and get prepared to begin populating that framework with the required content and technology.

In **Chapter 5, "Selling Versus Helping,"** I discuss the necessary sales strategy change you have to implement if you hope to achieve success. To win those invisible sales, you have to stop selling to prospects and start helping them make a buying decision. I talk about how this doesn't just affect how you sell via the phone or face to face; it drives *everything* you do online. I give you real-world examples of how to change a sales pitch or how to change your content based on a selling vs. helping mindset.

In **Chapter 6, "Social Agents,"** I discuss the second big mental leap you need to take to achieve success. I introduce you to the concept of social agents and the incredibly important role they play in your future success. I show you how you can use social media to find and network with your agents and leverage their goodwill to create new prospects and sales for you and your company. And I finish by talking about how social agents, can end up being your best, most valuable customers, even if they never buy anything from you.

Moving on, **Chapter 7, "Propinquity,"** talks about how this important scientific principle drives prospecting strategies and tactics in the invisible sale. I explain how propinquity thinking helps you select your outposts and social networks and can even drive your offline marketing efforts. The chapter ends with a discussion of the Propinquity Effect and how leveraging this established scientific principle helps you win over today's self-educating buyer.

**Chapter 8, "The Painless Prospecting Framework,"** puts it all together. Here's where the rubber meets the road. Drawing on the insights in the preceding chapters, I give you the step-by-step directions to create your own Painless Prospecting system. I explain how to create your *Home Base, Embassies,* and *Outposts,* and I discuss how to link all three to your existing sales Customer-Relationship-Management (CRM) system to build a highly automated qualified lead-generation system that finally puts you in a position to hear the invisible customers' buying signals and act on those signals to close more sales.

So now you have your framework in place, but you need a way to move your company or sales team to adopt this new framework. Also, you need to import your current database into this new, more efficient system. That's what **Chapter 9, "Making Every Call Count,"** covers. I show you how you can combine email marketing and your website content to systematically segment your entire existing sales database into hot, warm, and cold leads. This is an ideal first step that immediately shortens sales cycles and increases sales conversions.

To close this part of the book, **Chapter 10, "Social Selling,"** uses real-life examples from my own experiences, my clients' efforts, and others to show how you can effectively use social networks such as Twitter, Facebook, LinkedIn, and Google+ to build relationships, uncover hidden buying signals, and prospect for highly qualified leads that turn into customers. But I don't just talk about *what to do*—I dive deep into *how to* leverage these platforms to network at scale. There's elegance to proper social prospecting that I know you can learn—you just need someone to show you how. That's the purpose of Chapter 10.

When you have the framework built and you understand how to leverage social media to prospect inside the invisible funnel, you'll quickly realize that a successful data-based system requires a lot of digital content to function effectively. But don't worry—in **Section 3, "Creating the Content,"** I give you all the guidance you need to start your own DIY (do-it-yourself) content-creation program.

**Chapter 11, "Creating Video,"** kicks it off. Video is the one channel that most people understand the least and wrongly assume is the most difficult; I want to immediately show you why that isn't true. From picking out the right camera, to determining which editing software to purchase, to creating *right-sized content,* when you're done reading this chapter, you'll be ready to go out and start producing your own effective video content.

From video, I move to probably one of the most important content types in **Chapter 12, "Creating Photography."** From how to take better pictures with your mobile phone, to detailed directions on how to shoot professional quality photography using your own digital camera by simply buying one special camera lens, you will be able to put down this book and begin taking better photographs that will dramatically improve your marketing and sales efforts.

Probably the most underutilized tool in content marketing today is audio. In **Chapter 13, "Creating Audio,"** I explain the different ways to capture and edit audio, including dedicated audio recording devices, computers, and my personal favorite: mobile phones. I even show you how you can create a fully mobile recording studio that enables you to capture, edit, and publish audio content for less than $1,000.

In **Chapter 14, "Creating Text-Based Content,"** I show you how you can produce text-based content faster and more efficiently through innovative apps and approaches. Because text drives Google (and other search engine) indexes, it is imperative that you create a lot of keyword-rich text content to ensure top ranking results in search engines. This chapter teaches you the tips and tricks that I and other content creators use to win the textual content war online.

In **Chapter 15, "Creating Live and Recorded Webinars and Product Tutorials,"** I show you simple, low-cost systems and programs for creating these key self-educating buyer content tools. From using screen-recording software to create tutorials, to helping you select the best live webinar applications, I show you how to create and then leverage this high-value content in your digital prospecting system.

**Chapter 16, "Cornerstones and Cobblestones: The Content Creation Framework,"** pulls it all together via a real-world case study in content creation and dissemination. This chapter takes you through the process of creating one piece of cornerstone content such as a white paper and then helps you turn it into more than 20 cobblestones that will help you fill your Home Base and outpost content needs quickly and easily. Where available, I give you links to the actual content so that you can see for yourself how these Cobblestones work together to achieve the Propinquity Effect and ultimately help buyers self-qualify themselves as hot leads.

Finally, **Section 4, "Closing the Deal,"** discusses how this data-based approach creates the need for a different selling approach offline. Just as the self-educating buyer begins the purchase process differently, the process ends differently. Your sales team must understand how to craft a different kind of close. Team members need to understand how to approach the self-educating buyer differently, lest they kill the deal. In **Chapter 17, "The Invisible Close,"** I introduce you to Prospect Triage, Aikido Selling, and the proper Invisible Close.

Time to get started.

# Section 1

# Selling the Premise

The first step in winning the invisible sale is change. The buyer has changed, but your approach to that buyer hasn't. You have to fix this. After 20 years of trying to change clients' minds, I've learned that the most effective approach is evidence-based selling. You have to string together a story based on data. By combining real-world examples with recent third-party research, you create permission for your audience to believe you. That is the purpose of Section 1.

I take you through the real-world story (and pseudo case study) of my own first experience with the invisible sale and the power of a Painless Prospecting platform. That was a powerful moment in my life. It changed both the trajectory of my professional career and my entire point of view on sales prospecting.

But you can't just paint a perfect picture of a better future and expect your team to give up their old ways—nor should they. There is value to traditional sales approaches, and nowhere in this book will you find me telling you to simply abandon these proven practices. Instead, I show you tools and approaches that, when done well, reduce your reliance on traditional cold call-based selling. This is an important distinction here in this book, but also in any presentation you give to your team. You need to acknowledge the strength of your current approach to create permission for your team to listen and adopt your point of view. I map out that approach and a series of arguments for you.

But then it's time to dive into the abundance of available evidence supporting the existence of an invisible buyer and the invisible sales funnel, which together form the invisible sale. In this section, I don't just give you the statistics—I give you the statistics within the overarching context of the invisible sale. This gives you a storyline that you can use to educate your sales team or company.

Finally, I take you through the AdoramaTV case study. Adorama is a camera store in New York City that leverages the power of content marketing to win the invisible sale every day in more than 50 states and five countries. Thanks to the candor of Adorama's Vice President of Marketing, Brian Green, I give you an unprecedented behind-the-scenes look at what Adorama is doing today. More important, Brian tells you how he did it and gives you advice for starting your own Painless Prospecting effort.

# 1

# The Tweet That Changed My World

*Kuala Lumpur, Malaysia, April 13, 2010*

*"Ladies and gentleman, thank you for your attention over the last two days. I truly hope you feel like you learned something. If you need any help applying what we've talked about here, just drop me an email or we can schedule a Skype call."*

*And with those words, I concluded my first international social media workshop halfway around the world. Considering that 12 months before that, no one besides me even knew I possessed social media knowledge, that's no small accomplishment.*

So how did I get to Malaysia? And more important, why should you care? Simply put, I made it to Malaysia by changing the way I went about prospecting for business. I deemphasized my traditional, cold-call and outbound email marketing efforts. Instead, I spent 2009 and the first parts of 2010 building an inbound marketing program based on getting "known for knowledge," a process that I continue to use and that fundamentally altered my future forever. With inbound marketing, the prospect finds you via search engines, social media, and word-of-mouth. They research you or your company online and then contact you, most often by submitting a form you place on your website. In this book, I share that process with you so that you, too, can enjoy the same success in your sales efforts.

Let's start by exploring the story of how I made it to Malaysia.

## The Tweet That Started It All

It was January 20, 2010. I had just stepped off the stage at the Tulane Business Forum, where I had been delivering a talk about using social media to market family-owned and -operated businesses.

It had been a good talk that spurred a tremendous amount of Q&A and kept a number of folks hanging around to ask additional questions one-on-one. But after roughly 30 minutes of offering advice, answering questions, and agreeing to follow up with a handful of attendees, I finally got the chance to sit down and take a much needed breather.

As I sipped my water and nibbled on a bit of food the organizers had been kind enough to bring over, I did what I always do after a talk: I checked Twitter to see if anyone had been tweeting. As many speakers have learned, Twitter often becomes a live back channel during a conference presentation.

For me, checking this important back channel was a must after every talk. It provided instant feedback that helped me (and still helps me) improve my performance on stage. It's also a great way to see if any of my key points hit home with the audience. In fact, I often test new ideas, theories, or key phrases during talks. If I find that the audience gravitates to something, as evidenced by numerous folks tweeting or retweeting (for you non-Twitter users, that's the equivalent of quoting a speaker to your friends or colleagues) my key phrases or key points, I know that I've likely hit a hot button or accurately diagnosed a top issue or problem prospective clients are experiencing.

Thankfully, the immediate feedback was great. My audience had tweeted and retweeted a few of my test phrases, and I saw a number of "great speaker" or "really learning a ton" type tweets. But buried among all the normal session attendee tweets was a single tweet that literally rewrote the course of my personal life and professional career (see Figure 1-1).

It came from a guy that I didn't follow on Twitter—I'd never even seen him on Twitter or any other social network.

**Figure 1-1**   *The tweet that changed my life*

Holy crap. This complete stranger was offering to check off a Bucket List item for me. He was offering me an international speaking engagement. For a guy who had never left North America, this was the opportunity of a lifetime. Not to mention he was offering to help me punch my "internationally recognized expert on social media" ticket, which would have enormous implications on my life and professional career.

And I had no idea who this person was, how he'd found me, or who had recommended me to him. Needless to say, I was done nibbling on the food. It was time to put on my Sherlock Holmes hat and figure out what this was all about.

Luckily, Twitter gives you the ability to view conversation for a tweet to see the original or linked tweets. In this case, Brad had tweeted that he was looking for a social media speaker with a strong marketing bent, not a "here's how to use Twitter" speaker (see Figure 1-2).

**Figure 1-2**   *Brad's original tweet seeking speaker recommendations*

So now I had the first piece of the puzzle. Brad was crowdsourcing speakers. When you crowdsource, you leverage the power of large groups of people to more quickly achieve a goal. In this instance, Brad was asking his Twitter followers to tap their contact files to give him names of qualified social media speakers. Thus, instead of spending hours using Google to search for possible speakers, Brad was able to obtain recommendations from over 1,000 followers on Twitter in a fraction of the time.

After a few more minutes of research, I had my second piece of the puzzle. Two folks who followed me on Twitter also followed Brad. Upon seeing his tweet seeking a speaker recommendation, they had each replied that he should check out @TomMartin (my handle on Twitter).

I later learned that Brad had just contracted with a company in Kuala Lumpur to deliver a few workshops in Dubai. The owner of the company was interested in bringing an American-based social media expert to Malaysia to conduct social media workshops and had asked Brad for suggestions.

Now, think about this for a moment. Brad was looking to find a reputable speaker to travel from the U.S. to Kuala Lumpur and Singapore to deliver a set of rather high-priced two-day social media workshops. Furthermore, the workshops were being conducted not by his company, but by another company who had asked for his opinion. So whomever Brad recommended would become a reflection on him personally. And his first instinct was to ask thousands of folks he barely knew for their opinions.

He was crowdsourcing his research in hopes of finding someone he could offer up to the company. And in his mind, that was a perfectly natural thing to do. He didn't give it a second thought because it's a highly efficient methodology. Just as you might ask a friend for the name of a good plumber, Brad asked his "friends" for the name of a good speaker—and at the time, Brad probably had a few thousand "friends" on Twitter.

Now, I'm sure I wasn't the only person to get multiple nominations—but I was a guy Brad had *never* heard of who received two votes. Since at the time of the tweet I had been speaking publicly on social media for only a little over a year, the fact that two folks actually knew me, much less recommended me, is somewhat amazing. But it reinforces the power of social networking as a business tool. It's just like regular networking, only on a scale you could never replicate in the physical world.

At this point, Brad had the word of only two of his Twitter followers to go on, though, and he certainly wasn't about to recommend someone he didn't even know based on two tweets.

# Your Web Presence Precedes You

Let's retrace what Brad did because it's exactly the same process millions of self-educating buyers are following each and every day as they try to determine whom they will select as a vendor or partner.

Brad's first step was to review my presence on Twitter. He looked back over my Twitter feed to see who I conversed with, what I tended to talk about, and what kinds of content I shared, to get a general sense of who I am as a person. Twitter enables this kind of eavesdropping because, unless you set your feed to Private, all your communications are public and searchable. Thus, Brad was able to go back over several weeks' worth of my conversations to truly get a sense of who I am as a person and a professional.

He liked what he found, so he took the second step. Using the link on my Twitter bio, Brad connected with my home base, my blog, where he could see how I think in more detail.

On my blog, he found years of writing—literally hundreds of posts that helped him understand how I approach marketing, peek into my theories and ideas, and gain a general sense of my intellect and depth of understanding of marketing (especially social media marketing).

But more important, because I regularly record my conference presentations and upload them to both my blog and other social media channels like YouTube and Vimeo, Brad—and other buyers like him—could see how I present. So now he could go beyond a simple word-of-mouth recommendation to actually experience a handful of my presentations firsthand.

This is an important point. Technology is quickly making the world more global. *Local* not only means less today, but it often isn't nearly as powerful of a sales argument as it used to be. But even with technology making it easy to sell to and work with companies halfway around the world, there's still no substitute for actually "meeting" someone face to face.

Luckily for me, after reading a handful of my blog posts and scanning a few of my videos from presenting at conferences, Brad felt that he had "met" me. He sent me the invitation to connect and talk at greater length about the international speaking opportunity.

All of this happened while I was on stage presenting to the Tulane Business Forum. Until Brad tweeted to me, this was an invisible sales opportunity. I didn't know a thing about this opportunity. I didn't proactively sell my services or respond to his original tweet on Twitter (more on that tactic in a later chapter). *It all happened without me doing a thing.*

Well, not doing a thing *that morning.*

It's important to remember that what I experienced that beautiful January morning wasn't just a tweet that changed my world; it was a phenomenon that has repeated itself many times over the last four years.

I had just been introduced to a concept I now call the *invisible sale*, in which highly qualified leads find you instead of you spending time finding them.

And in the case of this prospect, I was about to close a deal that would send me halfway around the world, go a long way toward establishing my credentials as an expert on social media, and directly lead to my starting my own company, Converse Digital. That company has grown by 25% a year, every year, without me making a single cold call, running any ads, paying to attend conferences, or sending a single piece of unsolicited direct mail. The company is built entirely on finding and closing invisible sales opportunities.

## My Whole World Changed with a Single Tweet...or Did It?

Let's revisit that January morning for a minute. Yes, technically, that one tweet changed my world, and, yes, I didn't do anything *that morning*. But I had done many things that led to that moment.

I had created and uploaded a dozen conference presentations to Vimeo and YouTube, posted hundreds of blog entries, and shared another dozen copies of conference presentation decks on SlideShare. I had also developed a presence on Twitter, Facebook, and LinkedIn.

I had prepared my fields for rain. By building a rich digital content archive and freely sharing lots of information that others found valuable, I built a reputation. More important, I built a reputation that you could find via Google, and many prospective clients still do find me that way. In fact, according to Google Analytics (the free service I use to track website visitors on my site), Google Search is routinely the number one source of traffic to my site.

Even today, if you visit my website, ConverseDigital.com, you'll find a wealth of highly valuable, free information. Yes, I'm a consultant. Yes, I get paid to provide my insights and intellect to companies. And yes, every day I give away little bits and pieces of that insight and intellect for free. (We talk more about that in Chapter 5, "Selling Versus Helping.")

But that free information finds its way into the hands of self-educating buyers like Brad. They can then form an opinion about me—an opinion that is just as authoritative as any opinion formed from direct contact with me. And those buyers act on those opinions. They make decisions to hire me, recommend me, or ask me to speak.

In fact, in this particular case, even after I spoke to Brad and agreed to let him forward my name to the company in Malaysia, I still had to cross one more hurdle before I was hired to speak. I had to impress the Malaysian company's owner.

And how did I do that? The same way I had impressed Brad. Upon receiving my information, the owner did the same thing Brad had done. He reviewed my writings on my blog, watched a number of my previous presentations, and read past testimonials from previous presentation attendees on LinkedIn. Only then did he reach out and request a Skype call to get to know me better, explain the opportunity, and determine whether we both wanted to move forward with booking the engagement.

And that's what makes this process so painless. All that free content I'm creating and giving away lives on forever. Google forgets nothing. So unlike a traditional cold call, in which I have to spend 20 or 30 minutes selling myself to *one* person, I create content that sells to many people. Sure, it takes me an hour or two to write one good blog post, but that post sells me to hundreds, if not thousands, of people today, tomorrow, and for many days to come.

When I give a presentation to a conference, I routinely spend 20 to 40 hours preparing, rehearsing, and delivering that presentation. That's a lot of unbillable time. So to simply allow that presentation to live for only those 45 minutes I'm on stage would be criminal. The act of recording and uploading the presentation to my blog, YouTube, and SlideShare takes less than an hour. That's one additional hour of my time. But the content will live forever, helping to sell my services as a speaker and consultant day after day.

In other words, selling via content marketing and social media scales in a way that personal selling never could. And over time, it creates a painless prospecting platform that continually produces new qualified leads.

Better yet, with a small investment in certain types of marketing automation software, and by posting all my content on my own blog and website, I can track every prospect who comes to my site and downloads or reads my content. I'm not talking about just your standard web analytics of how many folks visit a piece of content or how long they stay on my site; I'm talking about creating a downloadable dossier at the individual lead level. This dossier shows how often that lead has visited my site, every piece of content that lead has consumed, every download, every webinar they've signed up for and every email they've received, and what they clicked on in those emails.

Think about that for a minute. How many times do you get the chance to read your prospect's mind? How often do you know—the first time you talk to a prospect—what someone's pain points most likely are and what that person most likely wants to purchase from you? Normally, that comes from your first one or two phone calls with a prospect where you ask probing questions to uncover areas of dissatisfaction that your product or service addresses. And as seasoned sales executives know, solving these pain points is the most powerful motivator to buy.

But when you leverage technology to listen for buying signals, you can reduce or eliminate the need for those qualification phone calls. Instead, you can reach a sort of sales nirvana where qualified leads come to you instead of you dialing for dollars to qualify prospects.

Thus, your sales team spends more time each day actually selling versus prospecting. And *that* is the key reason to augment your current sales approach with a digitally centric, data-based sales and marketing approach.

## POWER POINTS

- You can't win if you don't play. Every day buyers are online looking for resources, vendors, and partners to fill needs. If you're not playing in this digital sandbox, you're missing all those invisible sales.

- Data-based systems focus on sharing content today that creates sales tomorrow. By spending your valuable time creating and disseminating digital content that self-educating buyers can find, you are creating tomorrow's leads.

- The value of creating leads via content is scale. Cold calling and other one-to-one prospecting tactics don't scale. You can and always will be able to cold call or meet with only one prospect at a time. Conversely, an unlimited number of prospects can simultaneously consume content.

- Google never forgets and actually favors older content. Therefore, the content you create today creates leads not just for tomorrow, but for many tomorrows.

*Download all the Power Points at TheInvisibleSale.com.*

# 2

# Living Inside the Database

*One of my biggest regrets when I moved from using a PC to using a Mac was the loss of my beloved ACT! contact management system. Oh, how I loved ACT!. In my early days running business development at Peter Mayer Advertising (late 90s) in New Orleans, I discovered the power that a full-fledged contact management system such as ACT! can have on an ongoing outbound business development program.*

*I could program the first 18 months of a prospect's life in my business-development program. With the click of a button, I could assign a contact to the New Prospect outbound marketing schedule and create all the to-do items in my calendar.*

Then each morning, I simply needed to open my database and click on my To Do list. There in front of me was an entire day of outbound marketing activity—every cold call I needed to make, every email I needed to send, and every direct-mail piece I needed to address and send. Each of these touches was scheduled to occur at the same point in every prospect's life cycle in the database.

This brought order to the process and ensured that we were consistently touching our prospects in an orderly and methodical manner based on a strategically driven approach. It was effectively scheduling multiple ad campaigns to audiences of one.

Furthermore, I could search, sort, and merge to my heart's delight. I could almost hear my heart beat faster each time I opened my database. Oh, and the notation capability—to be able to capture and track every unreturned email, unanswered cold call, unopened letter, or politely ignored direct-mail clutterbuster (that was our name for those really expensive, time-consuming three-dimensional mailers we sent). And the part that warmed the cockles of my geek heart was that I could sync it with my Palm Pilot! It was heaven.

But before we finish with this story, let's stop here for an important distinction.

# Database Selling Versus Data-Based Selling

Let me be very clear: This book is not about destroying your database. Nor am I saying you should entirely cease outbound sales prospecting and marketing efforts. Some people in the online content marketing world will preach that to you, but I won't. There's a place for outbound marketing in this world because it works, and I expand on that thought in a few pages.

What I *am* suggesting is that you move from a database selling approach to a data-*based* selling approach. This is an important distinction. Database selling is about filling a sales funnel and working the funnel to qualify and ultimately close sales. But data-based selling leverages two important trends: self-educating buyers and the proliferation of high-speed internet service to create a Propinquity Effect. This Propinquity Effect creates qualified buyers who call you. We dig deeper into data-based selling, self-educating buyers and the Propinquity Effect in the following chapters. But before you can share all those ideas with your boss, sales team, or company, you have to create permission to be heard.

You need to create permission for them to believe there's a better, more efficient way to prospect for business. But you won't be able to tell them this. You need to help them discover it for themselves. Let's talk about how you might do that. And for that, we return to my story.

# Sales Inefficiencies

Back in my Peter Mayer Advertising days, when I was checking off my ACT! to-dos and methodically following up with my prospects, I was the king of my world—or so I thought.

In reality, I was working my ass off. The sales cycles (and my work days) were long. I was actively working 20 to 40 A-List leads, managing another 100 B-List leads, and trying to at least make contact with another 200 C-List leads—just in case one might throw their account into review and begin searching for a new ad agency partner.

On a good year, we were invited to a dozen pitches in which a prospect offered 10 to 20 ad agencies the right to submit elaborate, long, and detailed responses to an incredibly mundane and arduous Request For Proposal.

If we were lucky, we made the first cut, along with 7 to 10 other agencies. Then we were invited to a conference call or possibly a chemistry meeting with the prospective client. Luckily, the prospective client usually came to us, so at least we didn't have to pay for three or four agency staffers to travel to the prospect's offices.

Then if we were really lucky, we made the finals. Oh, joy. Our agency and two to four others had earned the right to create expensive verbal presentations, often complete with multiple speculative advertising campaigns. This easily cost the agency hundreds and sometimes thousands of nonbillable staff hours, not to mention thousands of dollars of travel, mock-ups, and other shock-and-awe tactics.

One was left standing: the winner. And if it was us, we rejoiced.

The timelines were grueling in their shortness. The process I just described often began and ended in as few as six weeks. All the other members of the pitch team had full-time jobs working on actual paying clients' accounts. That meant a lot of late nights and weekends.

Believe it or not, in the advertising business, I was always told that if you win 25% of the pitches you enter, you're killing it. Yes, that's right—win one out of every four pitches you enter, and you're kicking ass. Now, I've never been able to actually confirm that percentage (and, yes, I've tried), but after almost 20 years in the ad business, more than half of them spent pitching clients at different agencies, I can say that winning 25% of the pitches *was* considered a good year.

Looking back now, I can blame my youthful exuberance and workaholic tendencies for my love of that job and all the pitching that followed throughout my career. Only in the last few years have I truly come to realize where I was going wrong.

I was defining my world as my database—my ACT! database. That was the sum total of my activity. I was living inside that database every day and every night, under the belief that, if I just kept putting new leads into the top of my sales funnel and worked those leads methodically over time, enough of them would fall to the bottom and become qualified leads—and eventually invite us to pitch.

Furthermore, the manner in which I was acquiring leads—perusing marketing-oriented media for notices of executives changing jobs, buying lead databases, and attending conferences or other networking events—simply resulted in unqualified prospects. Sure, I had their names and addresses. And I could begin mailing, calling, and emailing them. I could use the Internet to begin researching the company for clues to its pain points and maybe even get lucky enough to schedule a qualification call with a key decision maker. But for the most part, I had a database of companies I wanted to do business with in the future. I had little to no evidence to indicate that any of them wanted to do business with our agency—or any other agency, for that matter.

What I needed was a database of highly qualified leads for which I had detailed knowledge of their pain points or marketing interests. Therefore, I devoted most of my time each year to handling outreach and qualification of prospects instead of actively engaging with qualified leads that I knew both needed and wanted a service we offered.

## POWER POINTS

- The biggest weakness of the traditional selling process is inefficiency. Detailing the waste in your current process is one of the first points you'll want to make to your boss, CEO, or sales team. You need to help everyone in your organization believe that the current process can be more efficient.

- To do this, deconstruct your prospecting, selling, and closing processes. Look for areas of inefficiency, and attempt to place a cost on each area. Don't look at just hard costs; also look closely at the soft costs of prospecting, such as manpower costs.

- Hopefully you can make this point in a single presentation slide or a series of them. However, if the traditional selling process is deeply rooted in your organization or you personally don't have the internal stature to quickly convince everyone, you might need to consider this step a phase in your overall transition plan.

- Remember, it is imperative that you gain complete and total agreement on this point before you try to move to the next phase of actually creating your Painless Prospecting system.

*Download all the Power Points at TheInvisibleSale.com.*

# Traditional Prospecting Works

As you were reading about my old ad agency business development process, did you start to see yourself in those words? Did you begin to relate the steps I was taking to the steps you take each day as you work your database?

Maybe you have a Rolodex instead of an ACT! database and a smartphone (the modern day Palm Pilot), or maybe you just keep your top desk drawer full of business cards with notes scribbled on them. The details of how you or your company manages a sales prospecting database aren't important. What *is* important is that you understand that you're spending your days filling and managing a database—and you're living inside that database.

And why do you continue to work this way? Frankly, it works. But as I noted earlier, the sales cycles are long. Sometimes I'd have to call on clients for years before we could finally find a pain point or get invited to pitch for their business.

I remember one such pitch before I left Peter Mayer Advertising. I was about to move an A-List telecom prospect to our B-List due to lack of responsiveness. This meant that, instead of a personalized, high-touch marketing campaign, this prospect would receive only ongoing mass direct mailings with follow-up calls to ensure receipt. While I was working to figure out which B-List prospect I'd move up to replace this prospect, my phone rang.

Guess who was on the other line? It was that A-List prospect asking us to submit a proposal to handle a small public relations project for him. We talked, and I joked that I had almost taken him off my list because he'd never returned any of my calls, emails, or letters. He laughed and said he had every single thing our firm had ever sent to him. In fact, he was calling us because of all those mailers, emails, and phone calls.

You see, we continue to prospect in this old-school manner and live inside the database because, darn it, it does actually work. It's like golf. You can have 17 bad holes, but if you get a birdie on hole 18, you'll be back out there next weekend. But it's painful, isn't it? After I hung up the phone, I looked back through this contact's electronic file in my database.

Not including the phone call I had just completed, I had contacted this lead via email, letter, phone, or direct mail 52 times in two years. That's a whole lot of prospecting for *one* small piece of business. In fact, figuring up all the hours I'd spent at my hourly rate, adding in the hard costs associated with all the mailings, and subtracting that amount from the profit generated on this new account would have shown that the agency spent more to acquire the business than it would profit on the actual account the first year.

In addition to those pitches, we usually picked up one or two projects or clients without a competitive pitch. We successfully identified the key decision maker(s) and began qualifying the prospect. At some point, we discovered a pain point that wasn't being satisfied and leveraged it to gain a meeting. If we did our job correctly, we could convince the client that a change in agency partners was warranted. Shortly thereafter, we had a new client.

But this process required tremendous effort on our part. In some cases, we developed and conducted field research studies to test a hunch. If the research results proved our hunch correct, we then had to find a way to get past the key decision maker's gatekeeper and share the information with our prospect.

In one such case, we noticed that a high-end barbeque grill manufacturer was using direct-response ads to invite consumers to request more information via a 1-800 number. Because our agency had significant experience in direct-response advertising, we thought we might be able to help this company. But first we had to see if the company had any issues we could solve. I had 20 agency staffers each call the phone number in the ad and request more information. Then I had them do the same process with three competitive grill manufacturers who were also using direct-response ads. Employees had to keep track of when they called and when the information from each company arrived. They also had to give me whatever the manufacturers sent them in the mail.

Luckily for us, what arrived from our prospect was a complete disaster. Very few staffers actually received the official product brochure. Others were placed on hold for long periods of time when they called to order their brochure. Still others waited for more than a week to receive their brochure. Meanwhile, the competitive grill manufacturers all performed flawlessly. All quickly fulfilled the phone requests with beautifully designed brochures designed to drive intent to purchase.

These are all deathblows to a direct-response advertiser. Luckily for us, we had a story to tell. But we still had to spend more than 100 agency hours on the project, and then we had to travel to the prospect's offices in another state to present the information.

And *that* is the problem with traditional outbound prospecting methodology. It's highly inefficient and truly painful.

But it does work.

## POWER POINTS

- No one likes to be told they're doing something wrong. So when you're trying to convince your company to adopt an inbound prospecting methodology, be sure to start your message with an acknowledgment that the current sales prospecting system is working.

- Take the time to acknowledge all the wins (new business) generated by your current sales prospecting approach.

- Acknowledge a key strength of outbound systems—their disruptive nature. Just as you saw in the stories about the barbeque manufacturer and telecom, an outbound system can create awareness where none existed because you send your marketing materials to the prospect versus waiting for them to find your marketing materials online. Don't ignore this in your arguments. This disarms your audience and shows that you are making a well-thought-out and properly balanced recommendation.

- Painless Prospecting systems work only when your prospect is actively searching for information online—inside the invisible funnel. If prospects aren't looking online for information or solutions, they don't become aware of you—you can't win the business because they don't know you exist, much less that you're a valid solution to their pain.

*Download all the Power Points at TheInvisibleSale.com.*

# You Don't Know What You Don't Know

Do you want to know the best part of the grill manufacturer story?

To our surprise, the marketing director wasn't surprised by our findings. He was pretty sure he had a problem, but he hadn't found a way to qualify it as we did. He also didn't know where to turn for help because he didn't know any direct response specialists. But he did know that his current ad agency wasn't one. Within a few weeks, we had a new client and he had the solution he had been looking for to solve his pain point.

However, if this same situation happened today, he most likely would have just turned to Google and searched for "direct-response marketing" or "direct-response advertising agencies" or some other related keyword string. And if he had found our agency and seen our work and our thinking, we might have had that same meeting without going through all the research pain. That would have been a far more efficient way to land a new client.

But if you're still living inside your database, inefficiency is really the least of your problems. Let's revisit a key point in the telecom prospect story. I said I was about to move an A-List prospect to the B-List, and vice versa. But what was I using to define A-List vs. B-List prospects?

Did I have reasons to believe that the A-List prospects were actually more likely to want to fire their current advertising agency partner and hire our firm? Did I know that they had key pain points that our agency was uniquely staffed to solve? Did I even know what their pain points were?

No.

Like many salespeople using outbound sales systems, I was placing a prospect on the A-List because A-List companies were the companies our firm most wanted to work with that were located within 250 miles of New Orleans and did business in categories in which the agency had at least some experience. Or the prospect was in a category that the agency wanted to penetrate.

For all I know, plenty of truly A-List prospects that really did need what we were selling were right there under my nose. But because I had that nose buried in a database, I couldn't see them. And if they weren't in my database, they didn't really exist. They were invisible.

Furthermore, the tools I was using to find and add new prospects to the database (scanning relevant trade for new hires, conferences, networking events, and purchasing lists) were not helping me add qualified prospects. I was just adding prospects.

Thus, after I placed a prospect on our lists, I had to begin the qualification process. Like salespeople everywhere, I cold-called every day in an effort to make contact with key decision makers and pry for information, clues, or insights to help me determine the most effective sales pitch. I don't know about you, but I hated these cold calls. They were emotionally draining because of the repetitive nature of the effort, an effort that usually resulted in leaving yet another voicemail that was never returned.

If I was lucky enough to get past the gatekeeper and establish direct contact with a prospect, I had to take the person through a series of qualification questions designed to help me tease out their pain points.

Sometimes the prospects would play along and dutifully answer the questions, provide the information, and basically help me qualify them as a potential client. But more often than not, as soon as they figured out I was simply trying to fish for information, they'd suddenly had to "jump on another call" or said "someone just arrived for a meeting," and the call quickly came to an end.

And then I'd move on to the next person on my call list and start the entire process over. Sound familiar?

## POWER POINTS

- Today we live in the age of the *self-educating buyer* who is using digital channels to develop a shortlist of solutions to pain points.

- Executives today are busier than ever. They don't have time to help you qualify them for 20 or 30 minutes via a phone call. But proper qualification is essential to creating a more effective sales prospecting system.

- It's important to help everyone in your organization understand that, with a data-based prospecting program in place, your organization will be able to let your prospects self-qualify by simply monitoring and recording what those prospects are reading, downloading, and viewing online.

- More important, by monitoring online information consumption, your company will be able to discover new invisible but qualified Self-Educating Buyer leads.

*Download all the Power Points at TheInvisibleSale.com.*

# Forgetting the Funnel

As you move away from database selling to data-based selling, you need to convince your boss, team, and company to adopt one more big mental change. They need to forget everything they've ever learned or believed about sales funnels. The idea that your prospect is moving through predefined stages of the sales process is antiquated. For non-sales executives, let me explain the traditional sales funnel.

While the individual stages of the sales funnel varies by company and industry, most will share a common set of core stages.

The first stage is **Prospecting**, where the goal is to locate possible customers. Second stage is **Contact**. The third stage is **Need Assessment**, where the salesperson attempts to qualify the sales potential of each prospect. The fourth stage is **Proposal**, where the salesperson presents the product or solution for sale. The fifth stage is **Overcoming Objections**, where the salesperson listens to a prospect's concerns and then attempts to overcome those concerns. And the sixth stage is **Contract Signed**, where the prospect agrees to purchase the salesperson's product or service.

Have you ever stopped to think about the sales funnel? Why did the sales industry pick a funnel? Why is it that sales looks at selling from a funnel point of view?

It's because traditional selling approaches all start the same way: soliciting and documenting the visible but unqualified prospect. The traditional sales funnel process in Figure 2-1 is precipitated on the idea that you're going to start with a big group of unqualified leads. Then through a series of marketing events, calls, mailers, and so on, you whittle down that list to a much smaller set of qualified leads. It also assumes that the first time you become aware of a prospect, that they will need you to move them through the various standard stages of the funnel.

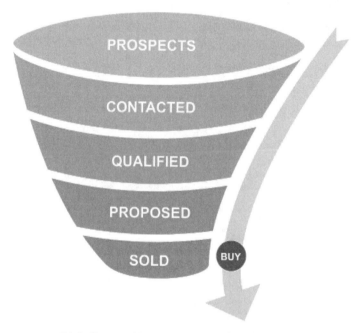

Originally created by Jason Keath, **SocialFresh.com**

**Figure 2-1**  *The traditional sales funnel*

When you have the qualified leads group, the law of numbers further reduces your list. The law of numbers states that you won't successfully close sales with all your qualified leads. Some percentage of those leads won't buy from you because of any number of factors, such as price, timing, or maybe the fact that your solution isn't actually the best solution for their particular pain point.

Thus, after all this eventual subtraction, we are left with a funnel-shaped database built on the belief that buyers move in a linear progression through it. At the top is a large group of unqualified prospects that we have added to our database. In the middle is a smaller group of qualified leads. At the bottom, the smallest point of the funnel, are the precious few who end up purchasing something from us. In fact, most sales management databases such as ACT! and SalesForce even have a standard Sales Funnel Report built in that segments all your leads based on where they fall on that linear progression of buying stages.

But what if you set aside the funnel approach? Instead of seeing your selling process as a funnel to be filled at the top with unqualified prospects, picture it as a radar screen that is constantly pinging the world around you and identifying qualified prospects worthy of being added to your database. But unlike with the traditional funnel, prospects enter and exit your sales radar constantly. Furthermore, the entrance and exit points change and do not always follow a strict linear path.

Let me help you visualize this by sharing my company's sales radar in Figure 2.2. Obviously, this isn't our actual radar, but a fictitious representation for clarification purposes only.

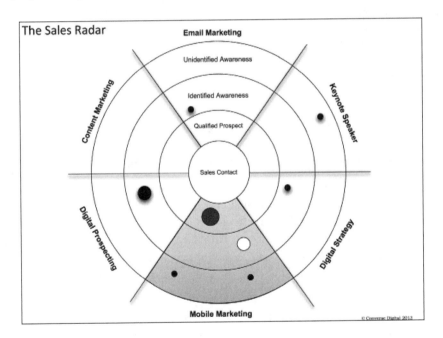

**Figure 2-2**  *The sales radar*

The biggest change to notice is that the radar is set up on a horizontal versus vertical axis. The second-biggest change is that the radar view plots prospects on three axes instead of one. Every prospect's place on the radar factors in three key data points.

First, we plot a prospect's position based on what type of information they are consuming on their most recent website visit or visits. In the case of Figure 2-2, I've associated each section with a major content area we cover on our Converse Digital website.

Second, we factor in what we know about that contact. In the outer ring, we know we have a contact that has consumed a piece of information, but that contact hasn't provided any identifiable information; they are still Unidentified. If the contact downloads something or subscribes to our blog or newsletter, they move into the second ring—Identified. Now that we have identified the contact we can track the contact's movements on our site. After being identified, if the contact consumes a particular amount of content or maybe performs a specific grouping of actions, the contact moves to the next circle and is designated a Qualified Prospect. Eventually, either the contact reaches out via a contact form or we reach out after a certain content/action threshold is met, and the contact becomes a Sales Contact.

Third, we calculate the total number of pieces of content the prospect has consumed since first identifying themselves by downloading something from our site or registering for something. That is indicated by the size of the contact's "blip" on the radar.

The key difference between the sales radar and the sales funnel is that, in the radar view, a new prospect can move methodically through the levels of the radar *or* can just show up in one of the inner levels. For instance, if you visited my website and, on your first visit, you downloaded a white paper, your "blip" would show up on the Identified Awareness ring even though it was your first time on my site. Conversely, other people might regularly come to my site but never download or subscribe; thus, they remain in the outmost ring of Unidentified Awareness. We talk more about using the sales radar to plan your content and digital marketing in Section 2.

Ten years ago, this approach wouldn't have been doable. Remember, the sales funnel process was developed because it worked. The reason it worked is that information wasn't as accessible as it is today. Thus, buyers actually needed salespeople to educate them about possible purchase options and solutions. The salesperson thus controlled those interactions and the information-sharing model.

But today, with all the world's knowledge at your fingertips and accessible at broadband speeds, buyers no longer have to rely on salespeople to educate themselves. The spread of always-on Internet connections, smartphones, and tablet computers is powering a critical shift in how humans buy things. From simple purchases for personal use to complex business purchases, buyers today are self-educating. And this self-education trend creates the invisible funnel.

To sell to prospects inside the invisible funnel, an organization needs to place significant efforts behind content creation and dissemination. By creating more content that prospects can find in more places, radar-oriented selling organizations create more opportunities for prospects to intersect with the company and its products or services. This then leads to the Propinquity Effect, which I talk about in Chapter 7.

So in your new data-based system, the top of the visible sales funnel is much smaller and the funnel itself is thicker. If done correctly, data-based selling leads to shorter sales cycles because you're starting with qualified prospects that are already well down the traditional sales funnel process before they've even talked to you.

## POWER POINTS

- Without constant, real-time data from your prospects, you don't know what you don't know. Instead, you are shooting in the dark, hoping to hit something or convince the prospect to help remove your blindfold.

- There's a new sales funnel in town, and you can't see it in any database. It's invisible to the naked eye but easily seen using digital technology.

- This new invisible sales funnel helps you because today's self-educating buyers are sending you their buying signals each and every time they interact with your content.

*Download all the Power Points at TheInvisibleSale.com.*

# 3

# The Self-Educating Buyer

In April 1998, Andy Grove, then president and CEO of Intel, the world's largest chipmaker, published his book Only the Paranoid Survive. In it, he introduced the idea of the strategic inflection point.

> For now, let me just say that a strategic inflection point is a time in the life of the business when its fundamentals are about to change. They are full-scale changes in the way business is conducted, so that simply adopting new technology or fighting the competition as you used to may be insufficient.

Today, companies that rely on a human sales force to discover, solicit, and close sales of products and services find themselves at just such a strategic inflection point. Gone are the days when buyers of products and services, especially high-involvement purchases, were forced to rely strictly on information provided by and from vendor sales teams. Technology, specifically the Internet, has created a shift in power from seller to buyer.

Buyers today, especially business buyers, have easy access to a wealth of online tools and information. This makes them much less dependent on potential vendors, their sales reps, and their sales literature to formulate purchasing decisions.

As a result, prospects are self-educating, and they're postponing face-to-face interactions or phone interactions with salespeople until the latest possible moment in the buying process. A recent study by the Corporate Executive Board[1] reported that B2B buyers get 57% of the way through the buying decision before they're even willing to talk to a sales rep. And Google's 2011 ZMOT Research Report[2] revealed that a consumer shopper consults an average of 10.4 sources before making a purchase.

That leads us to the question being debated in boardrooms and corporate sales offices the world over: Is this self-educating buyer phenomenon a fad or a trend that will only grow more prominent in the future?

I believe that this is most certainly not a fad or a trend, but a fundamental change and shift in the way people seek out and acquire information to make informed and intelligent purchasing decisions. Whether we are discussing a consumer purchase of a high-involvement item, such as an automobile, or we're looking at complex B2B transactions in which a buyer is purchasing on behalf of a corporate entity, the world has changed. The buying process is increasingly becoming invisible as the buyer hides behind the anonymity of a Google search.

## The Four Key Trends Driving This Shift

Four key cultural and technological trends are driving the strategic inflection point we find ourselves grappling with. It is vital that you understand these key trends and educate your boss, sales team, or company so that they can fully understand why it is important to augment or replace your existing sales methodology with a data-based prospecting system.

The first key technological trend that you have to understand is Google. Since its inception, Google has stated that it intends to index all the world's information and make that information readily available anytime, anywhere. We need only look around to see that although Google has not successfully indexed all of the world's information, it continues to march unabashed toward that goal and shows no signs of deviating from its stated mission. This, in turn, is creating a fundamental change in human behavior.

1. Corporate Executive Board Study, http://www.executiveboard.com/exbd/sales-service/the-end-of-solution-sales/index.page

2. 2011 Google ZMOT Report, http://www.zeromomentoftruth.com

There was a time when a person searching for information or answers to a question would have turned to a library, opened an encyclopedia, or maybe contacted a professional for the answer. Today that same individual fires up a computer, opens up a smartphone, or maybe grabs a tablet computer and immediately points that device to Google, Bing, or some other favored search engine. Once there, the person inputs the question or information need. Within seconds, not one, but many possible answers or sources of answers and information to the inquiry appear.

This leads us to the second key technological trend: the almost ubiquitous access to broadband Internet. Gone are the days of bulky desktop computers relying on telephone modem dial-up access to the Internet. According to the Broadband Progress Report[3] released by the Federal Communications Commission on August 21, 2012, 94% of Americans currently have access to broadband-speed Internet. This leaves a mere 6%, or 19 million people, without access to broadband. This not only makes the search for information faster, but it changes the type of information we can access. With broadband speeds, text, audio, video, and interactive applications are all accessible at the click of a mouse. Information that used to be delivered via mail or FedEx is now transmitted over the Internet and downloaded in a matter of minutes, regardless of file size.

In the case of our third key technological trend, that same content is accessed via a tap of a thumb caused by the rapid growth in smartphone penetration. A 2012 Nielsen Report[4] found that, as of June 2012, 54.9% of U.S. mobile subscribers owned smartphones. The same report indicated that two out of every three Americans that had purchased a new mobile phone in the three months prior (March to May 2012) chose a smartphone. We now have a rapidly growing population that is walking around with a computer in their pockets—and using it to do a whole lot more than just talk.

This rapid growth is powering the fourth key trend: the morphing role of smartphones from simple communication devices to what I call the *Encyclopedia Phontanica.*

With broadband access speeds at their smartphone-toting fingertips, people (your prospects) find themselves literally a click away from the answer to every question they can think of, delivered to the palm of their hand immediately after they pose the question. This instant access is creating the Google Effect.

Chances are, you have seen the Google Effect in action. Have you ever been at a conference, party, or gathering when two people have a disagreement over a

---

3. Broadband Progress Report, http://www.fcc.gov/reports/eighth-broadband-progress-report

4. 2012 Nielsen Report, http://www.nielsen.com/us/en/newswire/2012/two-thirds-of-new-mobile-buyers-now-opting-for-smartphones.html

mundane and often obscure fact? What happens next? That's right, one or both of them pull out their smartphone, access the Internet, and immediately locate the true answer or fact. This is the Google Effect. This is the Smartphone acting as *Encyclopedia Phontanica:* People looking for answers simply "Google it." Statistical proof even supports this phenomenon.

A 2011 Ericsson ConsumerLab MBB Service Quality Study[5] captured this fundamental shift in human behavior in a vivid and important chart (see Figure 3-1). Notice that, before they owned a smartphone, Internet access occurred a handful of times throughout the day and in chunks of time. However, when a broadband-enabled smartphone is included in the mix, notice how Internet access and utilization changes. We immediately see a reduction in the number of desktop access chunks. These are replaced by a much more staccato-looking utilization pattern, in which people routinely access the Internet multiple times throughout the day, for very short periods of time during each session. The researchers at Ericsson characterized the shift as humans moving to "spontaneous and unplanned" usage of the Internet.

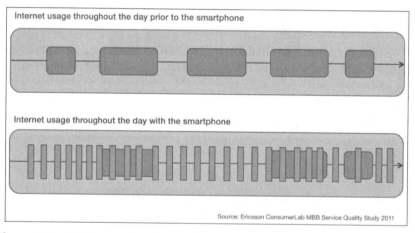

**Figure 3-1**   *Mobile broadband versus desktop Internet usage*

This graph is showing the Google Effect. We know what we want, we know how to find it, and we have access to the technology that can get us the information immediately. We are being trained by technology to expect that the answers to all our questions are available on the Internet. We are being trained that if we need information to satisfy a curiosity, meet an intellectual need, or provide a foundation for making a purchasing decision, we need look no further than a simple Internet search. We believe that a search will, in fact, deliver relevant, reliable, and actionable information to help us toward our goal of answering our question, solving our

5. 2011 Ericsson ConsumerLab MBB Service Quality Study, http://www.ericsson.com/res/docs/2011/silicon_valley_brochure_letter.pdf

problem, or making the correct purchase decision. The only question left is which device (computer, phone, or tablet) we will use to access that information.

## B2C Buyers by the Numbers

Google's 2011 ZMOT Research Report revealed that consumer shoppers consult an average of 10.4 sources before making a purchase. This increased from 5.2 sources the previous year. Even for relatively simple decisions such as picking a restaurant, consumers consulted an average of 5.8 sources. For high-involvement purchases such as a new car, the number of sources consulted rises to 18.2, the most of any category Google tracks.

And although the ZMOT research included online and offline resources, the online self-educating activity was significant. Fifty percent of respondents searched online via a search engine. Thirty-eight percent comparison-shopped products online, and thirty-six percent sought information from a brand or manufacturer website.

The 2012 Digital Influence Index[6] (an annual global study by Fleishman-Hillard and Harris Interactive) echoed the ZMOT numbers and, in some cases, corroborated them more loudly. The Fleishman-Hillard study asked consumers where they turned online for brand information. The results are telling:

| | |
|---|---|
| Use a search engine | 89% |
| Go to the brand or product website | 60% |
| Go to a product review site | 50% |
| Ask or post a question in a forum | 24% |

It's no surprise, then, that one of the biggest issues in retailing today is *showrooming*. In showrooming, a consumer visits a traditional retailer to evaluate a product, such as a big-screen TV, and then goes online to purchase the product for less at another retailer. A November 2012 Harris Poll[7] reported that 43% of Americans have participated in showrooming.

And although showrooming is really just a digitally enhanced version of the traditional price shopping consumers have done for ages, it reinforces a key point. Consumers have been trained to look to the Internet for product information, pricing, and reviews before they make a purchase. They have been trained that it's more efficient and more empowering.

---

6. The 2012 Digital Influence Index, http://push.fleishmanhillard.netdna-cdn.com/dii/2012-DII-eBook.pdf

7. November 2012 Harris Poll Holiday Shopping Extravaganza, http://www.harrisinteractive.com/NewsRoom/HarrisPolls/tabid/447/mid/1508/articleId/1128/ctl/ReadCustom%20Default/Default.aspx

# B2B Buyers by the Numbers

One of my favorite arguments in the B2B selling world is the one in which a sales director argues that consumer buyers are different than B2B buyers. That same sales director likely will set aside the Google and Fleishman data as irrelevant in the B2B sales world. But that sales director would be wrong.

Remember, a recent study by the Corporate Executive Board reported that B2B buyers are 57% of the way through a buying decision before they attempt to talk to a sales rep. And a 2012 DemandGen Report[8] found that 77% of B2B buyers said they did not talk with a salesperson until after they had performed independent research. Importantly, this research includes a significant online component that includes vendor websites. In Figure 3-2, you can see the results of DemandGen's *2012 B2B Buyer Landscape* study showing both *how* buyers are initiating the research process and *what* types of information they're searching for online.

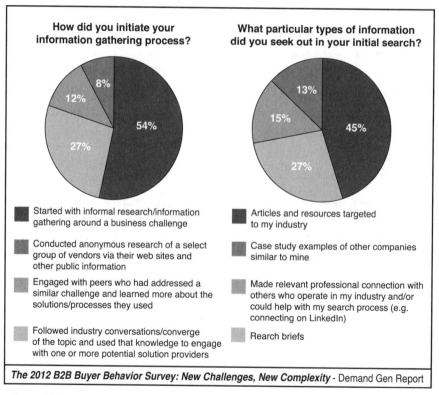

**Figure 3-2**   *The invisible B2B funnel*

---

8. Demand Gen Report, http://www.demandgenreport.com/industry-resources/research/1782-the-2012-b2b-buyer-behavior-survey.html

That DemandGen Report, *Inside The Mind of the B2B Buyer*, went on to point out a number of important points that reinforce the need to augment traditional sales prospecting models with digital friendly, knowledge-based programs.

According to the report, 67% of buyers said they were using a wider variety of sources to research their vendor options (up from 47% the previous year). Fifty-five percent said they spend more time researching purchases than they did in the past (up from 47% the previous year). And only 6% said they interact with a contact from a solutions provider almost immediately, as soon as they start their initial research (down from 22% in 2011). In fact, the number of respondents claiming to initiate contact with vendors only *after* compiling a short list of candidates jumped from 24% in 2011 to 51% in the 2012 study. Think about that last point. If your company isn't providing the kind of online information these buyers are searching for, the invisible funnel may be costing you sales opportunities, and you don't even know it.

Finally, the second most important piece of data to come out of the DemandGen Report was the response to this question:

> *At the start of your search process, what marketing/media channels influenced your selection of solution providers in this purchase. (Check all that apply.)*

As you can see in Figure 3-3, electronic platforms such as web search, vendor website, downloadable white papers, and social media all play significant roles in the early days of the invisible sale. Not only are these platforms the types of information the buyer is looking for, but they also play an influential role in the purchase decision process.

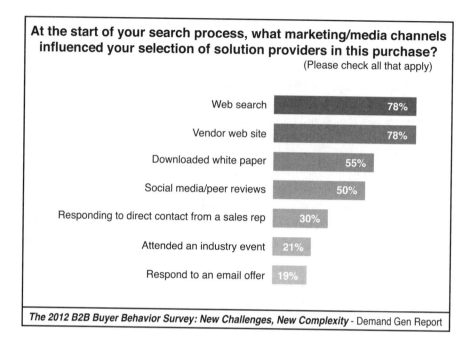

**At the start of your search process, what marketing/media channels influenced your selection of solution providers in this purchase?**
(Please check all that apply)

| | |
|---|---|
| Web search | 78% |
| Vendor web site | 78% |
| Downloaded white paper | 55% |
| Social media/peer reviews | 50% |
| Responding to direct contact from a sales rep | 30% |
| Attended an industry event | 21% |
| Respond to an email offer | 19% |

*The 2012 B2B Buyer Behavior Survey: New Challenges, New Complexity* - Demand Gen Report

**Figure 3-3**  *Marketing channel influence on B2B purchase selections*

# The Online Opportunity

All this data tells us that Woody Allen was right, although he might have been off on the actual percentage. With both B2B and consumer buyers secretly researching their purchase via online information and, in some cases, progressing all the way to short-list creation without ever speaking to a salesperson, being found online becomes essen-

> "Showing up is 80% of life."
> —Woody Allen

tial. Yet companies cannot expect their sales teams to create and post this online content. As it is, a CSO Insights[9] survey showed that salespeople are spending only 41% of their time on actual selling activities. Thus, to add online marketing activities on top of a sales team's current sales workloads wouldn't serve companies well. No, instead, marketing teams have to take the lead in impacting the secret sales research happening online and develop systems to identify and hand off qualified leads to sales for follow-up.

---

9. Optimizing Sales Effectiveness to Achieve High Performance, http://www.accenture.com/us-en/Pages/insight-optimizing-sales-effectiveness-achieve-high-performance-2011-study.aspx

The good news in all this data is that although today's buyers are committed to self-education, they are not necessarily finding everything they need and want. And that is where the online opportunity lies. On the B2B side, the DemandGen Report, *2012 Inside The Mind of the B2B Buyer,* asked respondents to consider their last purchase experience and indicate what information was generally missing from solution provider websites.

Thirty-seven percent felt that the sites lacked *relevant individualized content,* which is content presented by job role or industry vertical. Another 20% felt that the providers didn't give enough *valuable educational content* (such as helpful white papers). And 19% felt the breadth of information as it related to their search was suboptimal.

Yet when asked what they found most compelling about a chosen vendor's website, 30% noted breadth of product information, 29% cited valuable educational content, and 19% noted relevance of individual content presented by job role or industry vertical.

So the good news here is that even if your company website contains none of this, the current data suggests that you're not that far behind your competition. Not only can you quickly catch up, but the data also suggests that there's ample opportunity to pass up the competition and become the educational information leader in your product category or industry vertical. To do this, you need your sales and marketing teams to come together and create relevant, helpful, and impactful online content.

And the opportunity is even greater on the consumer side of the house. Think for a minute about all the consumer purchases that have high levels of risk and little to no opportunity to test-drive the purchase before making it. A few examples come to mind:

- Hiring someone to remodel your home
- Selecting a doctor, attorney, or CPA
- Installing a backyard pool
- Selecting a real estate agent
- Deciding on a private school or college

In each case, you can certainly see examples of prior work or, in the case of the schools, spend a little time there. But in the end, you're making a significant investment of money without any return policy. If you're unhappy after making the purchase, there's no returning the "product" for a refund. These are just a few examples of high-involvement purchases for which self-educating buyers are using the Internet to evaluate their options, create a short list of possible solutions, and reduce their risk.

# Now You See Me—Now You Don't

Let's finish with one last important point to keep in mind. In today's Internet-based world, the self-educating buyer is just a click away from your competitors' information. If you get the chance to serve as the information resource for a buyer, you have to live up to your end of the bargain.

This is probably the single biggest mistake most companies are making today. They continue to create content that isn't inherently helpful to the prospective buyer. Companies create white papers, research guides, or checklists that purport to provide helpful information and guidance. But after they download the information, the buyer is quickly disappointed. So what do buyers do? They just click the next link in their Google search. And if that link takes them to your competitor, who's providing helpful information, you might just lose that sale.

This is undoubtedly the most difficult hurdle for most companies to overcome. Too many companies continue under the misguided belief that if they can just get buyers to identify themselves, a salesperson can close the sale offline. These companies are still acting under the false assumption that quantity of leads beats quality of leads. But if you're going to win over the self-educated buyers, you have to be committed to helping them. Your information has to help them make the right buying decision, even if that decision results in the purchase of a competitor's product or service.

The intent of your content must be utility. You have to come to grips with the reality that the buyer's search will result in finding helpful information online. This information will help the buyer move forward on the buying journey and will affect who that person eventually buys from in the end.

The only question you have to ask yourself is whether you would rather have buyers find that information on your site (where you can track them to understand their buying signals) or on a third-party or, worse, competitor's site. We talk more about this topic in Chapter 5, "Selling Versus Helping"; for now, you need to understand that, in a world of invisible sales, your online content is your salesperson. And just like your offline salesperson, the content is making an impression that impacts the self-educating buyer's brand preference and ultimate purchase decision. In other words, your content is winning or losing sales.

## POWER POINTS

- The self-educating buyer trend is truly a trend, not a fad. The combination of ubiquitous broadband access via desktops and smartphones has changed human behavior, creating a new default. In the absence of knowledge, buyers just "Google it."

- Sales are becoming more invisible every day. Buyers are 57% of the way through the buying decision before they're even willing to talk to a sales rep, and consumers have doubled the number of sources they consult before making a purchase.

- Self-educating buyers are just a mouse click away from your competitors' online information, so if you want them to educate themselves on your website, you have to provide helpful information.

- Your online content is your online salesperson. The quality of that information determines whether you're winning or losing invisible sales.

*Download all the Power Points at TheInvisibleSale.com.*

# 4

# The Little Camera Store That Could

*As a content marketer, I've had to become proficient in creating photographic and video content. Although I've always been interested in these two topics, I've never taken a class or received any formal training. Instead, I've gotten my info from the "University of Google" and learned from some of the most accomplished photographers and videographers in the world. I got a lot of that education at AdoramaTV.*

*AdoramaTV is the fundamental content marketing tool for a camera shop of the same name located in New York City. Adorama currently sells products in all 50 states and five countries, including Canada and Brazil. Although ownership has contemplated physical expansion, the success of the company's online sales and prospecting efforts—combined with the current trends favoring online versus offline purchasing of electronics and photography products—prompted management to set aside those discussions and focus even more on powering sales through "originally produced educational content."*

I was fortunate enough to interview Adorama's vice president of marketing, Brian Green, who shared the Adorama success story with me. Brian studied marketing and economics while working at CNBC as a multimedia producer. The CNBC offices were located just down the street from the World Trade Center; after September 11, Brian left CNBC to pursue his master's degree and learn everything he could about e-commerce.

After graduation, Brian joined one of Adorama's biggest competitors, B&H Photo Video, where he ran the company's web channel department for three years. He then formed his own consultancy specifically for e-commerce, focusing on system integration, merchandising, and marketing. It was there that he first began working with Adorama.

At the time, Adorama didn't have a formalized marketing department. One person handled web content, email, and advertising development. Sensing that Brian's background could help Adorama leapfrog its competition by enhancing the company's digital efforts, Adorama ownership invited Brian to join the company and build out a full marketing department. After only four years, Brian and the Adorama team have built the content marketing juggernaut that is AdoramaTV. The little camera store has evolved into a multifaceted, multinational retailer. And it still has just the one store in New York City.

In this chapter, Brian shares valuable history, how-tos, and suggestions to help you develop your own content marketing-powered Painless Prospecting system to leapfrog your competition.

## Who Is Adorama?

Mendel Mendlowits started Adorama in 1975 with the goal of being more than just a camera store. He set out to create a silent partner for professional photographers at news organizations, modeling agencies, magazines, newspapers, and studios. He wanted to create a camera store staffed by people who "care about your images as much as you do."

Meldel also believed that Adorama should commit to inspiring and teaching: Whether in person via workshops or, now, by using online educational content, he believes the company has a duty to teach customers. Further, he believes educating consumers creates unique value for Adorama in the eyes of its customers.

In many respects, Adorama is a set of companies within a company that offer a host of services beyond simply purchasing photographic equipment. Adorama has an entire Rentals Departments for renting equipment ranging from television production studio equipment to regular cameras for weekend use. The store also boasts a professional printing lab that prints photo books, large-format photo prints, and metal prints (photos printed on metallic surfaces). In addition to new equipment, the store boasts a robust Used Equipment Department where customers can buy used merchandise or trade in their old merchandise for cash or a credit toward upgrades. Finally, the store features the Adorama Learning Center, which hosts free and paid workshops.

The Adorama Learning Center serves as an incredible case study for any company wanting to win the invisible sale. By combining offline and online educational content, Adorama creates a never-ending, self-populating database of leads for sales both today and tomorrow.

## Adorama's Content Marketing Machine

In the pre-Internet days of Adorama, content marketing involved in-store workshops. With the advent of the modern commercial Internet, Adorama moved some of their educational efforts online, creating the Adorama Academy. The academy was a collection of online articles similar to a blog. Basically, someone wrote a piece of content (most likely a product review or a photography tip) and posted it to the academy portion of the website. There wasn't any real strategic planning behind the content calendar—no emphasis on search engine optimization or effort to turn the reader into a subscriber. And because the blog was a separate site, prospective customers had a hard time finding it.

Today the Adorama Academy exists in a new, integrated form renamed the Adorama Learning Center. Powered by traditional blog posts, onsite workshops, and AdoramaTV how-to videos, the Adorama Learning Center has evolved from a poorly designed, stand-alone blog site to fully integrated feature content on the adorama.com home page (see Figure 4-1).

**Figure 4-1**   *Adorama.com home page featuring the Adorama Learning Center*

The Adorama Learning Center accomplishes three key marketing goals for Adorama. First, by offering free education and value-added materials to someone who is not necessarily in an active buying cycle, the Learning Center serves as a constant lead-generation and nurturing tool.

Second, it exposes a new audience to the Adorama brand. Although Adorama is well known within the professional photography world, it lags behind mainstream big-box stores on the amateur and consumer photographer awareness meter. With AdoramaTV (the company's video marketing) content available on YouTube and iTunes, and indexing well in search engines, new prospective customers can find, consume, and develop a preference for the Adorama brand.

Third, the Learning Center—and, specifically, AdoramaTV—makes Adorama more relevant to today's online buyer. Whether they're buying a television, a camera, a computer, or anything else electronic, Adorama estimates that 85% to 90% of buyers are doing research beforehand. Furthermore, Adorama estimates that more than 50% of that research starts on YouTube. Its data reveals a very high percentage of product-specific searches on YouTube, creating an effective and efficient acquisition channel, even more efficient than bidding on paid AdWords (ads next to Google search results).

## AdoramaTV

AdoramaTV grew out of a directive from Adorama ownership to educate customers in a more widespread fashion. When that effort was defined as a video, television style solution, Adorama personnel set out to find a host. Their research led them to Mark Wallace, who was already doing his own tutorials on YouTube. Adorama liked him because, in addition to being a talented photographer, Mark was very personable onscreen and would keep viewers engaged. He also had a great delivery and was very approachable. This was important because Adorama didn't want people to feel intimidated by the tutorials. The Adorama team approached Mark and explained their vision for AdoramaTV, and they invited him to serve as the host of the show for the first year. Mark loved the idea and signed on as the first host of AdoramaTV.

On April 29, 2010, AdoramaTV debuted on YouTube; the next day, it premiered on the Adorama website. The show contained three types of segments: *product reviews*, in which Mark reviewed cameras, lenses, lights, and pretty much anything a photographer might need to buy; *how–to* videos, in which Mark interviewed professional photographers and showed viewers how to apply the same techniques to their own photos; and *digital photography one-on-one*, in which Mark explained techniques and approaches specifically related to digital photography.

Today AdoramaTV's YouTube channel boasts more than 121,000 subscribers viewing more than 600 videos on the channel. Furthermore, AdoramaTV has expanded beyond its YouTube roots to Apple's iTunes podcast directory, where it publishes *nine* individual podcasts that have together captured more than 12 million views (see Figure 4-2).

**Figure 4-2**  *AdoramaTV podcasts on iTunes*

As the AdoramaTV effort continued to produce results, the company not only expanded platforms, but also developed new shows featuring new hosts. By expanding formats and hosts, AdoramaTV becomes even more valuable. As I discuss in Chapter 11, "Creating Video," one of the key how-to video success factors is the show host. Different viewers prefer different presentation styles, hosts, and information. For instance, my favorite AdoramaTV host is Gavin Hoey. I really like the way he breaks down his videos into discrete learning steps and then brings it all together at the end of the video. This step-by-step process works well for me. On the other hand, I get great tips for shooting sports pictures from Joe DiMaggio's podcast. In each case, Adorama provides me with exactly what I need and want from a photography podcast.

# Scaling AdoramaTV

As AdoramaTV grew more successful, Brian and the marketing team faced a content marketing challenge. They clearly had discovered a winning formula, trading well-produced, helpful video training for increased brand awareness, loyalty, and, ultimately, sales. And although the company was completely behind expanding AdoramaTV, Brian needed to develop a plan to successfully scale AdoramaTV without losing quality control.

First, the team created a strong support system of professional photographers, both famous and not-famous names in the industry, to serve as brand advocates and contribute original content to the Adorama Learning Center. These ambassadors promote Adorama online, on their blogs, and on social media networks. Adorama had already developed great relationships with them and was able to leverage those relationships when approaching the photographers to see if they wanted to contribute original video content to AdoramaTV. All the photographers were very receptive to participating because it would create exposure for their own personal brand. So the photographers received expanded brand awareness, and Adorama got incredible content at a fraction of the cost to produce it all in-house.

It's important to note one really important factor that excited the photographers and that Adorama felt was key to gaining participation. Adorama didn't limit the photographers creatively. It didn't provide scripts or rules for what the photographers could or could not say during product reviews or how-to videos. As Brian remarked during our interview, "We gave them complete creative freedom. Each photographer provided an outline of the different tips or tricks that they wanted to film or overview of the content they planned to shoot, and we would work with them to get their piece into the schedule."

However, the success created a new challenge: consistency. With each photographer filming his or her own episodes, AdoramaTV had to develop a system to standardize the episodes to build a consistent AdoramaTV brand. This led to outsourcing and digitizing the submission and approval process. Today AdoramaTV hosts film their episodes and electronically upload them, and then Adorama's outside production company cleans everything up and gives it a consistent AdoramaTV look and feel.

Additionally, content marketing success creates a second challenge: the need to create enough content. To keep feeding the AdoramaTV beast, Brian and his team are always looking for new talent to invite into the AdoramaTV family. They use a couple of free digital tools to simplify this process.

The Adorama team uses a combination of Google Alerts[1] (an email alert service Google offers that automatically notifies users when new content from news, web, blogs, video, and/or discussion groups matches a set of search terms the user selects) and different news readers[2] (web-based applications that aggregate syndicated web content such as news headlines, blogs, podcasts, and video blogs in one location for easy viewing) to find blog and web content on key subject matter and keywords to identify potential content creation partners.

The team also reviews Adorama.com website traffic to understand where incoming visitors were before they landed on the Adorama website. In some cases, this information can reveal an unknown brand ambassador who might be a candidate

---

1. http://en.wikipedia.org/wiki/Google_alerts

2. http://en.wikipedia.org/wiki/News_aggregator

to host AdoramaTV episodes or provide blog content for the Learning Center. The team also regularly searches avenues such as YouTube, Facebook, or even LinkedIn, with the goal of discovering other subject matter experts who have a large audience and create content that people are responding to and regularly consuming.

The successful scaling of AdoramaTV resulted from a key decision Brian made early on in the process. *He defined AdoramaTV as a platform to spread and showcase educational content and approached the project as producer, not creator.* He invested in content creation the same way companies invest in advertising creation: He hired professionals. In some cases, these professionals are compensated, with Adorama sponsoring them; in other cases, the photographic professionals trades content for the exposure AdoramaTV provides. Brian's decision to invest in processes, content creators, and outside production assistance allowed him to focus on the vision of AdoramaTV. In my opinion, that's one of the key reasons AdoramaTV has grown so quickly.

# Building Relationships with Content

One of the most significant and underappreciated uses of content marketing is vendor relationship development. As you create an audience around your content, you make yourself more valuable and more desirable to vendors and suppliers. At some point, these vendors and suppliers will offer to share their content with you for use on your platforms. This not only reduces your content creation needs, which is the biggest challenge most companies face, but also strengthens your relationships with that vendor or supplier.

The success of the AdoramaTV brand and the platform has definitely caught the attention of Adorama's suppliers. However, maybe even more importantly, AdoramaTV has captured the attention of the major photography associations in the industry—including a few of the biggest trade show events, which approached Adorama with offers to co-produce show coverage as AdoramaTV episodes. This effectively makes AdoramaTV the official broadcast producer of the shows and ensures significant, highly targeted marketing impressions that can generate awareness and future sales.

This "heard it here first" reputation is further enhanced when major photographic brands offer Adorama advanced access to new products. Adorama has a handful of professionals who have signed NDA's (nondisclosure agreements) to receive new products early. In return, these professionals agree to create product review videos for AdoramaTV, and AdoramaTV times the release of the video to the product announcement. Thus, if an item is released on the market at 12:01 a.m. on a certain day, Adorama has the video review published at that time as well. This perpetuates the circle of value: As Adorama strives to be more valuable to manufacturers and consumers, the manufacturers help make Adorama more valuable to the consumer. Everyone, including the prospective buyer, wins.

When I asked Brian how long it took Adorama to gain the attention of manufacturers and begin to shape the relationship Adorama currently enjoys, he answered, "Realistically, around seven to eight months. Once they got a sense of what the content was going to look like and they saw an audience building, they started to pay attention." And once AdoramaTV reached 1 million views on iTunes, the manufacturers became quite serious about working directly with Adorama in advance of major product introductions.

But the enhanced manufacturer relationship doesn't stop there. In what I've deemed a *reverse co-op program* (traditionally, a co-op program is a cost-sharing arrangement in which manufacturers provide financial assistance to help fund a retailer's paid advertising programs[3]), Adorama provides the manufacturer with content (unbiased product reviews and how-to tutorials) for use in the manufacturers' advertising. Thus, instead of a manufacturer helping Adorama create greater awareness by subsidizing Adorama's advertising, the manufacturer creates that additional awareness by placing Adorama-branded content directly in front of the manufacturer's customers.

After Adorama produces an episode that features their product or a tutorial that has their product in it, many camera manufacturers will incorporate the video file into their own marketing materials, whether it's on their web page or in an email blast. Photography magazines have begun incorporating AdoramaTV content in their editorial, too: Several popular photography magazines add Adorama videos as supplemental content. The publications include a QR code in the article inviting readers to learn more by scanning the code, which takes them to an AdoramaTV video. (A QR code is a black-and-white dot-matrix image that when scanned with a special smartphone app, provides additional information in the form of audio, video, or takes the reader to a predefined website.)

Ask yourself what kind of competitive advantage this type of access gives Adorama in the marketplace? How many more prospective buyers are finding Adorama? How much more trustworthy is the Adorama brand in the photographic consumer marketplace? Finally, do you think Adorama could ever buy this kind of access and trust? It's all a result of the strong relationships Adorama has developed with manufacturers.

---

3. http://www.sba.gov/content/what-co-op-advertising

## Adorama's Advertising

I'd be remiss in my duty if I didn't touch on the traditional advertising side of Adorama's marketing programs. Although enhanced inbound, content-driven marketing certainly can result in lowered outbound advertising spending, that is not the case here. Adorama maintains a healthy outbound advertising program that spans most of the traditional online marketing channels, such as paid search, email marketing, affiliates, and social media, along with offline channels such as print media, radio, direct marketing, and television.

Adorama has also begun using sports sponsorships. A new campaign for Adorama, which embodies a true multichannel branding strategy, is its status as the Official Electronics Retailer of the New York Giants. Utilizing branding assets and messaging, which are synchronized across live, in-game stadium promotions; social media; and television, Adorama leverages the partnership to drive new brand engagement and acquisition.

So although the focus of this case study is Adorama's content marketing, know that Brian credits Adorama's success to a multichannel program built around the success of direct marketing, traditional advertising, sponsorship, and inbound and online marketing efforts.

Interestingly, when Brian talks about his advertising efforts, he talks about how certain campaigns, such as the Giants sponsorship, focus on driving specific product categories, such as electronics and televisions, which Adorama has expanded into the last few years. He sees these advertising campaigns as a way to expand prospective customers' thinking and perception of Adorama as just a camera store. These expansion efforts resulted in a new tagline a few years ago: "More than a camera store."

So although Brian is an obvious proponent of content marketing, he's not quite ready to abandon the world of traditional advertising just yet—or maybe ever.

## How Adorama Wins the Invisible Sale

In my opinion, Adorama's success is based on two important and interconnected factors. First, the company creates truly helpful content. Second, its website is funnel optimized. I talk more about funnel-optimized website design in Chapter 8, "The Painless Prospecting Framework," but I would be remiss if I didn't show you how Adorama uses funnel-optimized design principles to turn its website into the company's best salesperson.

In Figure 4-3, you see a blog post from the Adorama website featuring an episode of AdoramaTV. This is a common content marketing approach—but less common is the list of products you see both to the right of and below the video file. These aren't randomly selected products or best sellers. These are the items that Joe McNally references in the video. These are the tools he uses to create the lighting effect in the video. Adorama smartly places those items one click away from the viewer.

**Figure 4-3**   *Adorama.com funnel-optimized blog post*

But Adorama doesn't stop there. Remember, this video is also accessible via iTunes, YouTube, and Vimeo, where it is viewed without the benefit of the product links to the right of and below the video. Here again, where possible, Adorama funnel-optimizes the content by embedding links to the products, as the host mentions them, directly in the YouTube video file (see Figure 4-4). This feature used to be reserved for a select few YouTube producers, but recently, YouTube made it available to everyone. You can learn how to embed these links in your videos by reading my blog post "How to Embed Website Links in YouTube Videos" (http://goo.gl/TQsoj).

**Figure 4-4**  *AdoramaTV embedded website link in YouTube video*

Adorama knows that often viewers of its content are not in an active buying mode. They're simply educating themselves or doing research for future purchases. Thus, the company looks for opportunities to provide content or services to invisible buyers in exchange for a valid email address. One way Adorama does this is its Wish List function. If a website visitor decides not to purchase a product immediately but wants an easy way to find the product in the future, the shopper can add that product to a Wish List. To do this, the visitor simply creates an account using an email address. Then the visitor (now visible to Adorama) clicks the Add to Wish List button. Here again, Adorama utilizes funnel-optimized design to entice the prospective customer to dive deeper into the website from the Added to Wish List page (see Figure 4-5). Notice the AdoramaTV content links in the lower-right corner of Figure 4-5. Those links take the reader to additional flash usage tutorials and technique videos.

**Figure 4-5**  *Adorama.com funnel-optimized added to Wish List page*

Finally, Adorama makes effective use of targeted follow-up emails. Instead of simply sending a generic lead-nurturing email, the company ties email content to the content viewed on its website and podcasts. While writing this chapter, I watched a Joe DiMaggio video on baseball photography techniques. A few days later, I received the lead-nurturing email you see in Figure 4-6. The email included a Father's Day offer, as well as links to waterproof cameras and smartphone cases (not shown in Figure 4-6). This makes sense—I viewed the video in June, and plenty of prospective buyers are hitting pools, rivers, lakes, and oceans as part of their summer fun.

**Figure 4-6**   *Adorama content-optimized email*

Throughout every stage of the prospective customer interaction, Adorama offers
helpful advice, tips, and content designed to make the buyer smarter and more
informed. This keeps buyers engaged and lessens the likelihood that they will
feel the need to reference non-Adorama websites to fully self-educate themselves.
Additionally, because every touchpoint is designed to help versus sell (I talk about
this in greater detail in Chapter 5, "Selling Versus Helping"), the prospect willingly
accepts the messages instead of viewing them as unwanted interruptions.

## Success Metrics

AdoramaTV launched in April 2010, and by every measure of success, the program
is a home run. Since 2010, Adorama.com has seen growth in overall traffic, return
visitors, and, most important, increased sales every year.

To preserve confidentiality, I removed any traffic or sales figures from these charts.
But even without the figures, the charts clearly tell a success story. Figure 4-7
shows the growth in overall website traffic from 2008 through June 2013. See how
the graph begins a noticeable uphill trend beginning in 2010?

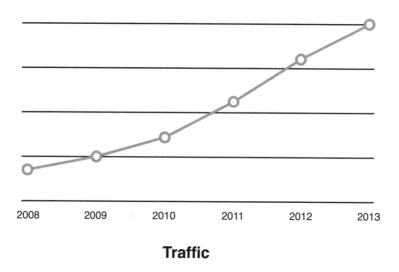

**Traffic**

**Figure 4-7**  *Adorama.com website traffic*

Diving into the traffic a little deeper, see how both new and repeat traffic has grown in Figure 4-8. More interestingly, notice that the percentage of repeat visitors almost equals the percentage of new visitors. This shows that Adorama's content is sticky—it generates brand loyalty instead of just capturing top-of-the-funnel leads. And don't forget to notice where you start to see that growth in both metrics.

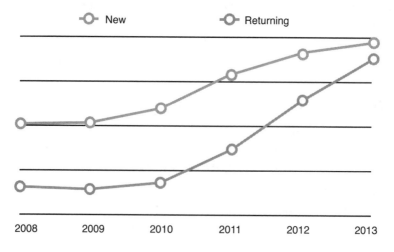

**Figure 4-8**  *Adorama.com website new versus repeat visitor traffic*

Finally, all this traffic growth is truly valuable only when it converts to sales. And convert it has. As you see in Figure 4-9, after relatively flat years in 2008 and 2009, 2010 began a steady upward sales trend that continues through 2012. *Note:* Sales figures for 2013 were not yet available at the writing of this chapter.

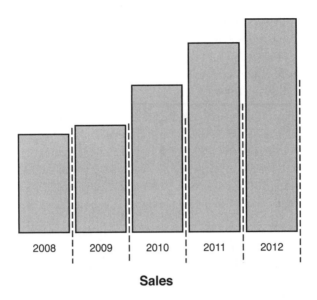

**Figure 4-9**  *Adorama sales growth, 2008–2012*

By any metric you choose—website traffic, brand loyalty, or sales—Adorama's "originally produced educational content" approach proves that investing in *helping* instead of focusing on *selling* produces meaningful, measurable results.

# Brian's Advice for You

When I asked Brian for some reader advice on moving sales and marketing efforts from an outbound, cold-calling or advertising-driven approach to a digitally centric, content- and education-focused one, he stressed two key points.

First, he advises listening both qualitatively and quantitatively. Listen directly to your audience—hear what they say, and aggregate and analyze how they engage with your content. Listen with your ears open, whether you have an online audience, customers calling your customer service lines, or customers coming into your store. Because so much of your content will come from the questions people are asking you, it's imperative that you hear every question and concern voiced.

An additional benefit of listening is that it keeps your prospective customers talking. They feel open to share and engage, whether it's with the content host (in the case of online video/audio) or with you directly. Always look at what questions are being asked, and pay attention to what people are trying to accomplish. Often the prospective customers don't know what question to ask because they are unaware that your products or service can help them. During these moments, listening is most powerful. By hearing the unspoken question attached to the spoken need, you can surprise, delight, and, most important, educate your prospective customers. If your content can continue to accomplish these three goals, you'll not only have an endless stream of first-time and repeat customers ready to do business with you today, but equally important, you'll have customers ready to continually engage with your brand even when they aren't looking to buy anything.

Second, choose your brand ambassadors carefully. Find people who are very relatable to the audience. Watch how your prospective ambassadors interact with an audience, especially when they are teaching the audience something. Ensure that they don't communicate in a very techie way or seem intimidating—they need to always recognize that the audience is smart and enthusiastic. This applies to how they write as well. It is absolutely imperative that your audience be able to relate to the ambassadors.

Follow Brian's advice, and learn from his efforts. Adorama is truly a company on the cutting edge of painless prospecting. I searched the globe for a company that is properly applying the Painless Prospecting approach—one that not only understands, but is also winning the invisible sale. I found it in Adorama, and I'm extremely pleased the company allowed me to share its story with you.

## POWER POINTS

- The key to successful content marketing is to create originally produced educational content.

- The content must be approachable. If you use video content, the host must be likable and approachable on camera.

- Your website and content must be funnel optimized.

- Great content doesn't just produce leads—it grows relationships.

- You can leverage great content to establish and grow manufacturer, vendor, and partner relationships.

- Choose to be a producer, not a creator of content. Create systems and partnerships that leverage expert talent to create the content that fulfills your vision.

*Download all the Power Points at TheInvisibleSale.com.*

# Section 2

# Capturing the Invisible Sale

When you've convinced your organization that the Invisible Sale is not only real, but also an area that you all need to focus on today and in the future, you're a quarter of the way to being finished. Next, you need to create an online (and, in some cases, offline) integrated content footprint to ensure that you can compete for today's self-educating buyer.

To do this, you need to set aside much of what you've been taught about how marketing and sales work to pursue a completed sale. You need to embrace a few thoughts and approaches that will initially feel foreign and, in some cases, downright wrong. But stay the course. If you commit to this brave new approach to sales and marketing, you'll create a prospect-generating machine that is committed to only one goal every day: creating new qualified leads for your company. You'll create an online machine that, in short order, will become one of the most important members of your sales team.

By the end of this section, you'll have the blueprint for creating this machine. But before we get into the details, let's take a 30,000-foot view of what we'll cover. It'll help you make sense of everything as you work through this section.

## Helping to Create Sales

The first area to focus on is a fundamental change you need to accept when creating marketing content. Traditionally, companies have felt that information is sacred. Information is power. And the company's marketing efforts should force prospective customers to call the company and talk to a corporate salesperson to gain the really useful information the prospect requires to complete the buying decision. You need to abandon that point of view if you want to compete for the Invisible Sale.

That thinking made sense once upon a time, but it's a very pre-search engine mindset. Today information is freely available on the Internet, and search engines such as Google and Bing are training society that all the answers and information in the world is now at the buyers' fingertips. So it's not a matter of wondering whether a prospective buyer will find the information without accessing a salesperson; it's a matter of where they'll find the information.

The impact of this information access shift on marketers wanting to win the Invisible Sale is profound. All that information you've previously kept hidden behind your sales force wall needs to become digitally accessible. No longer do you sell prospects. Instead, you use the plethora of insight and data that your company has to help the self-educating buyer realize that your solution is at least worth serious consideration, if not the perfect solution to their problem. As you'll see, in this model you aren't selling—as you're helping a prospect make a buying decision.

We spend Chapter 5, "Selling Versus Helping," talking about the difference between selling and helping. Specifically, we talk about why you need to create *helping* versus *selling* content. Most important, we discuss why this distinction makes the difference between winning and losing the invisible sales opportunity.

## The Social Sales Force

I'm sure you're quite familiar with the idea of prospects, customers, and non-prospects. Those are the traditional labels we use to categorize a person or contact we meet during the sales prospecting process. Basically, we salespeople today evaluate on a single variable: the likelihood of buying from my company or me. We tend to place everyone on one end or the other of that continuum. Then we promptly ignore the people we deem unlikely to buy from us. But in today's hyper-connected digital world, an important member of that nonbuyer segment has emerged as a powerful variable in the Invisible Sale: the social agent. And while social agents might never actually do business with you or buy anything from you, they might just end up being one of your most valuable *customers*.

In fact, much of the content you create for your digital footprint is written as much for your agents as your prospects. And much of the social selling ideas we talk about in Chapter 10, "Social Selling," focus on using social tools to meet and maintain relationships with your agents, as well as your prospects and customers.

## The Power of Proximity

Speaking of meeting folks, we need to do a deep dive into the social science of meeting people and see how those meetings affect a prospective customer's willingness to do business with you. In Chapter 7, "Propinquity," we dive into

Propinquity. Yes, it's likely a word that you've never heard of, but trust me—unless you're very different from the thousands of people I speak in front of every year, it's about to become one of your favorite water cooler words and likely will have an immediate impact on your sales and marketing planning.

The Propinquity Effect is at the heart of everything we talk about from this point forward. It's the strategic underpinning of the Painless Prospecting approach that I believe is the key to winning the Invisible Sale. Frankly, it's the natural evolution of marketing that enables you to move from trying to achieve simple top-of-mind awareness to working toward the far more powerful and effective top-of-mind preference.

# The Painless Prospecting Platform

When you understand the three key strategic underpinnings to winning the Invisible Sale, you get to roll up our sleeves and begin building your blueprint to create your own Painless Prospecting platform. In Chapter 8, "The Painless Prospecting Framework," I give you the blueprint for building an integrated content network of your own. We talk in detail about building a funnel-optimized Home Base. From there, I explain the differences between Outposts and Embassies and the role both play in your marketing.

Let me be clear on one point, though: Although I'll be frequently referring to the integrated content network as a Painless Prospecting platform, don't let that get in your way. The Painless Prospecting term is my firm's name for the approach, but our approach is just one of many. For the sake of convenience, I use my term, but the purpose of this entire section—and especially Chapter 8—is to give you the blueprint to create your own version of a Painless Prospecting platform. I want to make sure you understand the basic structure, strategy, and tactics required to build your own online sales machine that collects leads while you sleep.

# Making Every Call Count

Now, even if you're successfully convincing everyone in your organization to move to a Painless Prospecting approach, you're still going to have folks who will ring the "no leads in the interim" bell. They'll try to sabotage or undermine your momentum by pointing out (correctly) that it will take time to build a Painless Prospecting system. They'll point out (again, correctly) that it will take time for that system to begin to generate qualified leads, much less converted sales.

And that's fine, because I'm going to introduce you to behavioral email in Chapter 9. Not only is this one of the most effective and slickest uses of email marketing, but it's the perfect bridge campaign to move your company from an outbound, database-driven approach to the much more efficient inbound, data-based marketing and sales program.

Through the story of Amy Smith (not her real name), I'll show you how any sales force, no matter how small, can take that important first step toward a brighter data-based marketing future. Then we'll talk about how you can reuse this behavioral-based marketing machine to improve the effectiveness of your future inquiry-based advertising programs and your post-trade show and conference follow-up.

## Social Prospecting

Finally, we'll tackle the most debated (in my opinion) subject in the continuing marketing versus sales battle. We'll talk about the role of social media platforms such as Twitter, Facebook, Google+, and LinkedIn in the business-to-business (B2B) and high involvement Business-to-Consumer (B2C) purchase model.

This has been a hot topic since the early days of social media, and it shows no indications of abatement. Many leaders in the marketing world are pushing their sales teams to get active on social media, yet those same sales teams are questioning the value of time spent on these social networks versus time spent with traditional prospecting tools such as phone and email.

Further exacerbating the situation is the lack of reputable research on the subject. Current arguments are almost entirely built on personal thoughts and feelings instead of independent third-party research. However, I'm a believer in the power of social networks to drive B2B and high-involvement B2C sales. So although we discuss some of the available research, my intent is to prove to you that social networks play not only *some* role in today's Painless Prospecting, but often an integral one. You just have to understand how to leverage them for your particular category, industry, or prospect type.

To help you see that, and to give you more ammunition to make your point internally, we go through a few case studies and examples that clearly show the value of an active social presence. But we're not just going to make the argument. The purpose of this book is to be a guide, not a trophy, so we go through key examples step by step to show you what worked and what didn't. Then you can apply that learning to your own social efforts.

Okay, enough about what we're going to talk about. Let's get to work. Roll up your sleeves and turn the page.

# 5

# Selling Versus Helping

*Have you seen the movie* Jerry McGuire? *In it, there's a famous scene in which Jerry McGuire, played by Tom Cruise, implores his only client, Rod, played by Cuba Gooding Jr., to "help me help you, Rod." He's literally on his knees in a men's locker room begging Rod to "help me help you." In his soliloquy, he asks Rod to think less about himself and more "about the game" so that fans will love him. That will make him more valuable to the NFL and his team—and, ultimately, help Jerry (his agent) negotiate a better contract for him.*

# Helping Creates Buying Signals

Selling to self-educating buyers is a lot like that scene. The buyers are Jerry, begging you to help them help you. But instead of needing you to care about the game, they need you to care about giving them the information they need to work their way through a buying decision. In doing so, you give them what they need to help you: You create buying signals that the marketing team can analyze and then forward to the sales team when the time is right to close the sale. Each time you give buyers an answer to a question in the form of a blog post, email, white paper, or webinar, you're giving them an opportunity to send you a buying signal. That signal helps you understand their pain points, key decision drivers, and contextual details that, when forwarded to a sales team, result in a better, more targeted, and likely more effective sales presentation.

In a high-involvement or educational driven purchase, rarely does a single product attribute, pain point, or reason to buy drive a successful sale. Instead, a combination of these items creates the prism through which your prospects evaluate and determine the best product or service for them. By providing a variety of well-thought-out and well-planned helping materials, you give your prospects the opportunity to create those valuable buying signals. It's like your sales team can read their minds. Every time a prospect clicks an article or post, downloads a buying guide, or views a how-to tutorial, that person sends you a trackable, storable, usable buying signal that better informs your sales team and increases the likelihood of a successful sales call resulting in a purchase. But you can't create those signals unless you commit to helping and not selling. You have to anticipate questions and provide answers.

# Buyers Want Answers

When do you turn to Google? Is it when you know what you already want, but you just need to find the appropriate online destination to complete your purchase? Or is it when you're simply searching for options or more information to help you narrow your choices? The truth is likely both—but the big invisible sales opportunity lies in the latter.

Google's stated goal, outside of indexing the world's information, is to provide the best search results for every query entered into its search box. Ask yourself why Google cares so much about giving you the best results. Is it because Google just loves you? No. Is it because Google wants to sell more targeted advertising against the search queries? Possibly. But I think the reason Google strives so hard to give you, the searcher, relevant, accurate, and helpful results for each of your searches is that most searches do not start with an answer in mind. Most searches start with a question or a problem that the searcher is seeking an answer to. And they assume that Google can help them find that answer or solve that problem. Google knows that as long as Google Searches continue to answer questions, Google continues to thrive as a business.

This is why it is so important in online marketing—or, as it sometimes referred to, content marketing—to create content that answers specific questions. Your online content should function as the ultimate salesperson who neither eats nor sleeps, does not take vacations or holidays, and works 24/7/365. Creating online content is your opportunity to create a virtual salesperson who's ready to answer every question a perspective buyer poses, no matter how niche or unusual or mundane.

Your buyer needs you to anticipate questions, provide answers to those questions, and help them make a buying decision. Buyers don't need yet another channel filled with aggressive, high-pressure salespeople looking to do nothing more than fill a quota. They just need answers.

## Buyers Know What They Want but Not What They Need

Self-educating buyers don't always know the right solution before they start their online search. Often buyers simply know what they need to accomplish. They have a goal. They know that they want to save money, or they need a new kitchen. Or maybe their company wants to create a more efficient production process. Or they may simply need something more difficult to define, such as a marketing strategy to capture an entirely new target audience or customer base.

Goals like these can be the biggest opportunities for a helping versus selling approach. These self-educating buyers are in a purely research-driven, search-oriented mode of operation. They are educating in the truest sense of the word. Not only do they not have a short list, but they're not even familiar enough with possible vendors to begin to create one. In some cases, their problem isn't well defined enough to begin creating a long list of options, much less a short list. These buyers are looking for information that can help them craft a recommended solution or recommended strategy, or just put one foot in front of the other in an effort to get from where they are today to where they hope to be tomorrow.

In this environment, selling oriented content simply doesn't work. If you're lucky enough to rank that selling content high enough in search engines for self-educating buyers to find you, you will most likely disappoint those buyers when they land on your website. This disappointment will quickly turn into abandonment, often referred to as a bounce, in online statistical reporting. It's called a bounce because as soon as prospective buyers land on your website and realize that they have landed on a selling versus helping piece of content, they immediately leave your website without viewing any additional pages. They return to their previous search or simply close the web browser and move on. Either way, that prospective buyer is no longer engaging with your online salesperson (a.k.a your content). It's like the buyer walked into your office or retail location, took one look at you, and turned around and walked right back out the door.

And this is a huge problem because this self-educating prospect is your best prospect. That might seem counterintuitive, but stop and think about it for a moment. This prospect has no preconceived notions, no preconceived loyalties, and no favoritism toward any of your competitors, as might be the case in a normal sale. You have the best chance to convert these buyers if you simply approach them in the proper manner—if you help them.

## You Have To Give Before You Get

Every day, companies around the world give things away to consumers and buyers for free. They offer the promise of a free estimate, a product sample, or, my personal favorite, the free overnight test drive (also known as the puppy dog sale in the automotive world). Companies are accustomed to trading the consumer something of value (or, at least, perceived value) in return for the customer's contact information and, in the case of the automotive overnight test drive, an actual product ownership experience. But why do companies do this?

They do this because it creates the opportunity to engage a consumer and begin what is considered a traditional sales funnel process. They are willing to do this because, in the traditional offline world, where a consumer must reach out to you in a physical manner (such as a telephone call or possibly a face-to-face visit), companies feel that the trade is worthy. They do this because they believe that if a salesperson can begin to engage a customer either over the phone or face to face, that salesperson can "close the deal." Now, the veracity of this point of view is obviously up for debate and certainly has a lot to do with the quality of the salesperson, but it certainly does not hold true for all customers. However, the approach of giving before you get is valid and effective both offline and online.

The Internet actually amplifies this giving approach, whether it is a chance to give that customer a free estimate, a helpful tip sheet or buying guide, or a downloadable information packet. And that auto dealer can let a prospective buyer customize that car that they would love to come test-drive overnight. Giving the customer something of value online in exchange for some small bit of trackable data is not only encouraged, but also required.

It is required because, in the world of invisible sales, that contact information is the first step in moving the prospect closer to the center of your sales radar as a qualified lead. You need this contact information to begin correlating the digital buying signals into a detailed prospect dossier.

# Helping Is Easier Than Selling

Creating selling materials is hard because you try to anticipate every need, question, concern, and address in a single sales piece. Creating selling materials is hard because you often are working without the benefit of buying signals that will help you craft the better selling message. You're not really sure what the most important features are for each prospective buyer, so you talk about all the features. You're not really sure what problems the buyer is having, so you talk about all the problems your product or service can solve. Writing selling materials is hard because, too often, they are written without real-time, individualized buyer feedback or buying signals.

However, writing helping materials is actually quite easy. When you're writing helping materials, you don't need to have a clear direction—only a clear understanding. You don't need to know what each buyer needs, wants, and desires. You need only think about what all the possible wants, needs, and desires your product or service can fulfill. Then you break down each of those items into its finite pieces. If your product or service is a relevant solution for five different customer problems, then you write helping content around each of those five customer problems. And within those customer problems, you will probably find a number of questions, issues, or considerations that a prospective buyer has to think through more deeply. Answering these might require additional data or consideration. And then you write content to address each of those individual needs questions or concerns. Writing helping content is really not all that different than writing selling content—it's just packaged and delivered in a far different way. Instead of trying to put all the messages into a single brochure, you place all the messages over time on a single blog—not a single blog post, but a single blog. Each question you answer is another breadcrumb buyers follow until they've found their way down the path you've created for them and reached your front door.

For instance, imagine you own an air duct cleaning business. Every house with central air conditioning has air ducts but only a fraction of those homeowners ever have their air ducts cleaned. And they don't all decide to clean their ducts for the same reason. Thus, your air duct cleaning company can create multiple blog posts to address the various reasons.

Asthma sufferers are a big market for air duct cleaners. Here are three possible blog titles that appeal to that buyer:

- Can dirty air ducts trigger asthma attacks?
- Can you relieve asthma symptoms with air duct cleaning?
- Creating an asthma safe home for your kids.

Homeowners that see mold on their air duct vents are another big market for air duct cleaners. Here are three possible blog titles that appeal to that buyer:

- How to remove mold from your air ducts.
- Can mold in your air ducts make you sick?
- How much does it cost to remove mold from air ducts?

By publishing these blog posts over time, your air duct company increases the likelihood of appearing in search results for these keywords. The key to creating helping content is simple—put yourself in the buyers' shoes and write the blog posts that you would want to find.

Because writing helping materials is so much easier, the smart content marketer can produce infinitely more and better content if that marketer chooses to write from a point of view of helping versus selling. In fact, the Content Marketing Institute's *2013 B2B Content Marketing Benchmarks, Budgets and Trends—North America*[1] study found that the number-one concern content marketing companies have today is producing enough high-quality, effective content for use online. Could it be because those companies are thinking in terms of selling versus helping?

Let's use a hypothetical example of an auto dealership to help clarify this point. Imagine you're looking for a new SUV and you've narrowed your choices down to a Chevy Suburban and a Ford Expedition. You've never owned either vehicle, so you go online to compare and contrast the two vehicles.

First you visit the local Chevy dealer website. There you find a lot of information about the Suburban. There are pictures, features, videos and pretty much everything a salesperson will ever tell you about how awesome a Chevy Suburban is and why you should buy it.

Then you go to the Ford dealer website. There too you find all the standard sales information but you also find something else. The Ford dealer has a blog, and on that blog you find the following posts:

- 5 Features That Make The Ford Expedition The Perfect Family Car
- Ford Expedition vs Chevy Suburban: Which Should You Pick
- Is An SUV The Right Car For You?
- 3 Features Every Soccer Mom Should Have On Her Car
- How To Keep Kids Entertained During Long Road Trips

---

1. http://contentmarketinginstitute.com/2012/10/2013-b2b-content-marketing-research/

As you begin reading these posts, you realize that you're learning things you didn't know before. You didn't even know that two of the three features that every soccer mom should have existed. But now that you do, you agree that those are must have features. And as you review the Expedition vs. the Suburban, you find that only the Expedition offers some of the features mentioned in the "How To Keep Kids .... Road Trips" blog post.

The point here is that because your local Chevy dealer just wanted to make the sale, their content options are pretty limited. But because your Ford dealer is trying to be helpful, they have no trouble using products, product features, and customer challenges as jumping off points for keyword rich, helpful posts that lead their customer to the correct buying decision—buying a Ford.

## People Trust Experts

Every day, people buy products and services that they don't really understand. They hope that they're making the right selection, that they're buying the best option, and that they don't make a mistake. And the reason they're hoping versus knowing is that they are not well versed enough in the product or service to be able to really understand which option is the best. This fear, combined with on-demand access to information via search engines, is fueling the self-educating buyer phenomenon.

And I'm not just talking about complex B2B purchases such as software, computer systems, or enterprise relationship systems. No, I'm talking about simple, everyday consumer and business purchasing decisions. Buyers are researching common purchases—products and services that you likely have bought yourself—online.

For instance, imagine that you need to hire a new CPA. Maybe you've never had a CPA, or maybe you just don't like the CPA you have, or maybe you just want to confirm that you have the best CPA. Unless you have a degree in accounting or significant accounting knowledge, exactly how are you going to know who's the best CPA? If you know enough about accounting to properly evaluate the best CPA, chances are, you don't need one—then you could do your own taxes, handle your own books, and generally take care of your own accounting issues.

Or maybe you have a leaking window in your house. So you decide that you need to replace the window, lest you damage your house by getting water on your floors. Worse, maybe you have a bunch of leaking windows. Now you have a pretty expensive purchase on your hands that will affect the long-term value of your most expensive asset. How do you pick which window manufacturer you're going to select? Do you truly understand the difference among windows, window manufacturers, and window types? Chances are, unless you're somehow involved in the residential or commercial construction industry, you don't.

So how do you make these decisions? How do you decide what's the best when purchasing a product or service for which you are not really qualified to know what's the best? Think about that for a second.

You probably turn to your friends, family, and maybe even coworkers. You might call or email or post on Facebook, Twitter, LinkedIn, Google+, or wherever you choose to hang out online. You might utilize the efficiency of social media networks to ask all your friends at the same time for a recommendation on a CPA or window manufacturer. And if you're lucky enough to have friends who have direct experience with those kinds of companies, you might be done. You might have all the information you need to feel confident in making the best choice.

But what if your friends don't know? What if your friends don't have the experience, insight, or expertise to make a recommendation? If you're like most buyers, you turn to Google or another search engine. You go online and start searching. You begin looking for reputable resources.

But how do you determine that a resource is reputable? How do you understand or decide that the alternative you're looking at is, in fact, the expert on accounting, windows or any other product or service? That's where helping versus selling content really becomes valuable.

Let's return to the CPA scenario as a hypothetical example. Imagine that you're a small business owner, and from time to time, you have simple accounting or bookkeeping questions that you don't want to trouble your CPA with. Either you just don't want to trouble him or you might not want to be charged to have him answer the question. For whatever reason, you don't turn to your accountant. Instead, you turn to the Internet and pose your questions to Google or your favorite search engine. Over time, you find that one CPA firm consistently shows up in your search results. Better yet, quite often the answer you seek is located on that firm's website via a blog post, white paper, or some kind of presentation.

Over time, you begin to develop a *relationship* with that CPA firm. You begin to see it as an expert resource. Do you instantly think it's better than your current CPA? Maybe or maybe not. But if some day you felt unhappy with your current CPA, where do you think you would turn? Would you conduct an exhaustive search of your options, or would you just call the firm that always seems to have the answer to all your online accounting questions?

People trust experts. Why? Because expertise is defined by the buyer, not the seller. What makes one person or company an expert isn't the company telling you it's the expert. It's the customer, the buyer or the prospective buyer, forming that conclusion based on the information the company shares, the insights it provides, and the quality of work that you review. And part of what makes an expert is a willingness to help, even when that help isn't going to immediately or financially reward the expert. Helpful content, whose intent is truly to help, educate, or enable, creates a feeling of expertise in the mind of the reader. And that expertise can then be leveraged in the future and turns an invisible lead into a very visible customer.

# Help Buyers Realize They Need You

One of the most valuable uses of helping vs. selling content is in the service sector. Here I'm referring to businesses that provide services in lieu of buyers doing it themselves. This can run the gamut from plumbers and contractors to marketing consultants, CPAs, and real estate agents. When you stop and think about it, each of these disciplines involves delivering a service that buyers can do themselves. Thus, a buyer's decision of whether to buy those services often comes down to the level of difficulty associated with the need. If buyers feel that they can do the job themselves and save money, they opt for the do-it-yourself model. However, if before or during the attempt they realize that the job is beyond their capability, they turn to an expert resource to handle or complete the job.

In most cases, the buyer really isn't qualified to do what the company does—at least, not at the same level. Buyers turn to the Internet to try to acquire your level of knowledge in the form of a "how to" blog post, video, podcast, or free e-book. If you go to YouTube and type "how to [insert the name of anything you can think of that you want to do]," chances are, you will find many videos created by individuals, brands, and companies that attempt to provide the knowledge for prospective customers to solve their problems.

You might be thinking, "Why would a company do that? Why would they teach somebody how to solve a problem the company gets paid to solve?" Seems kind of counterintuitive, doesn't it?

But the beauty lies in the fact that, many times, as the prospect is attempting to follow the instructions the company has given, they realize that it's harder than it looks. Helping via an educational video, blog post, or e-book often helps prospects see the level of detail, intricacy, or difficulty they had never considered. That realization turns the do-it-yourselfer into a qualified prospect who hires the creator of the helpful content.

I've experienced this phenomenon myself. From time to time, I deliver half-day workshops around social media, content marketing, social selling, and other digital marketing topics. The cost of attendance is usually well below the value received or the cost to produce the content I share. And the people who sign up for these workshops arrive intending to apply my knowledge to do their marketing themselves. The vast majority *do* end up doing it themselves.

But from time to time, at least one company in the room fully intends to take the knowledge, return to their corporate headquarters, and begin implementing the ideas on their own. However, as they sit through the workshop and learn about the depth and breadth of the knowledge required to properly deploy content marketing, social media, email marketing, or any of the various digital channels we discuss, the company reps realize that they can't do it on their own. They realize either that the manpower required to effectively deploy digital solutions is beyond their staffing or that digital marketing is really quite complicated. They realize that, even though I'm teaching it to them, they don't fully understand it—and chances are, if they try to do it themselves, they'll be unsuccessful.

Usually within a few days, the company calls. After reminding me that they were in the workshop, they ask if I might schedule a time to come meet with them and talk about taking them on as a client. They go on to explain that although the workshop was very helpful, the biggest piece of learning they took away was that they're not equipped to do their digital marketing themselves. And a new client is born. See how that works?

## The World Needs Helpful Content

Although the explosion of the Internet combined with low-cost publishing tools has led to an unprecedented number of content channels available to consumer and business-to-business buyers alike, it has not provided an efficient mechanism for populating all these new media outlets with high-quality content. Thus, in addition to creating content for your own site, you can also create content for other websites that is attributed to you. Just as traditional offline media such as newspapers, magazines, television, and radio grapple with content production costs that cannot be profitably optimized via advertising, so do the new online channels. This creates a huge opportunity for you if you're willing to develop high-quality, helpful content that solves problems and answers questions buyers have today. These outlets need your content to populate their websites so they can monetize it via advertising. Thus, they will trade you exposure for content.

The benefit in crafting a guest post or an original article to appear on one of these sites is that it expands your presence while simultaneously reinforcing your expertise and reputation. Providing this content on these outposts exponentially increases your reach against the prospective target audience without the corresponding expense (advertising dollars). However, these media channels understand their value to you, the seller of goods and services. They understand that giving you the opportunity to guest post or guest author an article removes the impetus for you to pay to advertise to the audience they have spent time, money, and effort to acquire. Therefore, they will not extend this invitation to you or your company if you're providing selling versus helping content. The arrangement must have a *quid pro quo*.

To solicit guest post opportunities, you need to establish a track record on your own website first. You must create a portfolio of high-quality useful and helpful content. Then identify the websites and blogs that your prospects read and request guest-authoring opportunities. (We'll talk more about the specifics of this process in Chapter 16.) Someone from the sites you've contacted will visit your site and review your past content to see if your style and content fit their audience.

And if you're lucky and you do a really good job of developing an audience for your material, you might have some of these outposts contact you directly to request that you guest author a post or an article for their audience. This is a far rarer occurrence but it does happen. This phenomenon is not just limited to online entities. Offline media such as newspapers and magazines (especially trade magazines) are always seeking high-quality, low-cost or free content that they can publish. Many of these organizations even offer you an ongoing contributing writer role. Although they do not compensate you for your content, they give you a sizable built-in audience that you can market to in the form of educational content, positioning you as an expert or "best choice" solution.

## POWER POINTS

- Helping content creates buying signals that better inform your sales team's sales calls.

- Buyers, especially those that are still unsure of how to solve a problem, are searching online for helpful content.

- Providing helpful content on your website is the online equivalent of a product sample.

- Creating helping content is easier and more targeted than creating selling content.

- When you develop a reputation for creating high-quality, helping content, you can reduce your advertising and marketing costs by placing that content (with your byline) on targeted media content sites.

*Download all the Power Points at TheInvisibleSale.com.*

# 6

# Social Agents

There are two kinds of people in digital networking: social agents and prospects. You've probably already figured out what prospects are, but maybe you're wondering what agents—especially social agents—have to do with growing your business. Social agents are people that amplify your message by sharing your content online. They introduce you to prospective customers—both offline and online. Social agents may never do business with you but they love recommending you to others.

The single biggest mistake salespeople make is focusing exclusively on prospects and ignoring social agents. You see this every day online and offline. You meet someone at a networking or cocktail event. Eventually, the "So what do you do?" question is popped, and you answer. When you answer, the person you're chatting with immediately places you into one of two boxes: prospect or not a prospect.

If you're in the prospect box, the conversation continues as they try to qualify how good of a prospect you are for their company. They probably find a way to give you a business card and, well, you kind of know how this story ends, right?

As soon as your answer clearly places you in the second box, as not a prospect, the person continues polite chitchat and then usually develops the need for a drink, food, or a bathroom. You never hear from them again. This is a huge mistake.

Here's why.

Even though you might not be a true prospect for that person you just met, you can serve a far more important role in their prospect development plan than even the best future customer will today or tomorrow. You might never buy a thing from that person, but you can become his or her best source of revenue.

What that salesperson didn't understand is that a prospect is an opportunity to make a single sale. But befriending a social agent creates an opportunity to make lots of sales. And although you're not a prospect in that person's world, you might just be his or her next social agent. You could be the person who can help that salesperson make not just one, but many sales. But because you didn't have your special social agent clothes on, they didn't recognize you.

## Social Agents Are Your Social Sales Force

Humans have limits. When it comes to networking, selling, or any other one-to-one effort, there are only 24 hours in a day, 7 days in a week, and 12 months in a year. Subtract things like sleep, kids, wives and husbands, and a need to do something besides just working for a living, and you start to figure out that one person can contact only so many people in a meaningful manner. That's why companies developed sales forces to begin with and continue to field them today.

Science also tells us that humans have another constraining factor in their ability to network. It's called Dunbar's Number,[1] and an evolutionary psychologist named Robin Dunbar developed it. Dunbar theorized that "this limit is a direct function of relative neocortex size, and that this in turn limits group size.... [T]he limit imposed by neocortical processing capacity is simply on the number of individuals with whom a stable inter-personal relationship can be maintained."[2] Dunbar's research pegged this number at 148 (often rounded up to 150, for convenience). So according to Dunbar, you can maintain meaningful relationships with only 150 people at a time.

---

1. Drake Bennett, "The Dunbar Number, from the Guru of Social Networks," *Business Week*, www. businessweek.com/articles/2013-01-10/the-dunbar-number-from-the-guru-of-social-networks#p1.

2. http://en.wikipedia.org/wiki/Dunbar's_number.

You might be thinking that social media networks such as Facebook, Twitter, LinkedIn, and Google+ give you the ability to blow past Dunbar's Number. A 2011 paper[3] showed that although both Facebook and Twitter allow you to develop a network far in excess of Dunbar's Number, the average Twitter user only interacts with between 100 and 200 people on a regular basis. And on Facebook, which allows up to 5,000 friends, the average person maintains contact with 190. So it seems that our biology, not our technology, drives our ability to network in a meaningful manner.

But what does all this have to do with social agents? Glad you asked. Let's get back to that idea of building a social sales force. Dunbar's science is telling you that the only way you can effectively create a massive prospecting program online or offline is to leverage *your* network. And that's where the ability to build a social sales force powered by social agents can mean the difference between finding and missing an invisible sale.

Think about that for a second. What if you had a social sales force? One that you didn't pay to promote you, but that instead promoted you, your company, and its products and services just because they felt a sense of attachment to your company. We talk more about that sense of attachment in Chapter 10, "Social Selling"; for now, think about your Dunbar's Number. Take a moment to think about the 150 people you know well enough to strike up a meaningful conversation with as soon as you see them online or offline.

Now do the math. Dunbar's Number tells us that each of those 150 people have 149 other people (assuming you're included in their Dunbar's Number) they can strike up a conversation with at any moment. Let's also assume that each of the folks we're talking about here has strong enough relationships with their circle that they can influence that circle to take certain actions. We could continue opening wider concentric circles, but I think after you see the math behind just the first-degree social army, you'll want to think more about identifying your social agents.

1st Degree: 150 of your contacts × 149 contacts for each person = 22,350 contacts

To be fair, not all of your 150 might truly be able or willing to serve as social agents. But even if only 50% of them decided to work on your behalf and share your story with the world, that's 11,175 unqualified prospects that are just an introduction away. But remember, this is based on the strict one-to-one Dunbar's Number. We haven't even factored in the power of social media networking, which really begins to amplify the social agent effect through their weaker networking relationships on social platforms, where the agent can, at a minimum, create awareness of you by sharing your content.

---

3. "The Dunbar Number, from the Guru of Social Networks."

# Power Agents

In today's hyperconnect, social media-powered world, you don't always need that agent to have a close relationship with another person to create that all-important introduction. Social agents that are very active on social media networks and have established very large networks wield a great deal of online power. While they may not be able to maintain strong relationships with more than 150 people, they can maintain weaker, yet still persuasive, relationships with far more than 150 people.

This is important because every day, people are asking for help and suggestions to help them make a buying decision. And because your social agents are givers, they're often the first people to offer up help to anyone they see asking questions online.

Whether it's something as general as a person asking for a restaurant recommendation or as specific as a person asking for opinions of one company versus another, these online selling moments are happening every day. And although the receiver of the recommendation might not have a personal or close relationship with your agent, that person might consider the agent's opinion valuable and act on any recommendation provided.

In fact, as I write this book, companies are spending a lot of time and money trying to identify these kinds of social agents. They just don't call them agents—they call them influencers. But the value of the relationship is the same: to create more opportunities for your company to be recommended to a prospective customer at the point of need.

And that is the true power of social media networks. Not only can they turn a social agent into a power agent, but they also make it easy for that social-powered agent to reach out and provide help to an audience sized well beyond Dunbar's Number.

# Agents Want to Help

But the power of social agents isn't just that they have a network you can tap. No, the power of agents is that they *want* to help you tap their network. They want you to do well. They're rooting for you—sometimes even if you're the competition.

Let me take a moment to share a real-life story of how one of my competitors became one of my biggest agents, and I his.

Dave Serino (@DavidSerino on Twitter) was (and arguably still is) a direct competitor of mine. Dave does social media, email marketing, and such for tourism clients, mostly convention and visitors bureaus and destination marketing organizations. These are the folks who are responsible for marketing cities, states, and communities to tourists and meeting planners.

Like Dave, I focus on that market segment as well. But as luck would have it, Dave and I had a common friend: Theresa Overby, who, at the time, was in charge of marketing for Visit Baton Rouge. Dave was starting a new tourism conference and mentioned to Theresa (who promotes both Dave and me) that he was looking for good speakers.

Theresa suggested that he take a look at me, which he did. After vetting me on Twitter for a bit, reading my blog, and checking out some of my presentations that I had posted online using SlideShare (more on that in Chapter 15, "Creating Live and Recorded Webinars and Product Tutorials"), he reached out.

We chatted via phone. After hearing what he was trying to create, I agreed to waive my speaking fees and deliver the opening presentation at his brand-new conference later that year. That event led to a great relationship that has spawned numerous other leads for me. In fact, Dave went on to recommend me for a paid speaking engagement at a travel conference in his own backyard full of his prospects.

From his #SoMeT Conference, I met the incredibly giving Bill Geist, who has turned out to be a great agent and has helped me meet the right people and book important, influential speaking engagements. Bill speaks a lot at various tourism conferences around the country and has routinely referenced ideas and concepts he first heard at one of my presentations. He promotes me often and even passed my name along to the folks at DMAI (Destination Marketing Association International), who stage what is arguably one of the largest, most important tourism conferences in the country—and they booked me to speak. Speaking at these two conferences led to more speaking at other tourism conferences and resulted in new tourism clients for my firm.

You might read that story and think, "Tom, those aren't social agents working on your behalf—those are just routine referrals." And that's a fair argument, but here's the difference: Theresa passed my name to Dave because she wanted me to succeed. She knew that I had just started my business and that speaking at Dave's conference would help me. Bill didn't just refer my name to the DMAI. He followed up with me and even put in a good word on my behalf. You could almost say he campaigned for me to be placed on a stage.

And that is what makes social agents so important to your efforts to win the invisible sale. These social agents are hearing opportunities you can't hear. They are recommending you to people you don't know. Just as a Hollywood talent agent helps actors get parts, these social agents help you book sales.

The representation goes both ways. I tell everyone in tourism to attend Dave's annual #SoMeT Conference. I don't just tell them to attend—I tell them that if they can go to only one tourism conference, make it #SoMeT. I don't do it because Dave recommends me for something. I do it because I want Dave to succeed even if that means he'll end up working for some of the same clients I'd like to work with in the future. And that's okay; in the online world, all boats rise. Being a good person and helping others succeed even when you don't personally benefit is the undercurrent that powers social media networking.

So the question you have to ask yourself is this: Can you find folks like Dave, Theresa, Bill, and me in your network and then cultivate them to promote your company loudly and often?

## What Makes a Great Agent?

Suffice it to say that not everyone in your contact list will be a good agent. And if you don't invest in the relationships first, no one will want to represent you. But assuming that you're investing in the relationships in a real and genuine way, here are a few characteristics of a good agent.

- **Agents like you.** I don't just mean that agents like you on a personal level—that's a given. No, I mean that they need to be like you. Look for folks who share your worldview, who think like you do, and who value what you value. These should be folks you'd gladly spend a day with and genuinely look forward to being around or talk with over the phone. This is important. It gives them permission to promote you because, in promoting you, they are promoting a piece of themselves.

- **Background singers make great agents.** You want people with a strong sense of self, people who are comfortable in their own skin and don't feel threatened by the success of those around them. They believe that there is enough business to go around, and they're more interested in being around greatness than being that greatness. This comfort, this ability to see your star rise even at the expense of their star, makes for a powerful agent. Think about the relationship Dave and I have. Would it work if either of us couldn't be happy singing background vocals for the other?

- **They give more than they take.** Let's face it; if it's all about them, they're not going to be a very good agent. Great agents give first and take second. They love helping others succeed as much as success itself. That's why they end up working hard on your behalf. They see your success, or at least the part they helped create, as success for themselves.

## Which Is More Important—Agents or Prospects?

It's a trick question—both are equally important to your success. You need to have prospects to pay the bills today, but if you put your prospecting blinders on, you'll miss the opportunities of tomorrow.

Furthermore, you can't be everywhere. You can't hear every conversation. You can't know about every lead. You need a network of opportunity spotters. You need a network of folks who will gladly recommend you to a friend, colleague, or boss. And if you truly hope to build a Painless Prospecting platform, you need a big network of social agents who can and will amplify your content online so that you can create that all-important top-of-mind-preference among your prospects, both visible and invisible.

Let me finish with one last important point. When looking for social agents, don't disregard that wider social network you are developing. And don't ever, even for a second, think that you have all the agents you need. As you move through life, especially if you get active in the social networking space, you'll constantly bump into new people. Most of those people will remain weak relationships, but a precious few will escalate to become true friends and helpful agents—and it doesn't take long, trust me.

Cultivate those relationships at all costs. When someone tells you to quit playing on Twitter and start making a few phone calls, tell them you'll get to that in a minute. The time you spend tending to your flock of social agents will repay you many times over—and often at the times when you least expect it but most require it.

## POWER POINTS

- Just because someone isn't a prospect for your service or product doesn't mean that person isn't a valuable contact who should be nurtured.

- Prospects buy from you. Social agents tell everyone to buy from you.

- Social agents are your social sales force. They are on the social networks, hearing opportunities you can't hear and, more important, recommending you to people you don't know.

- The key to a great agent is that they desire to help you—it's personal.

- In a self-educating, digitally powered world, a good social agent might just become the most valuable customer you never sell anything to.

*Download all the Power Points at TheInvisibleSale.com.*

# 7

# Propinquity

The law of propinquity states that the greater the physical (or psychological) proximity is between people, the greater the chance that they will form friendships or romantic relationships. The theory was first crafted by psychologists Leon Festinger, Stanley Schachter, and Kurt Back in what came to be called the Westgate studies conducted at MIT.[1]

The study investigated how friendships developed among students at the new Westgate Complex at MIT. The results clearly showed the role of proximity in the formation of friendships. The strongest friendships developed between students who lived next to each other on the same floor. Where friendships developed between students who lived on different floors, one of those students tended to live near the stairways.

---

1. E. Hatfield, J. T. Cacioppo, and R. L. Rapson, *Emotional Contagion: Current Directions in Psychological Science.* Thousand Oaks, CA: Sage Publications, Inc., 1993.

In nonscientific terms, the Westgate Studies found that the ability to frequently "bump into each other" [my terms] led to the formation of friendships.

Numerous other studies confirm the Propinquity Effect. One of the more intriguing ones was conducted in Philadelphia.[2] James Brossard used the addresses found on 5,000 consecutive Philadelphia marriage licenses to determine whether proximity had a role in marriage partner selection.

Brossard found that 16% of the couples lived within one block of one another. Thirty-three percent lived within 5 blocks of each other, and 52% lived within 20 blocks of one another. (Note: The numbers do not add to 100 because of rounding.) In a later study in Columbus, Ohio, researchers found that 50% of married couples lived within 1 mile of each other at the time of their first date.[3]

Research has found various types of propinquity, including *industry/occupational propinquity*, in which similar people working in the same industry or company tend to be attracted to one another. I have this one to thank for my wife. There's also *residential propinquity*, in which people living in the same area or within the same neighborhoods tend to come together (such as we saw in the Westgate Studies). Finally, *acquaintance propinquity* is a form of propinquity in which friends develop a special bond of interpersonal attraction based on shared beliefs and attitudes.

With the advent of social media and other Internet-based platforms such as video conferencing, current research is exploring the concept of *virtual propinquity*. Interestingly, though, early research shows that physical proximity is still a powerful variable and predictor of friendship and influence.[4]

But for the purposes of this chapter and book, I want to propose a new version of propinquity: *marketing propinquity*. Similar to the other forms of propinquity, marketing propinquity results from increased interactions between a prospective customer and a brand or company that sells products or services that solve a problem for that prospective customer. In other words, the prospect "bumps into" the brand or company.

---

2. James Brossard, "Residential Propinquity As a Factor in Marriage Selection," *American Journal of Sociology* Vol 38 (September 1932): 288–294.

3. Alfred C. Clarke, "An Examination of the Operation of Residential Propinquity As a Factor in Mate Selection," *American Sociological Review* XVII (February 1952): 17–22.

4. "Distance Matters: Physical Space and Social Impact," *Personality and Social Psychology Bulletin* 21(8) (1995): 795–805.

# Marketing Propinquity

Two types of marketing propinquity exist: physical and psychological. The first, physical, also has two dimensions: time and place. The latter is strictly a subjective measure to the prospective customer. It's harder to formally define, but I think it's more powerful.

First, let's think about propinquity from a physical interaction point of view. If you consider all prospect interactions as physical (even those that occur online), we can agree that a physical interaction is simply a point in time when your marketing efforts, products or services, or salespeople come into direct contact with a prospective customer.

For instance, when a prospect reads an article about your product in a magazine or consumes an advertisement in another magazine, those two intersections are considered physical *bumps*. Likewise, when a salesperson meets a prospect at a conference or a prospect visits the trade show booth, a *bump* occurs. We could go through all the ways your marketing message can bump into a prospect, but you've probably got the point now. Each of these bumps is equal to a propinquity point, a place or channel where a prospective buyer is exposed to your company.

As I said, these physical bumps have a second dimension of proximity: time. I can thank my good friend Jim Elms for introducing me to the idea of propinquity scheduling of media impressions. Back in our Peter Mayer Advertising days (circa late 1990s), Jim began to toy with the idea of moving away from the standard top-of-mind awareness (TOMA) approach to media planning and buying for our Tanger Factory Outlet Centers client. Under a TOMA approach, a marketer seeks to maximize both the reach (number of buyers who hear/see a message) and frequency (how many message exposures are received) during a media flight (a defined time period during which an advertising campaign runs). The theory is that a brand wants to achieve consistent TOMA so that when buyers move into active buying mode, the brand is one of the top brands they consider.

However, because Tanger is a factory outlet mall whose customer traffic primarily occurs during the weekends, Jim suggested that we move from a TOMA approach to a propinquity approach. At the time, I had never heard of propinquity scheduling. Jim explained that this meant we'd run advertising only Thursday through Sunday afternoon. The idea was that we didn't necessarily need to be the most remembered brand (TOMA) all week; we just needed to achieve TOMA right before consumers decided on their shopping destination or weekend planning decisions.

In Jim's plan, propinquity/proximity is defined in terms of both the physical channel through which customers would bump into Tanger's message *and* their closeness to a decision-making moment. And if you're wondering, yes, it worked.

Moving to propinquity scheduling and shifting our media flights to better match the natural shopper seasonality produced some pretty impressive results.

# Psychological Propinquity

Studies also demonstrate the power of psychological propinquity. You've likely heard it stated as the Law of Attraction—more colloquially, birds of a feather flock together. Humans tend to spend more time with people they perceive to be like them than people they feel are not like them. And by "like," I'm not referring to demographic likeness. I'm referring to psychographic or attitudinal likeness.

Again, for our purposes, we need to consider psychological propinquity in terms of understanding and then aligning with our prospective customers' interests, attitudes, values, backgrounds, and even personality to create an optimum buying environment.

Probably no brand does this better than Apple. When Steve Jobs returned to Apple in 1996, he focused the company and the brand around "Think Different." The brilliant advertising campaign linked using an Apple product to being different, being brilliant, and changing the world. It gave Apple users permission to be unlike their PC brethren and, more important, wear that difference as a badge of pride.

It was a classic example of psychological propinquity. Everything Apple did in its marketing and product design celebrated the triumph of ideas and passion over compliance. This tapped a deep emotional undercurrent and perfectly aligned the Apple brand with its customers'—and prospective customers'—core beliefs and attitudes.

Furthermore, when you explore Apple's product development, the focus on key interest areas such as audio and video creation with products such as GarageBand and iMovie further aligns the brand with its customers and, more important, prospective customers. Since the '90s, Apple has become the brand for people who desire beautiful products that just work. And in doing so, the company has been able to continue to enjoy a higher price point and margin for their products versus the competition's.

This same psychological approach holds true for you as you consider how to market to the invisible sale. Because so much of your efforts will be content driven, which we cover in detail in Chapter 8, "The Painless Prospecting Framework," you have an unprecedented opportunity to establish psychological propinquity with your prospective buyers without having to spend millions on traditional mass media advertising as Apple did.

You need to map your customers' and prospective customers' various interests, beliefs, and personality preferences. In the case of Apple, that includes, but is not limited to, creative expression, individuality, and a preference for smart, confident people who are comfortable being a little different than the status quo.

You need to craft a simple Venn diagram such as Figure 7-1. First, you need to consider the entire prospect universe. Then look at your best clients and your highest conversion prospects, and deconstruct their interests, beliefs, and personality preferences. Next, look at your own company and your product or brand. Define what interests and beliefs your company holds dear. Look at your culture, your marketing materials, and your marketing and sales groups to deconstruct your corporate personality. Finally, look for the overlaps between your corporate circle and your prospect circle. In this overlap space, you have the opportunity to create psychological proximity by working those ideas and beliefs into your marketing content. The same holds true for the personality. Imbue your content with personality traits that your target prospects desire.

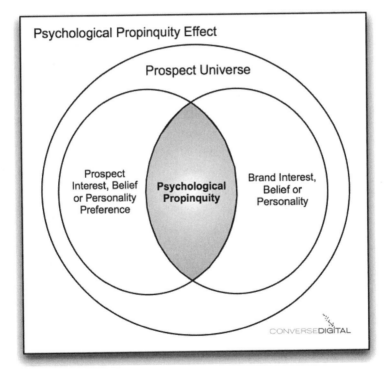

**Figure 7-1**  *The psychological propinquity map*

# Propinquity Is the New TOMA

Back in the 1990s, as Jim Elms and I were exploring propinquity- versus TOMA-based media buying strategies, we missed one important point. We were seeing the two as options instead of complementary ideas.

As I've continued to evolve my thinking on propinquity over the years, I've come to a new realization: Marketing propinquity isn't a replacement for TOMA; it's an evolution of the idea. Let me take a minute to explain where I'm going here because it will be important as you begin thinking through how you're going to build out your own Painless Prospecting framework.

As I noted earlier, TOMA stands for top-of-mind awareness. For many companies, it has long been the holy grail of marketing metrics because it is easily measured. To measure TOMA, you hire a research firm and field a phone study that asks each respondent to answer the same question. Usually the question goes something like, "When you think of [category, product, or service], which [company, product, service] comes to mind?"

The company named by the respondent is credited with TOMA for that respondent. Respondents are then asked if they can name any additional companies in the category; if they do, those companies also receive a secondary TOMA credit. Usually, these results are listed with the TOMA winner and the Top 2 Box companies—that is, the companies that received the second- and third-most mentions after the initial TOMA mention was recorded. This secondary TOMA is usually framed as a follow-up question after the respondent provides the initial TOMA answer. They're asked, "Do any other companies besides [TOMA mention] come to mind when you think of [category]?"

Why is this the holy grail of marketing metrics? Why do companies focus so much on achieving TOMA? Because before digital tracking of pre-purchase buyers, companies had no easy way to understand which prospects were and were not actively in buying mode. Therefore, the thinking was that if your product or service was always the TOMA winner (or at least Top 2 Box TOMA), then when that prospective customer did move into buying mode, your brand would be included in the consideration set. But although TOMA strategies are true and effective, they're traditionally expensive, especially for products and services that are purchased year-round compared to those with highly seasonal purchase patterns. Furthermore, TOMA strategies really only focus on the very top of the sales funnel: awareness. Before digital self-education capabilities, this was enough because, to complete their purchase research, prospective customers had to call and talk to your sales team. However, with the Internet and Google, that's often no longer the case, as we saw in Chapter 3, "The Self-Educating Buyer."

Enter propinquity marketing, which helps move a prospective customer from simple TOMA to actual brand preference. This approach leverages the Propinquity Effect to move buyers beyond awareness, to gaining knowledge, to liking, and, ultimately, to making a purchase consideration.

# From TOMA to TOMP

In today's overcommunicated world, simply establishing awareness among your self-educating target audience isn't nearly enough. Even top-of-mind-awareness just gets you invited to the search engine dance. If you want to win the invisible sale, you need to go beyond simple awareness to establish preference.

I call this goal top-of-mind preference (TOMP). (Don't fret if you haven't heard the term—I made it up.) But it should absolutely be your propinquity marketing goal. The propinquity model is quite simple:

To see me → To know me → To like me → To buy from me

So although TOMA might be easy to track, it only gets you two steps deep in the funnel. TOMP, on the other hand, gets you all the way to the third level, often before prospects have even raised a hand to identify themselves to your organization.

Because a propinquity approach is based on creating and sharing helpful content and advice, it's perfectly suited to create preference among your prospective customers. It's easy to ignore the hard sell. But when a person or company displays chivalry and honestly tries to help you make a better buying decision, it's hard not to like that person or company. Not only does that become the first company you think of, but it also becomes your preferred company—possibly the *only* company you will turn to for assistance.

# Propinquity in Practice

To better explain propinquity marketing and how it works with TOMP strategies, take a look at a hypothetical example for one of my pet passions: RVing. For this example, we select Thor, one of the biggest manufacturers of towables (those RV campers you tow behind your vehicle) and powered recreational vehicles (RVs).

At the top of the funnel, Thor wants prospective buyers to be aware of the Thor brand. This helps drive consideration and search. Thor would love for a prospective buyer to enter "Thor RVs" or "Thor towable" in the Google search query box. So for both of these reasons, a TOMA marketing strategy makes a lot of sense. But how might Thor go beyond TOMA to drive TOMP via a propinquity strategy?

First, by using offline research such as MRI (a third-party service media planners use to plan paid media buys) combined with primary research studies fielded against its current customer base, Thor can map out key propinquity points where it can most likely expect its message/content to bump into a prospective customer.

Second, using online research tools such as Google's Keyword Research Tool, Thor can determine how prospective buyers are searching to identify key category search terms. Google's tool lets you enter in a search phrase that you think prospective buyers use and find out how many monthly searches (on average) use that term.

Once Thor determines the top keyword search strings, they can identify the online media properties that show up highest in Google search results for each of those search strings. From there, Thor can leverage online traffic-projection tools such as Compete and Nielsen to understand how many prospective buyers and current owners of towables and RVs are congregating at each of these media properties.

Combining and cross-referencing this data develops a set of key propinquity points. For the purposes of this example, let's say that one of those propinquity points is guest posts on the Woodalls Blog (http://blog.woodalls.com)—specifically, reviews of common camping equipment such as stoves and grills.

From this data, Thor decides that it will create numerous camping equipment review posts that it can post on its own website and, more important, can submit as guest posts on the Woodalls blog. If those guest posts are accepted by Woodalls, prospective buyers will see the Thor brand at a key propinquity point. But the company doesn't stop here. It decides to share that Woodalls blog post on the Thor Facebook page, where fans can see, like, comment, and, most important, share the post.

Taking it one step further, Thor pays to advertise the Facebook post to married males ages 25 to 59 with children between the ages of 5 and 14 who profess to like camping because Thor's research shows that this group is an ideal prospect profile. Finally, Thor might post its product review on the product listings that appear on Amazon and offer to provide reviews to the manufacturers to use in their own content marketing and email efforts.

Now, assuming that Thor's research shows that the most likely buyers spend time on Facebook, like camping, read the Woodalls blog, and use Amazon to make camping equipment purchases, the company has just created the opportunity to have its brand bump into that prospective consumer multiple times. Each time, Thor is seen as a helpful, informed, and honest camping brand.

So with virtually no marketing spend, Thor can create enormous amounts of propinquity. But more important, when its prospects decide to invest in an RV or towable, Thor is not only the TOMA leader (hopefully), but it has established the brand as knowledgeable and helpful—the TOMP leader, too.

# Hurdles to Achieving Propinquity

The single biggest challenge to establishing an effective propinquity-based approach is the multichannel world we live in today. Not only do we have difficulty linking online and offline activity, but the online channel has fragmented into desktop, mobile phone, and tablet consumption. And as each additional channel is added to the mix, it becomes more difficult to track buyer activity and content consumption across all channels and devices to create a single prospective buyer dossier for the sales team.

Today companies in the online space are trying to create the über-cookie. A cookie is a small piece of code that websites place on computers and mobile devices to track a device as it surfs the website and, in some cases, even after it leaves the website to surf others. Tracking a single computer as it surfs the vastness of the Internet is fairly simple, but you need a second piece of information to create an identifiable dossier of that activity. The same can be said of mobile devices such as smartphones and tablet computers. You need something that is personally identifiable.

Most companies elect to use emails as the single referring record in their marketing database. Because an email can be "automatically" captured online via a download or subscription and then linked to a cookie, it is the preferred method. Additionally, capturing email at the point of an offline bump (such as a trade show or an event promotion) and then manually pushing associated information into the marketing database can help you link offline and online activity.

Where it becomes the most difficult is tracking self-educating buyers as they seamlessly move from desktop, to phone, to tablet in conducting their research. Unless you entice the prospect to download or subscribe to something on your site from each of these devices, correlating activities across devices becomes almost impossible.

Companies such as Drawbridge are trying to use highly sophisticated data analysis approaches to create the correlation and then place a cookie on each device. However, even if this is successful, it shows only that a single user is consuming content across each of those devices. It doesn't help you identify the buyer or link that buyer's data to offline activities. To do that, you still need either an email or a phone number to serve as the primary record field from which to develop a dossier.

# The Propinquity Solution

Luckily, an entire industry is trying to solve this issue. Commonly referred to as marketing automation, companies such as Marketo, HubSpot, ActOn,

InfusionSoft, and others have developed SaS (software as solution) platforms that help companies capture email addresses of self-educating buyers and then link those addresses to all content consumed on the company's website. These companies don't (and can't) address the entirety of the propinquity landscape to create a single source dossier, but they are likely some of the better-placed companies in terms of eventually creating such a solution. Their approach of enticing a file download in return for the prospect providing an email address, is a significant step toward turning that invisible site traffic into visible prospect dossiers.

Today their systems allow the tracking and reporting of all prospect contacts within your website and email campaigns. And although it's not a perfect solution, it's certainly a big step toward a true propinquity marketing dashboard. And it's a step that any company seriously chasing the invisible sale should be evaluating closely.

## POWER POINTS

- Propinquity defined: To see me → To know me → To like me → To buy from me

- The greater the physical or psychological proximity between a company and prospect, the more likely strong bonds will form.

- In a search engine-based world, top-of-mind awareness isn't enough to win the sale. Companies need to strive for top-of-mind preference to best position themselves to win the invisible sale.

- The biggest hurdle to tracking propinquity is the multidevice world we live in today. Because buyers are moving from mobile, to tablet, to laptop as they move through their research, establishing the traffic as the same buyer becomes difficult.

*Download all the Power Points at TheInvisibleSale.com.*

# 8

# Creating Your Painless Prospecting Platform

As we discussed in Chapter 7, "Propinquity," the key to winning the Invisible Sale is to create the opportunity for propinquity between you and an unqualified prospect. The heart of this strategy is built on creating helpful, relevant content that is strategically dispersed throughout the websites and social networks favored by your prospects—what I call your Painless Prospecting platform, or your digital footprint. As your unqualified prospects move through your platform and run into you and your content repeatedly, they begin to qualify themselves through their actions and interactions with you and your content. The Painless Prospecting platform has three legs. In this chapter, I take you through a step-by-step process to create them.

The first leg is your Home Base. Everything you do online and offline is designed to drive prospects to your Home Base. Your Home Base needs to be a corporate website, a blog, or both. If your company has multiple product lines, you might have multiple Home Bases. Regardless, your goal is to always drive prospects back to your Home Base, where you can use your content and tracking technology to qualify prospects and drive them down the appropriate sales funnel.

The second leg is your outposts. Two kinds of outposts exist: open and closed. Although they are different, they share a single similarity, which makes them important to you. Both types of outposts are places where prospects are hanging out or turning to for information they use to make better buying decisions or self-educate themselves. These outposts serve as prospect acquisition points in your Painless Prospecting platform, and you need to actively publish content to these outposts.

The third leg of your platform is embassies. Similar to outposts, embassies are places where you find and interact with prospects but in a much deeper and engaged manner. Embassies are where you'll plant a flag and plan to spend a good amount of time interacting with the people you find there. Unlike outposts, effective embassy management requires plenty of work and a hefty time investment on your part. You'll have only a few embassies in your platform, so you need to select them strategically to maximize the effectiveness of your prospecting platform.

The competition for your prospects' attention, especially repeat attention, is incredibly high and growing by the minute. So it is imperative to establish a digital footprint that extends far beyond your own corporate website or blog. However, simply building your platform isn't enough—you must be able to sustain your presence throughout your entire footprint. Just as a great army's advance is limited by the strength of its supply lines, you must think about how far you can stretch your content supply line to maintain an effective digital presence among the far-flung points of your prospecting platform.

Finally, keep in mind that your prospecting platform is not a static digital footprint. It ebbs and flows as you, or your company, emphasize different products or services. As you move in new directions or target new audiences, your platform morphs to match.

In some cases, that might mean adding new outposts or embassies. In other situations, it means reducing the footprint or abandoning certain propinquity points. There's no perfect science here; there's only trial and error. There's simply not enough history from which we can draw valid conclusions and say with absolute certainty what's right for every industry or every prospect target market.

So as you embark on this journey to build your own Painless Prospecting platform, know that you will make mistakes along the way. Failures will occur. Platforms or outposts will end up not making sense or not generating a big enough return on your time and investment to justify continued involvement. That's okay. Failure is the price of learning. The key is to fail small while simultaneously setting yourself up to win big. We talk more about that a little later. For now, let's talk about the first leg: creating your Home Base.

# Creating Your Home Base

The single most important thing to think about when crafting your home base—your website or blog—is not how beautiful it is, but how well it functions. Probably the biggest mistake companies and people make when crafting a website is focusing entirely too much on the physical beauty of the site. Does it look cool? Does it make them look smart? Does it make them look sexy, or up-to-date, or high end, or any of a host of attributes that they want to associate with the brand or company?

Don't get me wrong—I'm not saying that visual aesthetics aren't important in web design. I am saying that form should follow function, not vice versa. Contrary to popular belief, your website is not an ad. And although visual aesthetics can add to or detract from brand perception, the fundamental role of your website is not to brand your company. The fundamental role of your website is to serve as the ultimate salesperson. In your website, you want to create a qualified lead-generation machine that is committed to achieving only one goal: the constant creation and qualification of convertible leads for your company.

The best websites in the world are often not the most beautiful, but almost always the most functional. Think about your own favorite websites. Open them on your Internet browser and look at them to see if you find a common theme. I'm willing to bet that looking at the sites side by side will turn up the common design theme of easy navigation. The sites you like the most will almost always be sites where you can most easily find the information or services you desire.

If you need a real-world example, you need look no further than the world of search engines. Picture Google.com in your mind. What do you see? A lot of white space, a search box, and two buttons. One button says Google Search, and the other says I'm Feeling Lucky. That's it. The site is plain, simple, and easy. It's no wonder this is the world's number-one search site. Now contrast that visual to Yahoo.com. And although some might argue that Yahoo! isn't just a search engine (and I agree), even if you go back in time to look at Yahoo!'s original incarnations when it was a search engine, it still did not possess the cleanliness and simplicity that Google favors. The point I'm making here is that you can't get caught up in creating sexy. Instead, get caught up in creating useful. If you can make your website useful, you can turn your website into that lead-generation machine I mentioned earlier.

# Designing a Funnel-Optimized Home Base

Probably the most important design concept you need to understand and adhere to in developing your Home Base is the idea of creating a funnel-optimized website or blog. By "funnel-optimized," I mean websites and blogs whose information architecture, visual interface, and content strategy are designed to move a visitor down one or more qualification funnels. Funnel-optimized websites are built and designed based on the achievement of sales goals. They are built and designed to try to push visitors through static and dynamic funnels where software tracks their behaviors. This tracked behavioral data is then converted into buying signals, which are pushed back to you and your company's sales teams.

The core of a funnel-optimized website is its information architecture. *Information architecture* is simply a fancy term that means we're going to plan how someone will move through our information on the website. A past theory in web design, and one some people still adhere to today, stated that because we can't anticipate how every visitor to our website will want to move through the information, we should simply create relatively flat websites and make it very easy for the visitor to jump from one content piece to another without any direction from us.

I think that opinion is wholly wrong. I believe visitors prefer for us to give them some structure. And that's what information architecture does. Information architecture involves sitting down and cataloging all the various content you intend to put on your website. You then determine the organizational structure of the content. You want to make sure a visitor to the site can immediately begin sending back those buying signals via onsite behaviors.

To help make this idea of information architecture more clear, look at Figure 8-1. This figure shows an information architecture schematic for a window company website. Usually a company will develop this schematic with the help of a web developer or digital marketing agency. But if you feel confident in your ability to craft it yourself, it certainly is within your ability to do so.

The document lays out all the major content pieces that will appear on the website and maps out how we will construct the navigation system for our visitor to move through the various content pieces. Notice that it's a very linear diagram. However, the web and HTML are based on nonlinear consumption of information. So although we are trying to encourage a certain linear pathway, we must also provide a secondary, nonlinear path that still achieves our goal of generating trackable buying signals.

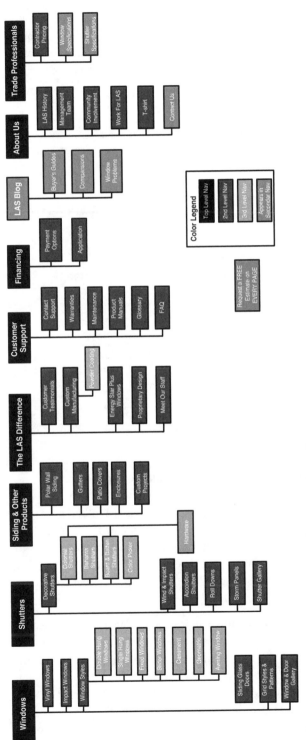

**Figure 8-1** *Sample information architecture schematic*

That's really the second layer of information architecture design. After you've laid out all your information in a two-dimensional grid and designated your navigation hierarchy (top-level navigation, secondary-level navigation, and tertiary-level navigation), you're ready to start thinking about the visual interface of your website, or what web designers often call a wireframe. See Figure 8-2 for an example of a basic wireframe.

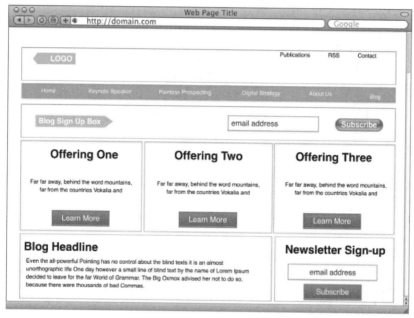

**Figure 8-2**  *Sample wireframe*

The power of a website and the Internet in general is that you aren't forced to read page 1, and then page 2, and then page 3, and so forth and so on. You have the opportunity to simply hyperlink, or click, from one page to another, even if those pages are not in any sort of linear order or even contained on the same website. This ability to move in a nonlinear manner has trained website visitors to expect you as the website owner to make finding related content easy. Think of the *Customers Who Viewed This Item Also Viewed* section on Amazon that appears each time you select a product on Amazon.

On your website, this nonlinear linking often appears as a related content area or section on each web page. This related content area forms the dynamic funnel that I just mentioned. I say that this creates dynamic funnels because any piece of content on a website likely has numerous buckets of related content. Thus, in your related content area, you can offer web visitors the opportunity to see related services, products, or knowledge. Depending on which content bucket they choose, you can begin to push them down one of your dynamic sales funnels. Let's look at an example of this dynamic funneling approach.

In Figure 8-3, you can see the related content block on a "How Much Should a Digital Marketing Strategy Cost" blog post from ConverseDigital.com. The primary content on the blog post is digital strategy and cost. Thus, if a website visitor is reading this blog post, we can safely assume that he or she is interested in digital strategy. What we can't necessarily understand is what aspect or aspects of digital strategy that person is primarily interested in. Thus, we use the related content section to let that prospect send an intent or buying signal via the content they click on next. In the related content area, you see links to additional digital strategy content that, once clicked, indicate interest in B2B marketing, B2B social media, mobile, email, or strategy. By clicking these links, the prospect sends a buying signal that we can track and eventually act on at the appropriate time.

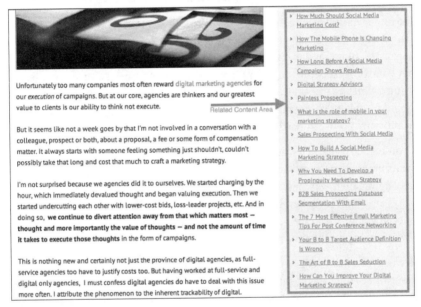

**Figure 8-3**  *Dynamic sales funnel example*

The last point to make here is that you have to build a Home Base that is mobile friendly. Visitors to your website or blog via a tablet or smartphone shouldn't have to pinch and squeeze or double-tap to zoom, or any of the other things we commonly do to view non-mobile-friendly sites on a smartphone. At the 2012 IAB Annual Leadership Meeting, Karim Temsamani of Google shared an interesting statistic. According to Google, upon landing on a non-mobile-friendly page from a mobile device, 61 percent of consumers[1] simply leave the website instead of attempting to manipulate the site through their phones so they can read it. We will

---

1. Karim Temsamani, 2012 IAB Meeting Annual Leadership Presentation, www.youtube.com/watch?v=uRR1dH5GFkw.

continue to see growth in the amount of content and information that is consumed on a handheld or tablet-based device versus a desktop or laptop computer. So do yourself a favor and make sure your Home Base is mobile friendly.

When you have your Home Base built and populated with relevant, helpful content, you're ready to begin building those other two legs of the Painless Prospecting platform: outposts and embassies. To begin that process, you first need to map all the relevant propinquity points where you can bump into your prospects. Usually two kinds of propinquity points exist: the obvious ones and the not-so-obvious ones. To succeed, you need to define both.

## Defining the Obvious Propinquity Points

The first step in defining your propinquity points is to start with the obvious ones. Ask yourself what are the key trade pubs, websites, trade shows, conferences, magazines, blogs, and even possibly television and radio programs or podcasts that your prospects turn to for information. You don't need any fancy research or third-party corroboration. If you simply pay attention to your prospects, you should be able to sit down with a pencil and paper and map out the most obvious propinquity points to reach your prospect.

If you're a B2B marketer, it's also important to remember that these propinquity points aren't always trade media channels. Your prospect is a person who reads the daily newspaper, watches the nightly news, and listens to local radio. This is especially important to remember if you're prospecting within your own geography, especially your own city—don't disregard your local media outlets. They can be powerful propinquity points.

So trust your knowledge of your prospects and their purchasing patterns. Think about where they might intentionally or unintentionally turn to for information about their industry or to purchase your specific product or service. Don't get caught up in trying to scientifically prove these propinquity points—just get them down on paper. Later in this process, you'll revisit each one to classify it. During that phase, you can always reconsider whether you want to keep or delete a particular point.

## Defining the Not-So-Obvious Propinquity Points

After you have defined the obvious propinquity points, it's time to take on the more difficult tasks of uncovering the points that aren't as obvious but are just as important. The technique for doing this varies by category, industry, and prospect type. And although there's no one way to do this, you can use this four-step process as your starting point. It's the same process I use with my clients, and we find it to be an excellent jumping-off point. As you work through this process, you might find certain steps more or less effective. That's fine and expected. Feel free to skip steps that don't generate good results for you, and spend more time with the ones that do. Chances are, you'll even discover a few new tactics or processes that help you discover key propinquity points for your industry.

The most important point is to be prepared to get frustrated. To map these less obvious propinquity points, you have to channel your inner Sherlock Holmes. And just like Sherlock Holmes or any other detective, you have to do the work, invest the time, and expend a lot of energy searching for clues you can follow. You need to piece together these clues to ultimately find those less obvious propinquity points. Often these searches require you to combine multiple tools and approaches. And that's why I'm warning you now that this is a frustrating process that's never fully complete. Stay the course, though: In the end, the results are well worth the effort. Now let's walk though the four steps one at a time.

# Step 1: Social Listening

You'd be surprised at what people will tell you if you just listen. And nowhere is this more apparent than in social media. Using special web-based software, you can eavesdrop on anything a person is sharing publicly via Twitter, Facebook, LinkedIn, or Google+; in blog comments; in forums; or on their own blog. Because you can cast such a wide information-gathering net, social listening is the perfect place to begin your investigation efforts.

You begin a social listening investigation in two ways. Traditionally, you begin by monitoring the Internet for mentions of keywords related to your product or service. The problem with this approach is that you are listening to the *entire* Internet. Thus, if you sell in only a specific geographic area, such as a certain city, you have to wade through a lot of noise to find the signal (the information you're actually looking for). Recently, new technology has emerged that allows you to focus your social listening to specific geographic areas such as cities, blocks, or even buildings. The downside of this approach is that you can't monitor all forms of digital communications. However, what you give up in breadth of listening, you gain in focus of listening. For the best results, plan to combine both versions of listening to get a complete picture of the online conversation surrounding your product or service.

To demonstrate how this works in the real world, let's revisit my Thor RV example from Chapter 7.

Using a tool such as Google's Keyword Generator Tool (https://adwords.google.com/o/KeywordTool), we can find all the terms people use to search for RV information online. By entering "RV" in the tool's search box, we can find hundreds of related keyword combinations and an indication of how popular each combination is in terms of Google web search volume. The theory here is that if people are using those terms to search for content, then those are terms they'd also use in their everyday online and social media conversations discussing RVs.

You can do your own search to see how the tool works. To demonstrate how this works in the Thor RV example, I ran a search, and the tool returned these words, among others:

- Toy hauler
- Fifth wheel
- RV rentals
- Campers
- RV park
- Travel trailers
- RV for sale
- Camping trailer
- Motorhome

With these keywords in hand, you can begin your investigation. As with anything in marketing, you can find free, low-cost, and enterprise (read: expensive) tools on the market that will help you conduct this research.

Two free tools that I like are SocialMention.com and Mention.net. Both enable you to create customized searches involving multiple keyword terms. Both supply results from all major social media platforms, including places such as YouTube and comments made on blogs and in forums. Social Mention is a completely free service. Mention.net offers a free trial, but it's ultimately a low-cost social listening platform designed to let you both listen and interact with prospects and customers. You'll probably want to check out both platforms, as well as any new ones that have sprouted since I've written this chapter.

You'll also find paid (enterprise) solutions such as Radian6, Sysomos, and a host of others. New ones seem to be popping up every day. These tools enable you to do more intensive searches and give you a host of more advanced analytical tools to make your investigations more efficient and effective. However, whether you choose paid or free tools, the goal is the same: You are trying to understand what online destinations your prospects are frequenting so that you can intercept them with your content or presence to create that propinquity bump we talked about in Chapter 7.

These online destinations include websites, blogs, and forums where the incidence of keyword use is high and where a significant number of prospects congregate.

In the case of microblogs such as Twitter, this might be relevant Twitter Chats[2] (ad hoc, real-time chat rooms created via the use of a hashtag on Twitter) where prospects and customers are coming together online to talk about RV'ing. In either case, you'll want to start a list (Excel is great for this) of the sites, forums, and hashtags where you find an abundance of these conversations. These data points are your first clues.

To find these points, you begin by using the listening software to create focused searches around the keywords. The software scours the digital landscape for blog posts, tweets, Facebook posts, and other entries containing any or all of the keywords. When the software has located all these posts, it displays them much like you're used to seeing in a Google search result. From there, you can review each post for the clues I mentioned. Specifically, you're looking for digital destinations that appear more often. This might be an Internet forum or an independent blog that shows up often in your search results.

The other thing you're looking for is social media posts that contain links. You want to look at the underlying content behind the links because if those links are shared on Twitter, for instance, they'll be shortened. Thus, simply looking at the link inside the tweet won't show you the real website that was shared. As you follow these links to see what websites are being shared, keep track of the sites. Again, you're looking for websites that are shared more often by a significant percentage of people using your keywords in their social sharing posts. This suggests that your prospects value those sites, and you might want to investigate publishing your content on those sites.

## Step 2: Geographic Social Listening

If your prospective customers gather in known places, such as a trade show, conference, sporting event, or festival, you can use special social listening software to monitor some of their social media posts while they're in these locations. B2B marketers can apply this same approach to a place of business: They can listen for most public social media information being shared by employees of a company while at the office. This can be especially helpful when your sales efforts are focused on selling to specific companies or you are trying to identify prospects within a company.

Location social monitoring platforms let you define a geographic area as small as a city block or even a building and then listen for all public social media posts on Twitter, Foursquare, Instagram, YouTube, and, in some cases, Facebook that emanate from within that geographic location. You won't be able to hear *everything* your prospect is doing online from these locations, but you will be able to filter out

---

2. Converse Digital Blog, "What Is a Tweet Chat and How Do I Participate," www.conversedigital.com/sales-prospecting/twitter-chats-b2b-sales-leads.

a lot of social media noise and just listen to what should be highly targeted customer and prospect conversations.

Let's talk about how you might use this to help define propinquity points for Thor RV. It's hard to know which social media profiles do and do not belong to a current RV owner. Unless a person uses RV keywords often or uses them in a bio, it becomes almost impossible to classify the person as an RV owner. But with location social monitoring, you can do so.

You can listen to all the social conversations emanating from RV parks and RV shows throughout the United States—or maybe just specific parks or shows that you know are favored by the customers you want to attract. By creating listening profiles based on geographic location, you create a single stream of RV conversations. Because these posts are all generated from inside RV parks and RV shows, you can be pretty confident that the people creating these posts are current or future RV owners.

Then by filtering through these conversations to find all the posts that include a hyperlink, you can begin to see which websites are repeatedly being shared via those links. By tallying instances of specific websites, you can begin to look for correlations among RV owners. For instance, you might find that a large percentage of links being shared or discussed point back to a specific newspaper, such as *USA Today*, or an online travel blog such as http://travelingmamas.com. This indicates a possible propinquity point.

# Step 3: Using Primary Research

Professionals always do the most accurate research, and if your company can afford it, I highly recommend pursuing that path. However, many people have to pursue a do-it-yourself model using an online tool such as Survey Monkey. The good news here is that the DIY model is just fine for defining propinquity points. Given that we are conducting exploratory research, I think the margin of error usually associated with DIY research is perfectly acceptable.

To field this research, you need to obtain a sample set of customers or prospective customers. You have three options for obtaining a usable sample. The first option is to simply buy one from Survey Monkey. Survey Monkey maintains a panel of people who have shared key demographic data with Survey Monkey and agreed to respond to surveys from companies. The company charges you based on the number of completed surveys you require. The cost per completed survey varies based on how specific your demographic targeting is for your survey, but pricing starts as low as $1 per completed survey. Given the cost of professional audience samples, that cost is quite reasonable.

Your second option is to field a survey to your own customer list, assuming that they read and watch the same things as your prospects. In my experience, this is a fair assumption. Again, we're looking for good enough versus perfect information here, so the risk is minimal.

Your third option is to partner with an organization made up of your target audience. This is an especially effective approach in the B2B world, where professional trade organizations have clean email lists of their membership. Offer to create, field, and analyze the entire study and share the results with the trade group. Given that the trade group likely wants to expand its member base, the resulting propinquity point data is as valuable to them as it is to you. So by partnering with these groups and sharing the results with them, you create a win-win situation that will help you define those all-important propinquity points. I've successfully used this approach with a number of clients myself.

Regardless of how you field the survey, you'll want to include both closed- and open-ended questions. Use the closed-ended questions to quickly let the respondents indicate whether they do or do not regularly consume information at a particular propinquity point you've already identified. This is a great way to help you validate those "easy" propinquity points that you defined yourself. It's also a great way to try to validate the destinations you discovered in the social listening phase of this process. But you also want to include open-ended questions, in which you ask the respondents to enter the names of the websites, media vehicles, and other places they turn to for information when buying your products or services.

The purpose of the open-ended questions is to help you identify all the online and offline propinquity points you haven't yet been able to identify through your own knowledge or through social listening. The difficulty factor with open-ended questions is coding the responses. This is a simple but laborious process that involves manual coding or tabulating of each open-ended response. Thus, if your sample has 500 respondents who each named five online websites visited for information, you have to code and tabulate 2,500 responses. Luckily, this is the perfect kind of activity to assign to a junior staffer, a receptionist, or even an intern. Just show them how you want the responses coded and set them loose. Because the Survey Monkey service is web based, the person doing the coding doesn't even need to be in your office. Survey Monkey also has a tool built into the system to enable you to conduct the coding and tabulating online.

## Step 4: Classifying Your Propinquity Points

Next, you need to classify each propinquity point as either an outposts or an embassy. In the simplest terms, an outpost is a place where you and your content show up from time to time and where your prospects congregate. A good example is submitting a guest post on a popular blog or authoring an article for a magazine. You create and post the content there, but you're not investing a lot of time in doing so because your goal is to generate awareness. You're trying to leverage the platform owner's audience to create awareness of you and your product or service, and give prospects a simple way to follow you back to your Home Base.

Embassies, on the other hand, are propinquity points where you elect to create a more continuous presence. Similar to outposts, these are propinquity points where your prospective customers congregate. However, based on your research, you feel that a focused effort and regular ongoing participation in conversations occurring at these propinquity points will result in increased business opportunities. Embassies might include platforms such as LinkedIn or Twitter, where you'll spend your time building and cultivating a community of prospects. But embassies can also be media based, as with my ongoing role as an author in *Advertising Age's Small Agency Diary*. Because I've developed a continuous presence and established a readership there, I classify that point as an embassy; it differs from the occasional post on a blog or in a tourism marketing publication, which I classify as an outpost for my firm.

It's important to point out that any propinquity point can vacillate between serving as an outpost and acting as an embassy. Often an outpost evolves into embassy, and an embassy might become outpost. This might be due to a change in your strategy, a changing business climate, or just a realization that a particular propinquity point is under- or overdelivering based on your current effort level.

As with most things in the digital world, outposts and embassies are fluid constructs. The only real difference between the two is how you interface with your prospects at each. So don't fixate on the initial classification of your propinquity points. It's okay to get it wrong the first time. You can make changes. There's no penalty clause for deciding that you're going to convert that embassy into an outpost, or vice versa. As with most things in marketing, there are no absolute rights and wrongs. Focus on trying to maximize your efforts instead of getting it *right*.

## Closed Versus Open Outposts

The digital world has two types of outposts. In open outposts, you are allowed to publish content simply because you registered to be a part of that platform. This might include industry content aggregator sites such as *Business Week*'s Business Exchange (http://bx.businessweek.com) or digital content platforms such as Slideshare.net and YouTube.com. In all three cases, no one needs to give you permission to publish on the platform. You don't need to develop a relationship with the owner of the platform and there is no need to ingratiate yourself to the platform community. Participation requires only that you sign up and publish. This does not make the sites any less important to your efforts, but you should factor it in from a time perspective as you plan your efforts. Because you simply need to register and post, utilizing these outposts as part of your digital footprint is relatively easy and efficient.

The other type of outpost you'll participate in is closed outposts. Examples of these include guest posting on a blog, guest authoring an article for a news medium, and, in some cases, publishing on certain aggregator sites as well. But before you can post your content on a closed outpost, you need the owner of the platform to grant you permission to do so. This is important because you're not just going to waltz in and start posting on someone else's outpost. You have to invest in some relationship building so that the owner feels comfortable allowing you and your content onto the platform. Understand that, by allowing you to post on their blog or website, owners are essentially vouching for you. It's a very public display of support and approval of you, your company, and your content. Always remember and respect that dynamic.

When you gain that permission and start posting, you need to think in terms of a breadcrumb strategy. Just as Hansel and Gretel used breadcrumbs to attempt to find their way back to their cottage, you drop breadcrumbs in every piece of content you publish to help your prospects find their way back to your Home Base.

Each and every time you post content on any outpost, be sure to include at least one link inside that content that points back to your Home Base. You'd be surprised by how long these links will continue to drive traffic for you. I still smile every time I see traffic coming to my site from a post that I wrote for SocialFresh.com in 2011. And although the amount of traffic that comes in today is nothing near what it was the day I wrote the post, it's still free traffic that I'm not really doing anything to gain. It still creates impressions and brings in people who might just be able to hire me. And most important, it garners prospects I might not otherwise bump into.

The last thing to say about outposts is they will likely change over time. Unlike an embassy, you're not planting a flag, participating in a community, or investing significant sums of time in the growth of that propinquity point. You're simply leveraging someone else's community or readership to create awareness of your content. But don't be misled into thinking that the work you do in an outpost ceases to have value if you change your outpost strategy and discontinue posting there.

The content that you create, share, and post today begets content opportunities to create and share tomorrow. What I mean here is that as you introduce yourself and request opportunities to post content to new outposts in the future, you will be able to point those new platform owners back to your current or past outposts. This gives them a sense of the quality of your work and the commitment of your spirit to not simply making it a one-way street. They'll be able to see that you contributed good, original content to those other outposts and that you also shared the content with your audience to help spread that content around the digital world.

This might be the single most important lesson I can teach you about planning and executing an outpost strategy. A lot of people in this world take the opportunity to guest post, create content, or participate in some other way on other people's platforms. They'll gladly take that awareness I spoke of earlier. But those people do not give back to the platform owner. And although that approach can work in the early days of an outpost strategy, eventually it catches up to you. And when it does, you'll find it much harder to convince outpost owners to let you publish your content on their platform.

## Manning Your Embassies

Now that you understand how to handle your outposts, you need to focus on your embassies. As I said, the difference between an outpost and an embassy is that an embassy is where you put down roots. For me, this is *Advertising Age* magazine, a private Facebook group full of tourism marketing professionals, LinkedIn, Twitter, and #TourismChat. Each of these platforms are places where I'm not only spending enormous amounts of time, but, more important, receiving a significant amount of value in the form of new business leads, reputation enhancement, or opportunities to connect with resources that enhance my ability to do my job on behalf of my clients.

Embassies are so much more than just a place to expose your content to new prospects. Embassies are the place for you to really network with prospective buyers. Embassies are the place you're going to meet people, introduce people to one another, and get introduced to people. When you create an embassy, you're telling the community and the world that it's important to you. Where you choose to place your embassies makes a statement about you and your company. It makes a statement about your commitment, your expertise, and your long-term plans to participate in digitally powered conversations between you and your prospects.

Let's take a look at an outstanding embassy strategy developed by Steve Woodruff. Chapter 10, "Social Selling," examines this strategy in more detail, but I want to mention it here because it's simply a great example of a successful embassy strategy. Steve's background is in the pharmaceutical world, specifically pharmaceutical training. When Steve set out to create his own company, Impactiviti, he decided that LinkedIn would be one of his embassies. At the time, pharma managers weren't using a lot of social media—in some cases, they were forbidden to access some social networks. But LinkedIn was the one network they all had access to and were utilizing at some level. So Steve chose LinkedIn as one of his embassies.

In the Groups section of LinkedIn, Steve created three separate groups. First, he created a private group for sales trainers—or, in Steve's world, prospects. He created a group where these sales trainers could congregate to talk with one another, without the fear of vendors or job seekers overhearing them. He created a safe place where these professionals could learn from each other and help one another do a better job, free from the prying eyes of outsiders—well, except for one outsider: Steve. That gave Steve a level of access with his prospects that most sales professionals can only imagine.

He went on to create the same for job seekers and also pharma training vendors. Steve often describes his company as the eHarmony of pharmaceutical client/vendor matchmaking. His job is to help pharma companies locate the right service vendors to solve their problems. Likewise, he works with pharmaceutical vendors to find unique and profitable opportunities to work with pharma companies. In short, Steve is a matchmaker. By establishing an embassy (actually, three embassies), Steve can network with key prospects, share helpful content, and build relationships that result in new customers for his company.

This is what makes embassy strategies such as the one Steve deployed here so important. By creating a safe zone that his prospects value enough to join, Steve ensures propinquity. Do you see how Steve is using his embassy to build his business? Can you see how you might be able to deploy a similar strategy on LinkedIn, Twitter, Facebook, Google+, or even your own website?

## Developing Your Propinquity Map

After you've successfully discovered, defined, and classified all your initial propinquity points, it's time to start connecting the dots. For instance, if most prospects that participate in a high-value Twitter Chat also tend to read certain blogs where you can guest post, you'll want to know and understand that relationship. Then you'll want to reach out to that blog and offer to guest post, preferably on the same day the high-value Twitter Chat occurs. That way, you increase your propinquity against the prospect audience in a very focused manner. This is how you prioritize your efforts and work efficiently to increase the prospects' awareness of you and your company so that you can begin to draw them down a path to your Home Base (your website or blog).

Just as all roads lead to Rome, all pathways in your prospecting platform should ultimately lead your prospect to your Home Base. And although you'd love for prospects to simply jump directly to your Home Base from an outpost or embassy, the greater likelihood is that they will pass through a number of outposts and/or embassy points on their way to your Home Base. That's why it's so important that you understand how your various propinquity points interconnect—you want to drop the right breadcrumbs at each point so that your prospects can follow the crumbs back to your home.

To begin the process, list all your propinquity points on a piece of paper. Next, plot those points on a propinquity map (see Figure 8-4).

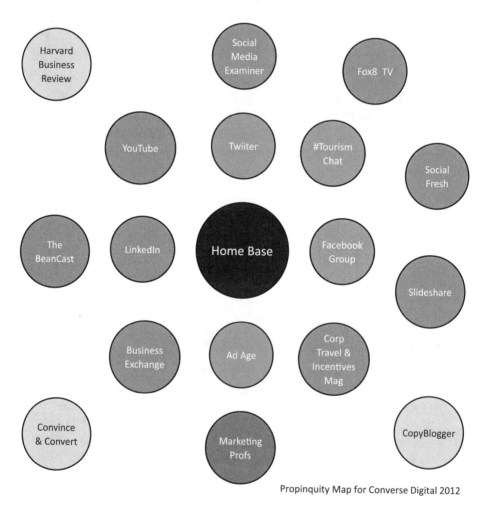

Propinquity Map for Converse Digital 2012

**Figure 8-4**  *Sample propinquity map*

Place your Home Base in the center of the map. As I've noted earlier, your Home Base is most likely your corporate website or blog. This is the place you want to drive all your online and offline traffic to visit. It's where you educate buyers and entice them to download something so that you can begin to track their behavior.

When you have this base map, you need to overlay all the interconnectivity among the various points. Visually, this starts to get a bit busy, so I've omitted that layer in Figure 8-4. You might even decide that you want to create multiple maps based on certain audiences, prospects, or industries, to keep the figure easier to read. However you decide to move forward, you'll want to connect the dots. Using lines of different colors, weights, or styles, connect the points in your propinquity map that have a high degree of prospect overlap.

For instance, in Figure 8-4, if I wanted to represent the key propinquity points for my tourism prospects, I would connect the Facebook Group bubble to both the Twitter bubble and the #TourismChat bubble; most of the members of the Facebook Group are on Twitter and regularly participate in #TourismChat. I would also connect the Facebook Group bubble directly to the Twitter bubble because most of the Facebook Group members are also avid Twitter users outside #TourismChat. By understanding how these three propinquity points work together, I can better plan my breadcrumbing activity to ensure maximum effectiveness.

The key here is to understand the relationships among your various propinquity points. Ideally, you want to be able to classify the connectivity between points as high, medium, or low and then focus on the points that have the highest degree of interconnectivity, as I demonstrated earlier in my tourism example. If I have very little time to prospect for new tourism clients, my propinquity map tells me that I should focus on being helpful in the Facebook Group and interacting on #TourismChat. If I have a bit of extra time outside of that, I should spend it conversing and helping those same tourism prospects on Twitter. That is the power of the propinquity map. Done correctly, it helps you prioritize your online prospecting efforts.

Now that you know where you'll be interacting and how often, let's turn to the final component of an effective Painless Prospecting strategy: breadcrumbs.

# Creating a Breadcrumb Strategy

The final piece of the propinquity marketing strategy is breadcrumbs. The breadcrumb strategy is the key difference between an outbound prospecting mindset and an inbound prospecting mindset. In outbound prospecting, you're never quite sure whether you'll get another bite at the apple, so you try to close the deal every time you get a chance to touch a prospect, whether it's in your ads, in a direct marketing mailer, or even during a sales call. (Note that when I say "sales call," I'm not including qualifying calls—I'm focused squarely on the calls designed to get a prospect to buy.)

But in a propinquity marketing mindset, you assume that you're going to get multiple bites at the apple. You assume that the prospect will see and interact with you and your content in multiple places and at multiple times. Because of this, the propinquity approach is far more elegant and patient. It's less about selling and more about seducing your prospect. And that's why you never try to tell the complete story in any one propinquity point. Instead, you tell the part of the story that's most appropriate. And like Hansel and Gretel, you've dropped a breadcrumb that prospects can consume and then follow to find another breadcrumb. With each breadcrumb consumed, your prospect is walking farther along the sales path until, eventually, he or she winds up at the front door of your Home Base, ready and willing to buy.

## POWER POINTS

- Use a combination of your own insights and secondary research to identify your propinquity points, the places where your prospects are congregating and where you can place your content in front of them.

- Classify each propinquity point as either an embassy (where you'll become part of the community) or an outpost (where you'll just post content).

- Create a funnel-optimized Home Base—your corporate website or blog.

- Your funnel-optimized website should consist of static, predesigned funnels that move your prospect closer to self-identification for follow-up and dynamic funnels based on constantly presenting the most likely "next step" content for your prospect to consume.

- Drop breadcrumbs to help your prospects find their way from your outposts and embassies to your Home Base.

*Download all the Power Points at TheInvisibleSale.com.*

# 9

# Making Every Call Count

As we discussed in Chapter 2, "Living Inside the Database," sales prospecting today is all about living inside your prospect database—a database that you populated by buying advertising, attending trade shows, purchasing prospects lists, and conducting general networking activities. This creates a fairly common problem for sales organizations around the world. They have huge databases full of prospects, and the sales teams really don't know a whole lot about each of those prospects. Sure, the sales team has a prospect's name, physical address, phone number, and likely an email address. But none of that is going to help a salesperson determine whether he should contact Prospect A or Prospect B today. None of that is going to help him sort the prospect database into hot, warm, and cold leads, much less know what each prospect is interested in buying.

This lack of knowledge has forced salespeople to qualify prospects via qualification phone calls. Thus, each day salespeople dutifully call on the unqualified prospects in their company's database, in hopes of getting a prospect to provide more context for the prospect's initial inquiry. To do this, the salesperson asks a ton of questions about the prospect's business, goals, pain points, and more. If the salesperson is lucky, the prospect will answer these questions, to help the salesperson properly qualify the prospect and develop a post-qualification sales strategy.

We've all been on the receiving end of these fishing expeditions. They're painful, and unless we are truly in need of the salesperson's product or service in the very near future, they're a complete waste of our very valuable time. So what do we prospects do? We screen our calls, create a plausible excuse to end the call prematurely, or, in some cases, rudely convey our lack of desire to be qualified and hang up.

But there's a better way. Most sales teams just aren't familiar with this new behavior-based qualification method. And that's what this chapter is about. I introduce you to behavioral email segmentation programs and show you how they're the perfect first step in moving your sales and marketing team into the Painless Prospecting world. I also explain how you can create a broader behavioral prospecting program by combining email outreach with strategically planned content. Both approaches are designed to achieve the same goal: to create a behaviorally qualified lead-generation database.

# Behavioral Segmentation Email Programs

When most people think about email, they think about it in a very transactional sense. You email a prospect or customer, and the measure of success is a sale. Yes, email marketers track and report email opens (how many people on your email list opened the email you sent) and clicks (how many people clicked a link in the email), but the return on investment (ROI) reports are always linked to revenue.

In behavioral email, you have to throw away that thinking! This approach is anything but transactional. You want your prospects to help educate you. The ROI isn't revenue, but knowledge. The goal of the program is to send prospects information and then have them read or click a link for more information, go to your website, and click on additional information presented there. And while they're reading and clicking, you're tracking every moment of their journey.

You don't care whether they buy right now. You don't expect them to buy. You don't even really care whether they make it all the way to the lead-gen form. You just want them to start clicking around and consuming information, because each and every time they do that, they're sending you a behavioral cue that you can then put into a profile where you segment them behaviorally.

# Why Behavioral Email Works

The Internet ushered in the ability for buyers to self-educate. And guess what? Buyers like to self-educate. They'd much rather talk to the Internet than you. They really don't want to call a salesperson because they don't want to get into the database unless they're really serious about making a purchase in the near term. However, they're perfectly willing to unknowingly send you buying signals by clicking content you send them.

Although I think it's safe to say that most people today understand that companies are tracking every email they open, link they click, and website they visit, most people don't really understand how much data their online activity reveals about them. They don't realize that companies aren't just tracking individual actions, but are compiling those actions over time to develop profiles and dossiers on each prospect. These dossiers are better than any qualification call because the information contained in them is unvarnished. Prospects often tell half-truths on a qualification call. They're guarded with information because they don't want a salesperson to have the upper hand in the selling process. But when these same prospects are online, they aren't actively thinking about the fact that their actions are transmitting information to a salesperson. They don't think about the fact that, with each click of a link or visit to a web page, they are sending trackable buying signals that clearly indicate their interest, intent, and need.

This unguarded display of intent makes behavioral email an incredibly powerful tool. Used correctly, this tactic creates more efficient and effective sales prospecting programs. Behavioral email not only helps you segment your database into hot, warm, and cold leads, but more importantly, it tells you exactly what you need to say or sell to each hot lead. It's like reading your prospects' mind.

# Behavioral Email: A Case Study

Let me tell you the story of Amy Smith (not her real name). Amy was a sales team of one; she was both the salesperson and the account manager. For every piece of business she won, she then had to manage it. So Amy had a very interesting challenge. The more successful she was at selling, the less time she had to actually sell. It's a common conundrum for small businesses and small sales teams everywhere.

When Amy was asked to define her challenge, she summed it up in seven simple yet powerful words: "I need to make every call count." To add emphasis, as if any was required, she went on to say that, when she called a prospect, she needed to know that the person on the other end wanted to talk to her and was interested in buying what she had to sell. And as long as she was asking, it would be really helpful if the marketing program could help her know what the prospect was most interested in buying or learning more about.

Now that's a heck of a marketing challenge. The only question left was what kind of data the marketing team would have access to for this campaign. The answer was a bit shocking. Amy had a couple thousand email addresses. That was it. Yes, the emails also included contact names, physical mailing addresses, company names, and a phone number. But beyond that basic information, nothing could aid the team in achieving the goal of "making every call count."

This is where the idea of behavioral email segmentation was really born. To help Amy segment her 1,600 prospect database, we needed to understand how interested each person was in Amy's products. This meant we needed to devise a well-planned series of emails designed to let Amy's prospects send us those important buying signals.

First, we developed a Behavioral Email Logic (BEL) diagram. Planning the BEL is the most important and most difficult step of these programs. To create a BEL, you first need to define the core message content of each email you plan to send. You don't have to develop finished creative executions—you just need to know the core content each email will include. Then you hypothesize what a prospect's behavioral pattern is telling you, based on how the person moves through the BEL.

Figure 9-1 shows a prototypical BEL (not Amy Smith's BEL). What makes the BEL so complex is the logic sequence that you have to build into it. In Figure 9-1, you think you're looking at a total of 19 emails, but in reality, it's only 8 unique emails that are sent in various predetermined sequencing patterns. For instance, notice that any time a prospect deletes two emails in a row, the prospect is terminated. That person receives no further emails under this campaign.

Likewise, if the prospect opens two emails in a row without a click, that person receives a specific third email message. Prospects who click on two emails in a row receive an entirely different third message. And so forth through all the possible delete/open/click patterns. The goal of the BEL is simple: By sequencing the messages in a predefined pattern, we attempt to hypothesize what the delete/open/click behaviors communicate. At the most basic analytical level, this delete/open/click behavior conveys interest. On a higher level, overlaying this activity with the content that produced the deletions/opens/clicks provides additional data points for segmentation.

Completing a campaign takes about six weeks because you have to give prospects time to act on the emails. I've found that prospects either act on an email almost immediately or save it and come back to it. In my experience, they come back to the email within three to five days. Thus, for behavioral email campaigns, I recommend sending each wave 7 to 10 days apart, to give respondents plenty of time to indicate interest through their actions.

In Amy's case, she had 1,600 emails. We processed those 1,600 prospects through the campaign and then analyzed the data. The results were very eye-opening for anyone who sells for a living. Out of 1,600 prospects, we identified 249 warm prospects who had opened emails, clicked on emails, and read a few items on Amy's website.

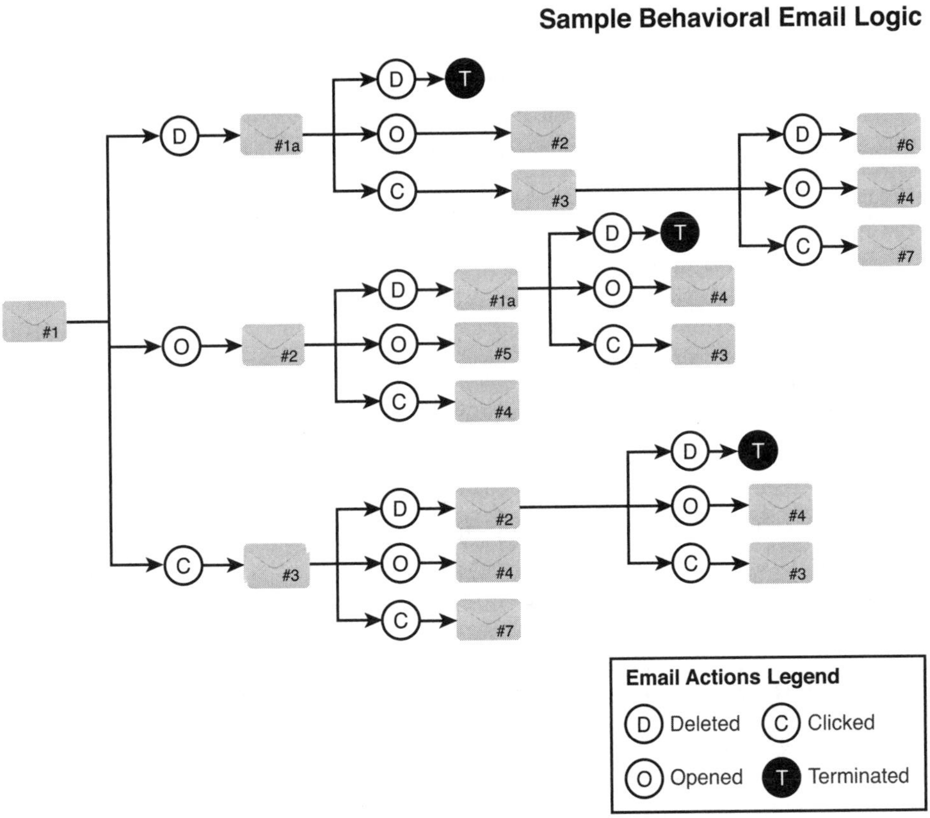

**Sample Behavioral Email Logic**

**Figure 9-1**  *A prototypical behavioral email logic diagram*

Additionally, we identified 12 hot prospects—12 needles in a haystack. Out of 1,600 people, we found 12 people whose behaviors indicated they were ready to buy. They not only opened emails, but also clicked on more than one email and/ or read *multiple* items on Amy's website. In some cases, these prospects visited a lead-generation form page on the website. That left 1,300 cold prospects. Those prospects hadn't interacted with Amy's content, but they also hadn't opted out of the campaign either. This is an important point. Cold prospects' behavior (not opting out of future campaigns) often indicate a willingness to receive additional email marketing. This creates opportunities to test additional behavioral campaigns.

Our recommendation to Amy: If you want to make every call count, call the 12 hot prospects first and then work your way through the warm list. Don't even bother calling anyone on the cold list until you've completely worked your way through the warm list. But the recommendation went beyond just whom to call. And that is the really powerful piece of a behavioral email program.

We recommended that Amy call the number-one person (Melissa Manthey—also not her real name) on the list immediately because she was very interested in Product A. We knew that because she had opened an email featuring Product A, read multiple case studies associated with Product A, explored the About Us info on Amy's site, and visited the Contact Form. The behavioral data was screaming "Hot Prospect."

So Amy called Melissa, who didn't answer. Amy left a message. Her call process was to leave a message, wait three days, and then call back. But she never got the chance to call Melissa back. The next day, Melissa called Amy and said [paraphrasing], "I am so glad you called me, Amy. I've been on your website reading about Product A, and I think my company could benefit from it." Within 90 days, Melissa was a new customer.

But it gets better. Within 30 days, Amy set 15 appointments! Amy's product had a long sales cycle. But even with her longer sales cycle, the entire campaign reached a 1:1 ROI within five months of completing the email campaign. That's the beauty of behavioral email: It helps your salespeople focus their efforts on your best prospects. That creates a happier, more effective sales team.

## Behavioral Email: The First Step Solution

When you build and optimize your BEL, you create a highly effective lead-qualification tool for qualifying trade show, advertising, and general networking leads. By passing these new leads through this behavioral process, you can quickly differentiate the truly interested from the casual inquiries. This is especially helpful for trade show leads if you ran promotions or giveaways in your booth. With behavioral email, you're immediately optimizing all your new database leads before you place them in your sales prospecting database.

Behavioral email is also your key to gaining permission to move your company or sales team to a Painless Prospecting approach. The single biggest hurdle to Painless Prospecting is the time it takes to create, launch, and then optimize the program. Understandably, sales teams that are compensated based on "making the numbers" every month, quarter, and year aren't willing to wait and see whether an inbound approach will work. They need to hit their numbers today. Enter behavioral email. As you just saw with Amy, this approach works. So although your sales team might balk at launching a Painless Prospecting approach, they likely will support or at least consider launching a behavioral email program.

Your behavioral email program is the ultimate Painless Prospecting Trojan horse. Because helpful, educational content is necessary for the success of the email program, launching a behavioral email program effectively commits your company to create the underpinnings (helpful, trackable content) for a Painless Prospecting approach. Thus, for any sales and marketing team trying to gain buy-in from the sales team for the movement to an inbound lead-generation and qualification system, behavioral email programs are a powerful first step.

# Behavioral Prospecting

The natural evolution of behavioral email is behavioral prospecting (BP). BP is designed to consistently qualify prospects over time. Under a BP program, the marketing department creates white papers, sales sheets, product comparison content, and more, all of which is stored in a database. This content is created for use by the sales force as part of a BP program. As the salespeople are nurturing leads in the database, they consistently email this educational and promotional content to prospects over time. What makes a BP approach different from most email marketing is the goal of the program. Unlike standard email marketing, the goal of each email isn't to create a transaction or sale. The goal is to create information in the form of a buying signal. All the content sharing is tracked and recorded to establish behavioral profiles such as hot, warm, and cold leads.

Various platforms can power a BP program. The common element of each approach is the capability to insert trackable links to digital content located on your website. Where the platforms vary is in price, tracking, and efficiency. Not surprisingly, as the platform price increases, you gain access to better analytics and systems that are optimized for BP. At the very upper end of the spectrum, the systems can even dynamically render your web content based on a prospects' past behaviors, further allowing you to segment your list into increasingly smaller, more targetable clusters.

At a minimum, you can use an inexpensive email tool such as Constant Contact, MailChimp, or Emma, three email marketing services. Each enables you to send out a mass email to your database with trackable links. These links are tracked down to the individual email address level. Over time, as you send additional campaigns, you can view your contacts' email open/click activity at the individual contact level. Thus, you can see all the content they've opened and clicked, as shown in Figure 9-2 pulled from my MailChimp account. You then can manually sort through the content to hypothesize buying motivations based on the content each prospect has consumed.

**Figure 9-2**  *Behavioral prospecting email click report*

If you have a small list, this approach is quite manageable. In Figure 9-2, from my own BP program, you see two emerging themes. First, the prospect clicked two tourism-focused blog posts. Second, they clicked on three sales prospecting posts. Without revealing the identity of this prospect, I can tell you that this person works in the tourism industry as the director of sales and marketing for a convention and visitors bureau. Additionally, what you don't see in Figure 9-2, but what my email system provides to me based on this prospect's email address, are his social network profiles. The system displays his Facebook page, his LinkedIn page, and a host of others. With all this data, I can determine how hot/warm/cold this prospect is and then quickly learn enough about him to craft a really focused and relevant personal outreach or phone call.

However, if your list is a bit larger, the necessary classification analysis is an outstanding job for interns, receptionists, and others who might have idle time on their hands. The analysis is simple. Using Google Tags and proper URL naming, you should be able to quickly place each link a prospect has clicked into a predefined content bucket. You might have a bucket for Social Selling, another for Trade Shows, or others for products such as Analytical Software or Family Sedans. The buckets will vary by your industry and classification system. The point is, by creating these buckets of like content, you can quickly score each prospect and assign them all to an overall behavioral interest segment.

You can do the same with detailed URL naming conventions, which is how you see it done in Figure 9-2. Notice that after the conversedigital.com/ you see a category such as "digital strategy" or "sales prospecting." This makes it easy to bucket those clicks into the appropriate buckets.

However, using a Google Tag is easier. A Google Tag is a short string of characters that you append to your base website page URL. One of the standard Google Tags is *utm_content=[content bucket]*. By using this tag and classifying each piece of content you create and share based on a predefined nomenclature, you can make it easy for anyone to perform the classification analysis. All that person has to do is run a click report (see Figure 9-2) and then look for the appropriate Google Tag on each URL. (You don't see the utm_content tag in Figure 9-2 because we used the detailed URL naming convention rather than the Google Tag for this example.) By tallying mentions of content tags, you can quickly define the prospect's interest level in your various products, services, or key categories. From there, you can begin offline prospecting secure in the knowledge that you are calling on prospects who have behaviorally shown an interest in the topics you intend to share with them.

# The Role of Funnel-Optimized Websites in Behavioral Prospecting

Tracking email click activity can help you build a prospect dossier, but it takes time. To speed up the process, you want to track your prospects' activity on your website after they click through from your email. To do this, you need to revisit your website design. The single biggest mistake most companies make with their website is valuing form over function. They build beautiful websites that impress the visitor visually. But that is absolutely not the role of your website. As we discuss in Chapter 8, "Creating Your Painless Prospecting Platform," the role of your website is to help prospects self-qualify themselves by sending buying signals based on the content they consume. What we didn't discuss was your website's role in BP programs.

If you visit ConverseDigital.com (see Figure 9-3), you might notice that we dedicate more than half of our home page to our behavioral prospecting funnel. Whether it's our latest blog post, the blog subscription widget (Never Miss An Update) or our email newsletter subscription widget (Insight & Information), we work really hard to acquire your email address and permission to begin an ongoing digital conversation with you.

**Figure 9-3**  *Converse Digital home page*

But we don't stop there. We include blog and newsletter subscription widgets on virtually every page of our site. Why do we place so much emphasis and use up so much valuable screen real estate pushing subscriptions? Because if I can get you into that funnel and you subscribe to my blog, I'm going to get to touch you about 52 times in the next 365 days. That's 52 brand impressions—52 opportunities to maybe get in front of you when you're making a decision that could result in hiring me, and 52 opportunities to read your mind by tracking your opens and clicks.

Think about that from your company's perspective. If your company was in front of a prospect 50 to 60 times a year, how many more qualified leads might you create? How many more times might you be sourced? Most important, how much better prepared would your sales team be when calling on that prospect? Keep in mind that those numbers are based on a once-a-week blogging schedule. If you blogged twice a week, you'd touch your prospects more than 100 times a year!

You're trading a bit of free information for insight here. And by varying the type and focus of your content, that free information you're sharing is creating a treasure trove of *open* and *click* data tied back to a piece of personally identifiable information: an email address. And with that email address, you can begin to understand who that reader is—what she's interested in and whether she should be classified as a hot, warm, or cold lead. This classification isn't arbitrary.

You create your segmentation schema. For instance, after reviewing past click and website visit data, you might determine that almost every new customer you acquire performs a series of actions. As an example, you might determine that they open at least 30% of the emails you send them and click on at least 20% of the links in those emails. Also, they consume at least 20 pages on your website other than the landing pages featured in your emails. Finally, they almost always visit a page on your site that explains your price/value relationship versus your key competitors. Thus, the standard antidotal hot/warm/cold schema transforms into a data-based continuum based on historical data.

Best of all, if you license certain marketing automation solutions (software that helps you track website visitors and automate your follow-up marketing), you can set up these systems so that as soon as a prospect trips the "hot" trigger (completes the action set you've defined as indicative of a "hot buyer), the system automatically emails your salesperson. That's right, the system automatically alerts your sales team when it's appropriate to reach out to a prospect *and* gives your salespeople the suggested content for that sales call based on the prospect's click-through and website visit history.

But none of this works if you don't have an active BP program powered by the proper email marketing software pushing prospects to trackable content.

# Advent Global's Behavioral Profiling Program

Advent Global Solutions, Inc., a global IT solutions provider based in Houston, Texas, utilizes a behavioral profiling program to ensure not only that leads are qualified and nurtured, but also that prospects and customers receive only solution information that is pertinent to their needs.

Beth Harte, Director of Marketing, shared how Advent Global utilizes a third-party email/content marketing system to nurture leads, along with a CRM system to capture responses. This powerful combination helps ensure that the sales team follows up on leads based on the prospect's real need versus the salesperson's perception of that need.

Via the email/content marketing system, prospects and customers receive appropriate and targeted emails offering "a free downloadable white paper or collateral." In one click, the prospect can download the white paper or collateral (see Figure 9-4). When the prospect downloads the white paper or collateral, an email alert is immediately sent to the marketing team, who then alerts the sales team and tracks the response.

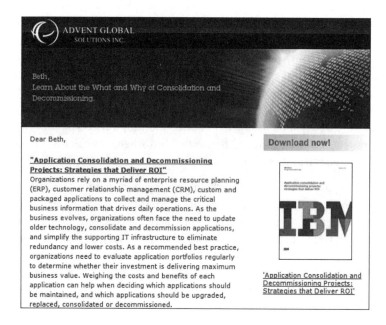

**Figure 9-4** *Advent Global Solutions white paper email sample*

This email/content marketing system also provides salespeople with their own account as well. If a sales call uncovers a perceived need, the salesperson can easily select the appropriate white paper and proper content, and send it to the prospect or customer. The email/content marketing system tracks every action the prospect or customer takes, starting with clicking the link in the email. This newly captured information is then added to each prospect in Advent's CRM system. This combination of responses—along with other relevant details—gives the salesperson a holistic view of the prospect's behavior, which is important for both selling and cross-selling.

Beth shared that the biggest challenge with content-based marketing is separating the interest signal from the buy signal. You have to develop a process to understand whether the prospect simply wanted free information or whether he or she had a reason for wanting that free information. For Beth and the Advent sales team, this has required a close sales and marketing working relationship, a lot of testing and refining, and a commitment to tracking every prospect as they move through the sales funnel from initial lead to final conversion or nonconversion. Most important, it's still a work in progress.

One of the most interesting points Beth made, though, had little to do with technology and everything to do with approach. In Beth's view, successful BP-oriented selling requires the sales team to value the prospect/customer relationship more than the individual sale. A salesperson who is driven by quota instead of relationships simply will not find the increased success that a BP program creates. She even noted that Advent's most successful salespeople (and not by a small margin) are the ones who have most enthusiastically embraced the BP approach.

Finally, if your company is not investing heavily in BP programs right now, change that. BP programs are the heart of a successful social selling approach. Salespeople are comfortable with email, and it's a highly trackable medium. Thus, by giving your sales team good, relevant content that can be shared on demand with prospects via a simple email (as Advent Global Solutions does) or deployed via mass mailings on their behalf, you improve the efficiency and effectiveness of your salespeople.

And if you're trying to convince your sales teams to adopt inbound marketing techniques, a behavioral email approach will help you quickly create the proof you need to convince even the biggest skeptic.

# 10

# Social Selling

*I don't have time to play on Twitter, LinkedIn, or Facebook—I have sales calls to make.*

Ever hear that one or maybe mutter it yourself? If you answered no, either you're a liar or you're not listening closely. It's the most common thing social media consultants have been hearing from sales organizations for as long as social media has been around. And in that one statement, we have identified the key reason sales organizations still haven't embraced social media.

They don't realize that, at a minimum, social media is the new phone. It's both an inbound and an outbound way to contact and communicate with prospects. Is it the best phone to use for all contacts? Certainly not, but it does allow you to call more people in a day than you'd likely be able to call in a week using a standard phone.

So why is that? First, social media favors short conversations. Led by Twitter's famous 140-character limit, buyers who use social media are being trained to accept and often favor short, episodic conversations. You'd never pick up the phone to call a prospect and just ask, "So how was the trade show last week? Pick up any good information?" and then hang up, but doing so via a social media channel is perfectly acceptable.

Want to wish a happy birthday to 10 prospects whose birthdays are tomorrow and with whom you've successfully connected via Facebook? No problem—Facebook makes that a snap. Not only does Facebook remind you of the important date, but it also gives you a simple, single window to type a quick happy birthday message to each and every person without ever leaving your own Facebook page. In less time than it takes you to dial and leave a voicemail for the first person, you've left a personal message for all 10 people on Facebook.

Twitter, Google+, and LinkedIn are no different. In each case, it is perfectly acceptable—even expected—that you will drop in and touch people with one or two short little messages. Maybe you're saying hello or sharing a quick piece of information you think they'll find helpful, or you see a question you can answer. You can do it all in a fraction of the time it would take you to accomplish the same through phone or even email.

You and your sales team have to understand that the time you spend on social media isn't goofing off or playing. It's every bit as important and impactful as the time you spend cold calling or following up with leads via the more traditional channels of phone and email. You're still on the phone—it's just a more modern version. It's sort of like when you dumped your old rotary phone for a fancy, speedy push-button version. Only this new phone is not only faster, it's actually better at helping you locate and seduce prospects down the sales funnel.

## Social Selling Is About Seduction

Seduction isn't about what you say; it's about how you say it. Yes, that goes for B2B and B2C sales prospecting as well. Anyone can belly up to the bar and ask for someone's phone number, just as any salesperson can hand you a business card and say his or her company has the perfect solution for your need. But what's desirable about that? What makes you want to offer your number or actually keep that card? Nothing. Nothing in that kind of direct "I want to sell you something" approach creates any level of desire.

And the creation of desire is what seduction is all about. Yes, seduction is linked to sex, even in the dictionary definition, but set that aside. Don't think about the common end game of the seducer. Focus instead on how the seducer attempts to achieve his or her goals. Seduction in practice creates desire by sensing the needs, wants, and desires of the seduced and then pandering to those needs, wants, and desires to achieve a goal.

Seduction begins and ends with the seducer paying attention to the seduced. The dance is initiated not by the seduced, but by the seducer. And although we most often link seduction to physical beauty or sexiness, we should be linking it to attention because that is the secret weapon of the seductress.

And that is why seduction selling is the most powerful sales approach you'll ever use, and social media might just be the best-kept secret in the seduction selling world. Social media lets you pay attention to more prospects than you could ever hope to in the physical world. All you have to do is find them and then be seductive.

# How Can You Be More Seductive?

**Truly hear prospects.** You know the most seductive act you'll ever perform? Giving someone your truly undivided attention. Don't be thinking about what you want to sell—just listen intently. Pay attention to what the person is saying and, more important, what he or she isn't saying. Then engage in an open and honest manner that's designed not to sell, but to support, help, or inform.

**Care more about the prospect than your sales quota.** Chivalry is seductive—and, yes, girls can be chivalrous, too. If you don't believe me, pick up a *Cosmopolitan*; you'll see it right there on the cover. Okay, I made that up. I have no idea whether *Cosmo* has ever written about the sexiness of chivalry. Maybe it's because I grew up in the South, but when people place your comfort, interests, and needs before their own, that gets your attention and makes you want them around more often. That kind of attention gets noticed in a good way.

**Learn to enjoy the journey as much as the destination.** Too many salespeople live for the victory, and too many marketers live for the lead. It's not their fault—it's how sales and marketing is taught and reinforced. We ring bells when we close a deal; we celebrate with big dinners, drinks, and bonuses. But the salespeople who practice the seductive arts realize that seduction is about creating anticipation, and anticipation builds over time. So slow down, take your time, and bring the prospect down the funnel just a little bit at a time.

**Don't be a one-night stand.** Great salespeople understand and love that the sale is the beginning, not the end. They understand that the seduction process takes longer but results in a stronger bond between salesperson and customers. So build on that strength and leverage your first sale to create opportunities to seduce again, and again, and again.

# Hearing Your Prospect Online

One of the reasons social media is such a powerful tool in the sales and marketing toolbox is its ability to cast a long, wide antenna or as a friend of mine prefers to say, it lets you grow big ears. In fact, casting that antenna is a primary goal of a rather unlikely (in my opinion) social media marketer: Caterpillar. Would you believe that a company could sell Material Handlers, Backhoes, and Off Highway Trucks (the big ones they use in mining operations) via social media?

Kevin Espinosa is the social media manager for Caterpillar's Global Marketing Services Group. In an interview, Kevin shared some of the thinking that is powering Caterpillar's current social media efforts. Caterpillar defines its social media activities using four pillars: social listening, customer support, promotion, and thought leadership, which are very focused on helping develop deeper customer relationships.

Let's take a second to look at two of the pillars as Kevin describes them and their role in helping Caterpillar truly hear their prospects online.

First, with social listening, the goal is to understand the customer's needs. Caterpillar uses its social listening tools to understand what customers and prospects are saying about Caterpillar and its products. They not only hear what is being said, but they also determine the sentiment of those conversations. They can quickly determine whether prospects and customers are speaking well or poorly of the company and its products. Even better, they can determine who is talking about Caterpillar and its competitors, where those conversations are occurring, and how influential the people having the conversations are in the world of heavy machinery.

By intently listening to the voice of the customer and the prospect, as well as the overall industry conversation happening online, Caterpillar can (and does) use all that information to see the bigger trends or issues. This data also helps the company determine what content it might be missing in its digital marketing arsenal.

Second is customer support. Caterpillar treats social media as the new telephone and handles it the same way. Any question submitted on its social media sites is automatically entered into Salesforce.com and routed directly into the social media call agents' queue. Caterpillar has set up guidelines for social media call agents directing how they are to transact with people over social media.

By delivering on these two key pillars, Caterpillar gets closer to its prospects and leverages that closeness to build and strengthen relationships. They hear challenges before they become full-scale problems. They sense market opportunity. And they better prepare their sales teams for possible sales objections. All because they use social media to hear the prospects voice.

# Defining Your Social Selling Approach

The first thing you need to determine is how you'll actually present the company in the social space. Will you engage at an individual level, a brand or company level, or possibly both? Let's look at how this might play out in the real world.

What if you owned a funeral home? How would you approach setting up your social selling strategy? Given that seduction is probably the last thing you think of when discussing funerals, let's set that aside and focus first on the listening and engaging part. You could set up listening software to capture any public mention of funeral or death, but would that really give you actionable intelligence? Would it be socially acceptable for you, the funeral home, to reach out at that moment and offer your services?

Just as it probably wouldn't be acceptable to reach out, it would be highly unlikely that you'd get a lot of folks to follow a funeral home on Twitter or like it on Facebook. It's just odd to the ordinary consumer to think about liking a funeral home, much less liking a post about death. Because of this, your strategy likely wouldn't include a brand-level effort. So does that mean social selling can't play a role in your sales and marketing efforts? I don't think so. Let me explain.

What if your strategy was instead to have each funeral home director establish a social presence on places such as Facebook, Twitter, Google+, and LinkedIn? What if they used these platforms to connect with members of their community? What if they used these as opportunities to reframe the idea of a funeral not as a sad occasion marking the end of a life, but as a joyous celebration of a life well lived by a person who left the world a better place than before he or she entered? Or maybe the directors could find opportunities to talk about the business side of funerals, answering the most common questions asked by people online and offering to help with advice. Or maybe they can just be social and helpful.

Would those funeral directors be able to develop a few friendships? Not as a funeral director, but as Bob, the really nice guy who does a lot for the community and happens to be a funeral director. Would that person achieve TOMA (top-of-mind awareness) or, better, TOMP (top-of-mind preference) the next time one of his friends or followers experienced a death in the family? Would that translate into future business for the funeral home?

Just because you're developing a company-level social selling strategy, don't always assume that you have to execute it at a corporate level or that you can't consider individual sales team member efforts. In fact, I can think of few instances when individual social profiles for sales, marketing, and pretty much any employee aren't justified strategically. Social selling is just a new way to network.

When you have determined the form, figure out the function. Remember, seduction is slow and requires an elegance that isn't always the hallmark of sales teams.

So ask yourself about the most likely opportunities to create that first propinquity *bump*. Then focus on helping your sales team establish that first—and maybe second—bump.

# Developing Your Corporate Social Brand

Now that we've looked at an uncommon example, in which a corporate-level social sales effort may not be warranted, let's consider the more common approach: use of a corporate brand.

After you've established that you will utilize a corporate-level presence you need to make one more really important decision. You need to decide whether that corporate presence will be a person or a brand. And if it's going to be a brand, will you let it behave as a person and maybe even identify the person or persons running it?

Let's return to Caterpillar—specifically, its Twitter account, https://twitter.com/CaterpillarInc. If you visit Caterpillar on Twitter, you'll see that it's decidedly corporate in its approach. The company doesn't follow back most of the folks who follow it. Instead, the company uses the account largely to answer questions, field customer inquiries, and, of course, promote products, events, and happenings at Caterpillar.

When asked why Caterpillar chose that path, Social Media Manager Kevin Espinosa shared the company's strategic approach. Given limitations on manpower, Caterpillar chose to keep the account activity at a more corporate, publicity-based level. But the company also uses the account to field, direct, and, in some cases, answer questions from customers and prospective customers. This lets the company be helpful and begins to position Caterpillar for TOMP with prospects. Eventually, as it grows further in its social strategy, the company hopes to eventually use the account as a place for Caterpillar's own thought leaders to engage with the Caterpillar community, much as Dell does with its employees and customers. This will make the account even more helpful to prospects and customers and continue to drive TOMP for Caterpillar.

But as with most things in life, there's no one right way to do anything. To help reinforce that point, let's contrast Caterpillar's approach with the MarketingProfs approach. MarketingProfs is a very interesting B2B content company headquartered in Boston. It bills itself as the one source for online marketing resources, marketing strategies, marketing articles, online seminars, case studies, conferences, and events for marketing professionals.

Unlike Caterpillar, MarketingProfs believes that social channels, especially Twitter, give it an opportunity to personify the brand. To be fair, MarketingProfs also has a bit more staffing devoted to social media than Caterpillar does. Being personable takes more time than being corporate. You have to invest in conversations with people and that takes time and manpower. So maybe this greater staffing gives them permission to believe that social profiles and platforms should be friendly and give a sense of who MarketingProfs is (as people), not just what the company sells. To this company, the strength of social channels is the ability to be personable versus personal. You might think it's mincing words, but there's a big distinction between *personable* and *personal*.

For instance, during a social media conference, a social meme (an idea, behavior, or style that spreads from person to person within a culture) began that directly references MarketingProfs' chief content officer, Ann Handley. She serves as the company's primary evangelist and, as you can see in Figure 10-1, is also literally the face of the company on Twitter (https://twitter.com/marketingprofs).

**Figure 10-1** *The MarketingProfs branded Twitter home page*

Before and during the conference, a few of Handley's fellow social media buddies began to wonder aloud and on Twitter, "What would Ann Handley do?" This quickly became a hashtag, #WWAHD, on Twitter throughout the conference, and it continued well after the conference. Although it was no "McKayla Maroney isn't impressed[1]" (the infamous American gymnast caught with the *I'm not happy* face during the 2012 Summer Olympic medal awards program), #WWAHD and its iterations—such as #WWAHS (What would Ann Handley say?)—both began linking Ann to humorous thoughts and situations.

And although some brands may have been on edge with their public face being associated with an outside meme, MarketingProfs wasn't. It even helped the meme along, with Ann herself adopting the hashtag in all its glory (see Figure 10-2). But then that's not surprising, given Ann's belief: "MarketingProfs believes we should

1. *Los Angeles Times*, August 9, 2012. http://articles.latimes.com/2012/aug/09/business/la-fi-tn-mckayla-maroney-not-impressed-20120809.

let some personality come through because it creates a relationship with our followers and members, and it's that relationship that gives us an edge in a highly competitive environment."

**Figure 10-2**  *Ann Handley embracing the #WWAHD meme*

So which approach is the best for your company? As with so many things in marketing, it depends. But what's important is that you think through how you intend to communicate on social media platforms at the corporate level and then develop your social communication guidelines, strategies, and tactics appropriately.

# Social Warning

One of the biggest arguments against personifying your company brand at the level that a MarketingProfs does is the danger of very publicly associating your brand with a person. People are human, and humans tend to make mistakes. So before you decide to let a person represent your company—or even if you choose to have your company exist as a brand but publicly identify the person behind the brand—you need to consider the dangers.

First, you must establish who will own the followers and fans. Ann currently maintains a personal account on Twitter, but that wasn't always the case. For many years, her personal and professional account was @MarketingProfs. That was the only way consumers could reach Ann on Twitter, and it was the only account she actively monitored. So what happens if Ann leaves? Many of those followers chose to follow @MarketingProfs because they were really choosing to follow Ann. This might seem inconsequential when you're starting up your social selling effort, but if you're successful, it could become a real issue.

Second, you need to set the ground rules for the brand. As I said, there's a difference between *personable* and *personal*. Think through exactly how much personal information about the person behind the brand you will share on social platforms. This will avoid any misunderstandings.

Third, always try to utilize an owner or someone with significant professional or financial investment in the company as the face of the company. This helps alleviate the ownership of followers issues. It also minimizes the chances that you will have to one day change the person who manages the social accounts and thus change the overall brand voice. This can prove problematic and derail a successful social effort.

Finally, because you might have to make a switch, and that switch might need to happen immediately, always have someone waiting in the wings who can take over your social media accounts. This person should have access to all the passwords, be familiar with the current discussions, and, in general, be ready to step in at a moment's notice. You'll likely want this person to handle some of the social media efforts while your primary person is on vacation, on weekends, or on holidays so that he or she gets a working knowledge of the social media platforms, audiences, and conversations.

# Social Rules of Engagement

When you determine how you'll set up your social media presence, you're ready to begin engaging prospects on social channels. Learning the customs and laws of each social media platform you choose to participate in online is important.

Just as different countries have different laws, cultures, and customs, so does each social media platform. Facebook is primarily a private platform, except where fans of brands publicly like a brand and then publicly post on that brand's Facebook page. Twitter, on the other hand, defaults to public posts. Unless users restrict their Twitter handle, all posts are public by default and, thus, anyone can see them.

This creates a unique culture on Twitter versus Facebook. Facebook is the place you go to talk to people you already know; Twitter is the place you go to meet new people. Twitter is the ultimate cocktail party, where it's perfectly acceptable for a person or even a company to strike up a conversation with pretty much anyone over even the most mundane of topics. By understanding and embracing this cultural nuance of Twitter, a company can painlessly prospect for new business.

A former client, The Drake Hotel in Chicago, successfully used this approach to meet and win business from Chicago Twitter users. Figure 10-3 shows an example in which The Drake struck up a conversation with a highly influential Chicago Twitter user, David Armano, by simply talking about the weather.

**Figure 10-3**   *The Drake Hotel engaging David Armano on Twitter*

The resulting exchange both ingratiated The Drake to David and also resulted in David booking a room to celebrate his 40th birthday at the hotel (see Figure 10-4).

**Figure 10-4**   *The Drake Hotel booking a room on Twitter*

Notice that multiple times during the exchange, The Drake, which is presented as a corporate brand instead of a personified brand (such as MarketingProfs), engages with David in very human terms. From kidding with him about his Klout score (a Klout Score is a number between 1-100 that represents how influential a person is online based on a proprietary formula developed by Klout) to making a reference to David's love of Harley-Davidson, The Drake has fun with him instead of striking a professional tone. If you read the exchange out loud, it sounds like two people talking instead of a consumer talking with a brand. This is a key component to social selling. As I noted earlier in this chapter, social media is just a new phone. Just as you wouldn't talk like a press release when talking to a prospect on the phone, you should extend that same personal touch to your social profiles. If you do, you will find ample opportunities to win new business on these platforms.

# Creating a Sense of Attachment

Now let's turn from looking at how you can engage from a brand perspective and think about engaging at the individual salesperson level. Social selling at an individual level is about networking at scale, as I often refer to it. Having lived with a foot firmly planted in the old way of networking (doing everything face to face or by phone or email) and one planted in this brave new digital, social-powered world, I can tell you that it's so much easier to network in the new, virtual world than the old.

To demonstrate, let me share with you how a friend of mine, Steve Woodruff, who you will remember from Chapter 8, uses social media (specifically, LinkedIn) to create what he calls a sense of attachment between his prospects and himself. I love the phrase "sense of attachment" because it so perfectly explains the odd, in non-social media users' minds, social dynamics that rise from virtual relationships. Steve is a great example of a guy who understands that dynamic and is probably one of the best at working under it. Steve and I first met face to face via a video chat on Skype after we'd tweeted with each other for more than a year. That call was just as much a call among old friends as any I've experienced. That's the power of networking at scale via social media. You can use these platforms to create that sense of attachment, even without ever having met in real life. So let's see how Steve does it.

Steve is probably one of the best ambassadors on the Internet. He routinely establishes embassies on various platforms. Whether it's his Circle of Trust (a private Facebook group), his #LeadershipChat (which was cohosted with the brilliant Lisa Petrilli—they've stopped doing the chat) on Twitter, or his various private groups on LinkedIn, Steve creates virtual gathering places and serves as the glue that connects like-minded people in holding conversations and establishing relationships that make everyone more successful.

And that is the great value of embassies. An embassy enables you to create a sense of attachment between your prospects (with each other) and between you and your prospect. Just as many of us have a favorite author, musician, or band with whom we have an almost unnatural attachment, you can create this as well by simply being helpful and striving to make others more successful at what they do—by doing nothing more than joining you at your embassy.

This idea of attachment is the most powerful aspect of a propinquity strategy because you are not trying to create TOMA, as has historically been the case with advertising and traditional outbound marketing. Instead, you are trying to create something more important, something more impactful. You're trying to create TOMP. Restated in the language of the traditional RFP (request-for-proposal)-based sales process, you're trying to create a top-of-stack relationship. You want to be the person, company, or proposal placed on the top of the stack of proposals because it's the one that the prospect is predisposed to want to sign.

Achieve TOMP, and you are more likely to be sourced by prospects when they are at the point of purchase. If their purchasing process requires some sort of RFP or multibid process, not only will you be invited, but you'll enjoy most favored nation status during that process.

So let's revisit how Steve does this with LinkedIn. Steve's company Impactiviti, helps pharmaceutical executives source qualified vendors for outsource services and helps high-quality vendors establish relationships with qualified pharmaceutical executives that can hire them. In his words, he's the eHarmony of pharmaceutical vendor/client relationships. Steve's success depends on being top-of-stack. He needs his prospects to call him when they need a connection. To do this, he creates those embassies we talked about in Chapter 8. But he goes even further.

His embassies are private LinkedIn groups where Steve has to approve every person that applies for access. This gives Steve a couple great opportunities from both a creating attachment and sales prospecting perspective.

First, the group is generating inbound leads for Steve. Unlike Facebook, where private groups are basically invisible, LinkedIn's Group Directory displays all groups, both open and closed (LinkedIn terminology for "private"). Thus, simply having a group turns invisible leads into visible connections for Steve. And as members of the group tell their peers about the group, Steve just has to sit back and wait for the leads to appear in his Group Administrator panel. This is the prospecting opportunity.

Second, remember that Steve isn't creating this group just to find new leads. He's committed to creating a valuable, safe place that his members actually want to frequent. He's trying to be more seductive by focusing not on a quota, but instead on being chivalrous. Thus, he doesn't let just anyone in. He vets new members by visiting their LinkedIn page. He could even email or call them to welcome them to the group and understand what they hope to get out of their time in the group. Steve reaches out directly to certain key individuals to establish more direct contact, opening up communication channels that eventually could turn into a discussion about vendor needs.

Did you read that last sentence? *He is using a LinkedIn group to create a warm sales call with a new prospect.* That's a brilliant use of social selling. When he has someone on the phone or even email, he can quickly begin to build that sense of attachment. He can probe deeply to understand the person's pain points, goals, or needs and then use that information to immediately begin doing what he does: connecting vendors to executives and executives to executives to make everyone more successful.

Third, Steve has created a safe zone free of vendors. Well, that's not exactly true, because Steve is there. He sees and hears every conversation and participates in a good number of them himself. He has created some mighty big ears that only he can use to hear. If you believe that information is power or that having better information gives you an unfair selling advantage, ask yourself how much power and advantage Steve has over his competitors.

And to think, Steve is generating new leads and creating a sense of attachment every week by playing on LinkedIn.

Ask yourself how many of Steve's phone calls and emails get returned. Ask yourself who holds the vaunted TOMP place (what Steve calls "becoming the go-to") in the minds of Steve's group members. Ask yourself if Steve could ever create that TOMP position using cold calls and emails?

And I can tell you from personal experience this phenomenon isn't just limited to LinkedIn. I have had the good fortune of belonging to a tourism-based, private Facebook Group for a few years. The group is primarily made up of client side marketers in the destination marketing space—a space where my firm does a good amount of work—and includes only a handful of vendors. The rules are pretty straightforward. Vendors are allowed to stay, as long as they participate fully and don't outright prospect. But that doesn't mean prospecting isn't happening in that group.

I know from chatting with a few of the other vendors that like me, they too can source significant amounts of business to the group. They understand that by being active and helpful in the group they can be sexy, seductive, or maybe even thought of as #Pretty. Regardless of the term of endearment, by putting the needs of the client-side marketers ahead of sourcing new deals, these vendors, like myself build that same sense of attachment that Steve talks about. And when the client-side members of the group have a project that needs doing, we vendors usually get first shot or in some cases are the single source provider that is contacted. It is easily the highest return-on-investment social selling tool in my toolbox.

So do you still think you don't have time to play around on Twitter, Facebook, and LinkedIn? Are you sure about that?

# Six Ways to Get Started in Social Selling

Social selling isn't brain surgery. But often folks who aren't used to doing it just need a little push. That's what this section is for—just a list of little pushes to get you started. So give one, a few, or all six, a try, and then let me know how they worked for you. I've even created a place where you can share your war stories, ask questions, and chat with other folks who are exploring just like you. Visit TheInvisibleSale.com and check out the Community page. Till then, here's your homework:

1.  Join a few clubs. Go to LinkedIn's Group section and search for key-words for your industry or the industries of your prospects. See which groups show up in the search results. Then head over and check out those groups to see if any of them look like a target-rich environment. If they do, join the group and then go be nice, helpful, and focused on providing service to the other members.

2.  Twitter Chats[2] are a great way to meet new people on Twitter. We've posted a number of Twitter Chat lists on TheInvisibleSale.com. Head over there and see if you find one that might work for you.

3.  Use Twitter Search (https://twitter.com/search) to conduct keyword searches. Think about the customer problems your product or service solves or what kinds of questions your customer might be asking on Twitter. Then search for those words and see what you find. If you find tweets from prospects you can help, go ahead and offer to do so. If you find tweets from folks you can't help (maybe you don't serve their geography), but you know where to point them for that help, do so. Karma is good to have on your side.

4.  Do you attend trade shows or conferences? Live Blog or Live Tweet the conference sessions. This just means that you can take notes using tweets and then share those notes with anyone who is following you. You can do the same with your company's website. At the end of each day, consolidate your notes and create a blog post on your website with a rundown of the most important points made during educational ses-sions or announcements made at the conference.

5.  Another great trade show tactic is to interview attendees or speakers at the conference on video. We talk more about this in Chapter 11, "Creating Video," and I share an example of how Emma (an email marketing firm) used this tactic to meet prospects and create a year's

---

worth of video content. For now, just know that it's a great way to provide really helpful, interesting content that you can push out through your Painless Prospecting platform to help position you and your company to win the invisible sale.

6. Be the conference concierge. If you're attending a conference or trade show in your home town or a city you know well, monitor Twitter for other attendees who are asking questions about where to eat, drink, or pretty much do anything attendees often need help with when traveling. Then point those folks in the right direction. Be the "go to" person on the ground with all the inside scoop. Everyone likes that person.

## POWER POINTS

- Social selling is like cold calling, except that the calls are warm and welcomed.

- Social selling is about seduction. It's not a quick close—it's about building a relationship with prospects before they're even ready to buy.

- Social selling aids in the selling process by making it easier for a company or salesperson to hear the voice of the prospect.

- You need to develop a plan for presenting the company online—decide whether the company should exist as a brand or a person.

- If the social brand is a person, you need to define ownership of platforms, followers, friends, and contacts. The company, not the individual, retains those if the social face of the company leaves.

- Brands can be human on social networks. It's okay to talk about the weather; it might just result in a new customer.

- The goal of social selling is to create a sense of attachment to the company or to a salesperson.

*Download all the Power Points at TheInvisibleSale.com.*

# SECTION 3

# Creating Your Content

As you've been reading through the book, have you been thinking that there's no way you can possibly pull this off? That there's no way you and your team can produce all the content you need to fill all those propinquity points you just finished mapping? Are you thinking that you and your team are already working at full capacity and you simply don't have time to produce more content? It's okay. I used to think that, too.

I used to think there was no way I could blog once a week, travel to and deliver 20 to 30 speaking appearances a year, handle client work, and find time to be a half-decent dad and husband, much less find the time to write this book. Yet here you are reading that very book I never thought I would have the time to write. And yes, I still blog once a week and average about 20 speaking appearances a year on a slow year. I continue to handle the client work and well, you'd have to ask my wife and kids about my success at being a good husband and father.

I tell you this not to brag about myself, but instead to help you see that I am like you. I had those same doubts and challenges. I, too, used to complain that I didn't have enough time to write more or create more content. In fact, those very feelings led me to create all the tips, tricks, and shortcuts I'm about to share with you. What you're about to read is the sum total of almost five years of successes, failures, tests, and experiments as I tried to find the magic solution. And while I still search for new and better processes and tools to optimize my content creation efforts, I think you'll be quite content with the abundance of information we're about to cover. Through these pages, you will come to realize that creating the enormous amounts of content required to power your Painless Prospecting system is actually a lot easier than you think—once you know what you're doing.

In this section, we cover the nuts and bolts of how you can create do-it-yourself marketing content in every format. When you're done with this section, you'll understand how to create *right-sized content* (RSC). RSC matches the level of content production to the usage situation—and the failure to create RSC is the biggest mistake marketers make today. You'll understand tools and production techniques for optimizing the efficiency of your content creation, and you'll have a disciplined system for creating and disseminating all that great content.

# Creating Right-Sized Content

The first big concept we need to talk about is the idea of creating right-sized content. In the content creation realm, most marketers fall victim to two huge challenges on a daily basis. The first is that they create content at the wrong level—they choose to focus on single content pieces instead of creating an ecosystem of content. We cover that in detail in Chapter 16, "Cornerstones and Cobblestones: The Content Creation Framework." The second challenge is that these same marketers misspend on production quality.

Marketers traditionally fall victim to a cycle of overspending on the production quality of their online marketing content, resulting in unsustainable content marketing programs. Then when the shock of overspending wears off, they swing the pendulum too far the other direction and underspend to the point of producing ineffective content. Or worse, they simply abandon the idea of creating sharable content to drive in-bound leads.

The answer to this challenge is RSC. The RSC concept is based on matching the quality of your content, in terms of production quality and cost, to the content need you are filling. Simply put, a Facebook video doesn't need to be shot or produced at the same quality level as a television commercial. The digital world has trained the buyer to accept—or, in some instances, desire—lower-quality content. In fact, overproduced content often can be just as ineffective as underproduced content.

But with that said, you're still probably not going to use your mobile phone to record your company's most important video assets. But as you'll see in this section, you don't necessarily have to hire a professional video crew either. When you understand your technology and production quality options, you can make informed decisions on which content creation solution to deploy for each content opportunity. Armed with this knowledge, you can right-size your content every time.

# Content Creation Types

We start with what is arguably one of the most persuasive but least utilized media: video. Video's power is its ability to combine sight, sound, and motion to truly leverage emotional selling points like no other medium. Traditional advertisers value and invest in this power via television commercials.

If you've ever been on the set of a video shoot, you know that it can be an overwhelming situation. Everywhere you look, you see people, cameras, cables, and a controlled chaos that makes the average person feel that video creation is outside his or her capability. Add to this the computer knowledge and tools needed to effectively edit video, and you can understand why most people don't consider video a Do-It-Yourself (DIY) medium. But in Chapter 11, "Creating Video," we change that. I show you there how my 10-year-old son creates, edits, and publishes video using nothing other than an iPad or an iPhone—and I tell you how you can, too. We also talk about the different types of cameras you need to consider when creating RSC. And we finish up with a thorough discussion of lighting and audio, to round out the necessary education you need to get started producing your own DIY sales and marketing video content.

From video, we move on to photography. Here again, too many people believe that the only solution for creating high-end photography is to hire an expensive professional photographer. Don't get me wrong: Although some instances certainly warrant a professional, DIY photography shot by you or your team suffices in plenty of instances. The key is to know the tools of the trade, techniques, software, and apps you need to elevate your shots from nice home photo to a professional-quality marketing tool.

I also want you to strongly consider adding audio to your marketing toolbox. We spend a chapter talking about the power of podcasting and how mobile tools such as iPads and mobile phones can help you quickly create interesting and effective audio content. For instance, did you know that, for about $100, you can turn an ordinary iPad into a powerful mobile audio recording and production studio? But I don't stop there—I also introduce you to a professional podcaster who offers step-by-step instructions for creating your own professional-level podcasting studio at your office.

And we can't forget the most commonly used content: text. But I don't talk about how you can type more text—no, I talk about how to use tools such as speech-to-text software to turbo-charge your writing abilities. I show you how to combine mobile phone apps with inexpensive computer software to turn your morning and evening commutes into highly productive writing sessions. I discuss services to turn any audio file, such as an interview with an industry thought leader, into a fully formatted and largely ready-to-post piece of text content. And I introduce you to a simple, proven writing process to write higher-quality content faster than you've ever imagined. If you've ever told yourself that you don't have time to write more, this might just be the single most valuable chapter in the whole book for you.

From the common content types, we move into less common formats, such as webinars, product demos, tutorials, and how-to videos. Again, too many people think that these content forms require expensive professionals or technical know-how that is beyond their ability. That's simply not true. I show you how you can create live and recorded webinars with nothing more than a laptop and a couple pieces of cheap software. And in what is probably my favorite trick, I show you how to turn your next PowerPoint presentation into a streaming webinar using nothing but a mobile phone and a free Internet website tool.

 *Note*

> I need to share one important note with you before we go much further. As you've probably already noticed, when I talk about content creation, I mention a lot of i-devices. I'm a devoted Apple fan, and many of the apps, techniques, and shortcuts I discuss are Apple device centric. But if you're a PC user, don't worry. I used to be one, too, so wherever I can, I give you the PC or Android (if it's mobile-oriented) solutions to create the same content types. In some cases, there's no PC or Android option to accomplish what you can with an Apple product. In those cases, I simply let you know that; you can decide whether the solution is worth the expense of becoming a Mac user.

# A Disciplined Content Creation Framework

Finally, this section finishes with an introduction to Cornerstones and Cobblestones. The single biggest lesson you're going to take away from this section is how to create content at the right level. Far too many marketers focus on creating content at the blog post or individual content piece level. That's why the idea of creating tons of content seems so daunting to most people. They see all the various content types and channels and think there's simply no way they can produce all those content pieces. That's because they're planning and creating their content at the wrong level.

In Chapter 16, I show you how to strategically create big pieces of Cornerstone Content such as white papers, major presentations, and eBooks that are predesigned to break down into easily distributable Cobblestones. But I don't just talk about it; I walk you step by step through an actual Cornerstone and Cobblestone example. You'll follow my every move as I create an actual piece of Cornerstone content and then break it down and distribute it to my various propinquity points. And at multiple steps, I share the actual URLs where you can go see the final results so that you can better understand how I use this process to seed content throughout my digital footprint to painlessly prospect for new clients and position my firm to win the invisible sale.

Up to this point, we've been talking more theoretically. This section gets very utilitarian. My goal here is to give you your MBA in DIY marketing content creation. And although I give you a lot of really good step-by-step examples here, I've included even more at TheInvisibleSale.com, along with a complete list of all the software and hardware I discuss in these chapters. That way, you get a simple, one-stop shopping destination so that you can go from thinking about the ideas you've read in this book to acting on those ideas and creating your sales and marketing content.

Now, let's get started.

# 11

# Creating Video

*I love sharing the story of the making of the USS Duct Tape. (You can see the video at TheInvisibleSale.com/ VideoTools.) The video shares the successful inaugural floating of a handmade boat created by three young boys. Over the course of a week at Tinkering Camp in Austin, Texas, those three boys, with the help of a few adult counselors, made that boat out of materials they found. Finally, on the last day of the camp, the boys took the boat to the river to see if it would float. As you see in the video, the USS Duct Tape sort of floated. The boys learned that the weight limit was around 180 pounds, so as long as only two boys were on the boat, it floated. If they crossed that magical number, the bailing began.*

*You're probably starting to wonder what that summer camp video has to do with marketing video creation. If you have that video accessible, look at the video thumbnail. Do you see that victorious 10-year-old with the orange flag? That's my son, Hayes.*

Hayes is the producer of the video. That's right, a 10-year-old boy made the video. He made it from pictures and videos that I took with my iPhone as I watched him and his team attempt to launch the *USS Duct Tape*. But from there, he did all the editing, inserted the music, added on-screen titles, and assembled and produced the entire movie. Impressed?

Wait, I'm not done yet. He did all that editing on my iPhone while riding in the back of my car on the drive back from Austin to New Orleans. It took him about three hours, and if I had been willing to let him blow up my data plan, he could have published the video to YouTube, too. And all that would have happened before we even arrived home in New Orleans.

But this isn't just a story to show you how easy it is to create video. There's more. The camp in Austin liked it so much that it republished it on their Facebook page. My wife and I shared it on our Facebook pages, and the response was a bit surprising.

After sharing the video, I cannot tell you how many parents asked me about the camp. They wanted to know where they could go to learn more about it, find out pricing, view dates for the next year, and so on. That little iPhone video that my 10-year-old son created in the back of a car was the perfect little piece of right-sized content (RSC).

Yes, it was obviously amateur video. No, it wasn't perfect. But it was engaging, it was funny, and it showed kids having a ball doing something truly unique and interesting. What more could a parent want in a summer camp? That little iPhone video is a perfect example of an effective marketing video.

Now, granted, my son isn't your average kid. He's very inventive, he's technologically adept and he has an uncanny ability (for his age) to remain focused on projects for long periods of time. It didn't hurt that, the previous summer, he attended film camp and learned how to make a movie with Final Cut Pro. But he's still a 10-year-old boy creating a video that makes parents want to send their kid to a Tinkering Camp. He's a 10-year-old boy who used DIY video to capture the invisible sale and convert it to the very visible customer.

And if my kid can do it, I promise you that you can, too.

## Let the Equipment Do the Work

What Hayes and I have learned is that today's technology and equipment can pretty much make anyone a movie director. The power of mobile phones and the plethora of video apps for those phones is mind-boggling. The combination of the two makes it easy for anyone to create stunning videos.

For instance, go back over to TheInvisibleSale.com/VideoTools and watch the *Man on the Mound* video. It's a nifty little time-lapse video I created watching my son Davis' baseball game. In a brief snippet of video, you see multiple innings of pitching condensed into a minute or so of time-lapse video. Normally, to create this effect, you need to shoot still photos and then stitch those photos together in a video-creation program. It's incredibly time consuming but an absolutely awesome way to create interesting video from what might otherwise be a repetitive or elongated process.

I created that video by simply affixing my iPhone to a tripod that I placed behind the backstop. Then I used an inexpensive iPhone app (Lapse It) to capture the pictures. To do this, I just activated the app, set the photo interval (time between pictures), and clicked the Start button. After a few innings of watching the game, I walked back over to the iPhone, clicked the Stop button and then clicked the Render button. In a few short minutes, I had the time-lapse video you can see at TheInvisibleSale.com/VideoTools.

Another great example is creating depth of field[1] in video using an inexpensive ($100) lens on a standard digital camera. I shoot a lot of my video on my Canon 7D camera. And when I'm shooting interviews or any video and I want the viewer to really focus on the onscreen talent, I always use a 55mm f/2.8 prime lens. We talk more about lenses in Chapter 12, "Creating Photography," but this particular lens creates a visually interesting effect. Because it has a very shallow depth of field, it keeps your onscreen talent in crisp focus while simultaneously rendering everything in the background out of focus. The resulting effect looks very professional but requires no real talent or understanding on your part. The lens does *all* the work for you. To see an example of the effect, visit ConverseDigital.com/ContentMarketing/Making-Better-Interview-Videos.

# Focus on Storytelling

The power of video is its ability to tell a story using sight, sound, and motion. It is one of the only marketing channels that lets you combine all those elements to tap a buyer's emotional triggers. And although that used to be out of your reach, as I just showed you, it isn't anymore. But to really leverage the power of video marketing, you have to focus on telling a story with your video, because if you do, you can work miracles.

Chris Yates is the founder of Huddle Productions in Dallas, Texas. Chris is an Emmy Award-winning producer that worked in sports broadcasting for more than 12 years. During that time, Chris covered the Super Bowl, the Masters, the NBA Finals, the Daytona 500, and countless other events. His company, Huddle

---

1. http://en.wikipedia.org/wiki/Depth_of_field.

Productions, creates social video for companies such as Bud Light, Verizon, Spectrum Properties, and many more.

But when I interviewed Chris for this chapter, he didn't speak about any of that work. When I told him that the purpose of this chapter is to help people understand that they can do video themselves using affordable tools and techniques, he immediately jumped to his work with DeleteBloodCancer.org and the story of Danielle Stephens. Danielle needed a stem-cell transplant to live. This required a donor match, and she didn't have one. So DeleteBloodCancer.org asked Chris to create a YouTube video for use in a social media-powered campaign to create awareness of a "swab event" where people can provide a DNA sample for matching. The goal was to get a couple hundred views on YouTube and help get a few strangers through the door.

The result was a video that did almost 5,000 views and resulted in 2,188 strangers showing up for swabbing, including Dallas Cowboys Super Bowl quarterback Troy Aikman (who shared the video on his own social media channels). All that came from a video that Yates shot on an iPhone with a simple iRig microphone combined with still photos from the family. The entire video was edited together with Final Cut Pro, and Yates found a piece of free music to use as background music for the video.

When I asked Yates why the video had so successfully motivated strangers to action, he had one answer: It told a story. By combining family photos with on-camera interviews and candid family togetherness video footage, Yates helped the audience see Danielle as more than just a blood cancer victim. He transformed her into a living, breathing devoted mother of two young boys who deserved a fighting chance. You can see the video at http://youtu.be/wQjhEGbiPoI, and I encourage you to watch it.

Whether you're creating a video to save a life or sell a product, your goal needs to remain the same. *You have to make the viewer care about the subject matter.* So as you begin your video creation project, think about the story surrounding your product or service. Don't just tell the viewer that your product can solve problem X. Tell them how it solved problem X for customer Y and led to a meaningful change. Focus on the drama behind the story of problem X.

For instance, what will happen to customer Y if the company doesn't fix problem X? Will it go out of business? That is a great starting point for a story but probably not a compelling enough point. Instead, focus on what having customer Y go out of business means for the people who work there. Then tell the story of how your product saved the job of employee Z instead of how your product fixed the problem for customer Y. The latter point is important but hard to relate to. The former makes it personal and compelling and lets you tap deeper human emotions, which is where video really excels.

# Video Creates Relationships

Video also has an uncanny ability to generate relationships between the viewer and on-camera talent. If you look at any talk, cooking, or DIY television show, you'll find that the more successful ones tend to have very likable hosts. The hosts inspire us, enamor us, or somehow just connect with us as viewers. And this is probably the most overlooked detail in corporate or sales-oriented videos.

Brian Matson, Client Strategist at Think!SocialMedia and himself a former on-air personality, said it best. When I asked him how companies can create better "talking head" video, he answered, "Find on-air talent that is passionate and can convey their passion for your brand or company." He went on to say, "Maybe you or your CEO isn't the best person to serve as the on-air talent for your brand." Brian makes an incredibly important argument. So often, especially in the B2B world, companies use the vice president of marketing, the director of Sales, the brand or product manager, or the president or CEO as the on-air talent because those people make the most sense, given their product knowledge.

Don't make that mistake. That person on screen is as much your brand as the product or service you're marketing. The on-air talent needs to come through the screen and capture the viewer's attention. He or she needs to make you want to keep watching that video. Otherwise, that person is just taking up space on the screen, and your video efforts will likely be less effective. In some cases, this may be one of those key executives. But if none of those folks can convey their passion, recruit a passionate employee or hire professional talent.

# Creating Better Video

If you want to make your video appear more professional and be more effective, you need to understand some of the finer points of good video. Like any talent, a little bit of coaching goes a long way. Let's discuss some of the tips Chris and Brian shared with me, along with a few lessons I've learned along the way.

First, from a content perspective, focus on educating your viewer. Viewers want tips, information, or to learn how to do something. No question is too small or too niche. Think of video like an enhanced version of the FAQ (frequently asked questions) section of your website. Salesforce does a great job of this. In Figure 11.1, you see how it's using videos in place of standard text/photo-based "how to" guides. This makes it very easy for customers (or prospective customers) to answer their own questions and gives Google a wonderful piece of content to index and then serve up in its own search results. You can see the actual Salesforce page at www.salesforce.com/smallbusinesscenter/demo-videos/.

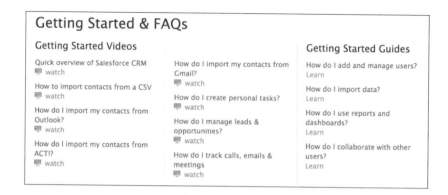

**Figure 11-1**   *Video FAQ page from Salesforce.com*

Next, from a style perspective, pay attention to your video framing. If you're filming someone talking directly to the camera, frame the shot from the belly button to the top of the head, leaving a little room in the frame above the person's head. Also, don't necessarily arrange the person directly in the center of the screen. Experiment with placing the person in the far-left or far-right portion of the frame, especially if you're shooting in 16:9 ratio (widescreen) versus 4:3 (square screen). This has two benefits. First, it looks professional, especially if you're using a lighting kit to create a more professional lighting effect. Second, and more important, having the empty frame area gives you room to include text overlays in the final video file. This might include logos, key quotes, or hyperlinks.

Another talking head video tip that Chris shared is to have the subject look at a point 2 to 3 feet to the left or right of the camera instead of directly at the camera. He usually just holds up his hand and asks the person to look at his hand instead of the camera. Alternatively, you can mount your camera on a tripod, frame your subject, and then simply stand or sit next to the camera and ask the person to look directly at you. This has two positive effects. First, it makes the interview look more like what consumers are used to seeing on the news. The reporter in an interview never stands directly in front of the camera, so the interviewee's eyes are never looking directly into the camera. Second, not looking directly into the camera makes many interviewees relax a bit more and feel more comfortable. It's odd to look directly into a camera and talk; that discomfort will come through in the final video product.

While we're talking about interviewing tips, another great one is timing. It may be terribly difficult, but never cut off your interviewee by asking another question on top of his or her answer. Force yourself to wait for the person to finish, allow for a few seconds of quiet, and then ask your next question. Likewise, before you start an interview, encourage the person to keep a few seconds of quiet between your question and the answer. In both cases, having these few seconds of dead air gives you a clean edit point. Nothing is more frustrating than trying to clip a quote out of an interview and find that you can't get a clean cut because there's no dead space.

Another big point that both Chris and Brian drive home is that audio is probably the most important piece of any video. It doesn't matter how incredible your video looks—if the viewer can't hear the people speaking, your video just failed. As a video marketer, there are tricks for covering up bad video, but you're powerless to cover bad audio. So invest in good microphones. Most likely, you'll want to have at least three or four different types of microphones. For basic interviewing, you'll want a wired lavaliere mic (the kind that clips onto a person's shirt), a handheld microphone, and a shotgun mic (a long, cylindrical microphone that excels at picking up sounds in front of it, while rejecting sounds to the sides and rear). You will probably want to invest in a wireless lavaliere microphone too. We talk about each of these in more depth in Chapter 13, "Creating Audio."

Regardless of what kind of microphone you're using, when you set up a video shoot, listen to your surroundings. Do a few audio samples (video anything so that you can hear how much background noise you're picking up) to understand the impact of the background noise on the audio recording. If you're getting too much background, move the shoot. This becomes especially important when you're doing interviews at conferences or trade shows, both of which can be notoriously loud environments.

Lastly, pay attention to your lighting. If you can't see your subject, you've lost one of the most powerful aspects of video: sight. Numerous lighting options are available. From simple LED lights that mount directly to a camera, to more elaborate three-point lighting kits, there's a solution to fit every budget and need. But make no mistake—you need to invest in lighting, especially if you're shooting video with a mobile phone, which magnifies the effect. For an example, visit www.converse-digital.com/iphone-lighting for a video demonstrating the difference. We talk more about lighting in Chapter 12, and I share a few specific lighting setups you might want to consider.

# Cameras for Video Creation

One of the biggest decisions you'll make each time you create RSC video is camera selection. Not only does camera selection drive cost (you actually need to own the various camera types), but more important, it affects your workflow and production timeline. And although investing in multiple cameras isn't necessary, I recommend having at least a smartphone and one additional camera—a DSLR (digital still photo camera) or traditional camcorder—to give yourself some creative freedom.

One of the greatest benefits of using mobile phones and tablets to capture video is their ability to capture, edit, produce, and publish video directly from the device. From a workflow standpoint, this can be ideal when you're creating real-time video coverage of an event, conference, festival, or product launch. So for those times when you're "running and gunning" with a very small content creation crew, the mobile solution is often your best choice. But smartphones have one big drawback: their inability to zoom. So if you need to zoom, you'll have to invest in a camcorder or DSLR option.

If you're budget challenged, you might opt to purchase a high-end DSLR to capture your video content. This gives you one device to shoot both professional-grade video and photography. Personally, and I'm not alone in this, a lot of people think the DSLRs capture better video quality than even high-end camcorders. The video seems to have a more filmlike quality to it. And with the ability to quickly swap different types of lenses on a DSLR, you gain a nice amount of creative latitude. But the trade-off is that DSLR cameras can have issues with recording longer pieces of material. If you shoot very long (20 to 30 minutes or more) video, the sensors in DSLR cameras can overheat; this results in audio dropout, and the camera stops recording the audio. I also find that although the cameras can zoom, unless you invest in additional lens adaptors, the zoom isn't nearly as smooth as with a camcorder.

Even within the camcorder solution, you have to think through what level of camcorder you really need. In some cases, a standard high-end consumer version might be just fine, given that these camcorders record in HD, accept external microphones, and, in some cases, can accept external lenses to increase the creative latitude. They also tend to be very compact in form, making them much easier to travel with when capturing video on location.

In other instances, you definitely want to opt for a professional-grade video camera. The benefit of the professional-level camera is recording range. A consumer-level camcorder might have issues with lowlight recording, but a professional camera has manual settings to compensate. The professional cameras offer extensive manual settings that, in the hands of a properly trained user, allow for the capture of truly great video. However, the power of the professional-level camera is also its greatest weakness. If you opt for a professional-grade video camera, you need to invest time and possibly money into proper training for whoever will operate the camera.

Regardless of the option (or options) you choose, every camera you use needs to accept an external microphone. Because audio quality is so imperative to good video, you simply cannot use the onboard microphone of any camera. Also be aware that the iPhone uses a special headset jack, so if you want to attach an external mic to the iPhone, you need to purchase an inexpensive adaptor cable. But don't worry—I've placed a link at TheInvisibleSale.com/AudioTools where you can learn more about the cable and visit the manufacturer's site to purchase the cable.

# Desktop Video Editing

After you've captured your video, you need to edit it into a finished product. When I started my advertising career, video editing meant a trip to New York City to sit with the video editing team in a high-tech Avid Video Editing Bay. There was literally a room full of hard drives with digitized video and an entire switchboard of monitors, dials, and keyboards to make the necessary video edits. And as you can imagine, it was all quite expensive.

Fast-forward 20 years, and pretty much everything we did in those Avid bays can now be done on a laptop by you and me using programs such as iMovie, Final Cut Pro, Pinnacle Studios, Microsoft Movie Maker, Adobe's Premier Elements, and Avid's Media Composer. Each of these applications lets ordinary folks perform incredibly complex, professional-grade editing to both the visual and audio aspects of our videos.

If you're using a Mac user, you'll probably want to start with iMovie. iMovie's easy drag-and-drop editor is drop-dead simple to use and will probably be all you ever need for the vast majority of videos you create. If you find you need to step up to something more powerful, Final Cut Pro and the simpler Final Cut Express are both great options. A word of warning, though: These two programs are more advanced, so if you're not using them often, it becomes easy to forget how to do even the simplest editing tasks.

If you're looking for a higher-end editing option that is fairly intuitive to use, you might want to consider Adobe Premiere Elements or Pinnacle Studios. Premiere is available for both Mac and PC, but Pinnacle is PC only. Both are great applications for straightforward editing such as adding titles, adding soundtracks, slowing down or speeding up footage, and outputting in a variety of formats. These two apps are powerful, easy to use, and priced for even the tightest budget.

When you're ready to step up to truly professional level tools, Final Cut Pro is probably one of the most-used and most well-respected Mac editing products on the market today. It is incredibly powerful, but as I noted earlier, it's not the easiest program to use—if you won't use it often, you might forget how to do things. It's also a Mac-only program. On the PC side of the world, there's Avid Media Composer and Avid NewsCutter. As with Final Cut Pro, these apps aren't for the meek or untrained; they're serious, professional-level editing applications. But in the hands of someone who knows the programs, you can do pretty much everything.

Whichever solution you choose, the main point here is the same. With a little effort, you can create professionally produced videos on your laptop while you fly home from that next sales call or client meeting.

## A DIY Video Blog Case Study

As I alluded to earlier, I'm a huge fan of using mobile devices to record many types of video. Their small format, ability to both capture and edit on one device, and vast array of apps that make creating good video a lot easier open up a world of creative opportunities for the DIY video creator. And in some cases, a mobile phone could be the only device you need to create and produce your own video marketing content.

Believe it or not, you can create, publish, and maintain an entire video blog using nothing other than an iPhone. In 2011, Emma, an email-marketing firm based in Nashville, Tennessee, did just that. The company partnered with my firm, Converse Digital, to launch an innovative marketing campaigned designed to raise their profile among social media thought leaders. The resulting campaign was a 52-week video blog series called TalkingWithTom. Each week, the blog featured a short interview with a leading social media or digital marketing thought leader answering one question: *What's next?* The videos and a short text description (see Figure 11-2) of the thought leader were published every Monday morning during 2011.

**Figure 11-2**  *TalkingWithTom.com weekly video blog*

*All videos were shot, edited, and produced using my iPhone and the iMovie video-editing app.* Each blog post was written on the iPhone with a mobile blogging app, and every Monday morning we uploaded the post and video to the TalkingWithTom website. We even managed any comments on blog posts from the mobile app. The entire campaign, including agency fees, the iPhone, my travel expenses, iPhone data, and website hosting plans, cost about 1/10th of the average cost to produce a single television commercial.[2] And although we certainly could have done this with traditional cameras and workflow, using the iPhone made capturing on-location interviews with these thought leaders cheaper, faster, and significantly easier. Instead of having to carry a ton of camera and audio tools, I just had an iPhone and a wireless lavaliere microphone that fit nicely in my gear bag.

Mobile technology, smartphones, and tablets have fundamentally changed the world of video creation. They have democratized video production in a way that previously wasn't possible. Mobile technology, the hardware and software, has brought the power of video to the masses. For the cost of a smartphone or tablet plus a few accessories and apps, you can assemble a fully functional multimedia production center that fits in your briefcase or your pocket. And because mobile video will likely be where you find it easiest to begin incorporating video into your marketing efforts, I want to spend the rest of this chapter talking about the apps and tools you need to be most successful.

# Mobile Video-Creation Apps

To really access the power of mobile phones and tablets as video content studios, you have to invest a few dollars in apps. The great news is that you get a ton of editing power for very little money. In fact, the most expensive app I cover here costs less than $15. Lots of video-creation apps exist, so don't think that the list I'm giving you is the technology bible. I'm constantly discovering new apps and don't foresee that changing anytime in the future.

Let's start with video capture. Certainly, the base camera app that ships with your mobile device is just fine. But as I learned in my TalkingWithTom project, often you're forced to shoot in suboptimal lighting conditions. You might not have enough available light, and in the case of the iPhone, the flash is entirely too harsh for use in video. This means you have to bring along your own lighting, which we talk about in Chapter 12. But sometimes you can use an app to capture what you need without having to pull out the lighting.

In these cases, I favor FiLMiC Pro, which, unfortunately, comes in only iPhone and iPad versions. What I like about this app is its ability to give you enormous

---

2. 2011 Executive Summary of the 4A's Television Production Cost Survey, www.aaaa.org/news/bulletins/Documents/7480.pdf.

control over video capture frame rates. When you're shooting in low light, one way to counter the lack of light is to simply slow your frame rate. This doesn't fix every situation, but it often saves the day. Also, these slower frame rates can add a bit of drama to regular videos to give your product videos extra pizzazz. Lastly, you can add film slates to the beginning of each video. Film slates are those little wooden things you always see production people snap right before they shoot a scene on a movie. Film slates give the video editor key information, such as the name of the footage, the scene number, and even the camera number if more than one camera is being used. Having this information captured on your videos can be a huge time saver when you've shot a ton of stuff and then have to go back and start editing it all into something usable.

When you're ready to try something more creative, think about how you can use time-lapse videos. A time-lapse video such as *The Man on the Mound* is a great way to show ongoing activity or change that happens over time. Time-lapse videos are great for showing how something is built, like a home, building, art exhibit, or other complex assembly activity. But they're also a great video marketing tool to have in your toolbox for pretty much any product or service because the resulting videos are just cool. If they're done correctly, it can result in viral shares of your content.

My favorite app to use is Lapse It. This app is available for both iPhone and Android for a few bucks, and it makes creating time-lapse videos super simple. This is the app I used to make *The Man on the Mound,* which I mentioned earlier. The app lets you add music from your iTunes library for background music (be sure you have legal permission to use any music you select) on your video and has a nice set of filters you can use to adjust the look of your video. Lastly, the app gives you a lot of control over settings such as focus, white balance, and contrast, so if you're doing outdoor time-lapse videos, you can maintain a good visual even as the lighting changes or your subjects move within the video frame.

## Mobile Video-Editing Apps

After you've shot all your video, it's time to edit it. Most of the time, you'll want to transfer your footage to a computer and edit via one of the apps previously mentioned. But sometimes, due to timelines, you'll prefer or need to edit the video right on your mobile device.

On the iPhone, you have a few different editing apps. For simple videos that involve a person onscreen talking to another person or directly to the camera (such as in a how-to video), you can use iMovie. iMovie makes it easy to add media clips to the editing timeline, apply simple transitions between clips, and add music or audio background tracks. It also makes creating simple titles easy, as long as you're comfortable with iMovie's built-in title treatments. This is the app I used for almost all my TalkingWithTom interviews.

If you need a bit more power or fine-tuned editing, you'll want to opt for Reel Director on the iPhone. The disadvantage of Reel Director is usually render time. Some folks think the app takes too long to render and save their finished video. On the positive side, the app gives you a lot more control of titles in terms of style, location, and effects. It also enables you to make very exact scene splices with its dial wheel that lets you scroll through your scene to find the exact spot to make that splice.

You can't go wrong with either app if you're looking to quickly edit and upload or publish your captured video. Both apps will surely get the job done and allow you to include branded title cards with logos, phone numbers, and URLs. Both apps render HD-quality video, and both apps cost less than $10 in the App Store.

If you're really looking for power editing on a mobile platform, I recommend that you check out Pinnacle for the iPad. This powerful video-editing tool is based on the Pinnacle Studio video editor for PC product. The app gives you precise control—from frame-by-frame trimming and flexible audio editing, to customized motion graphics and picture-in-picture effects. And with Apple's Camera Connection Kit, you can easily import photo and video files that you've captured on another device. You can also use that connection kit to attach a USB microphone to your iPad and then use Pinnacle to directly capture video interviews or add high-quality voice-over right in the editing program, to further speed up your workflow.

The iPhone and iPad world certainly seems to have a far more robust video capture and editing app marketplace. However, if you're using an Android-based mobile device, you're not completely out of luck. One app that comes highly recommended for Android phones and tablets is AndroVid Video Pro. It's a full-fledged mobile editing app that even lets you convert your video files to MP3 audio files, which can be useful for turning video interviews into audio podcasts.

Hopefully, you see now that DIY video isn't out of your reach. Like most things in life, you just need to start. Think about creative ways you can use video or key sales points that could be made more effective with video assets. Then experiment. Don't get caught up in the tools—just focus on telling a story that will move your prospective buyer one step closer to buying from you. Then go make that video.

# 12

# Creating Photography

Let's begin this chapter not by talking about how to shoot better photos but instead, by focusing on how to think more strategically about the photos you intend to use in your marketing and sales program. They say a photo is worth a thousand words. The problem is, as a marketer, you don't know what those 1,000 words are, and you don't understand which of your prospects uses which words. Let me explain.

I first became really interested in the science behind photography as a marketing tool about 10 years ago. For most of my career, I've spent countless hours in conference rooms and behind the two-way glass in focus groups trying to figure out whether the images we were using in our ads, our websites, or our collateral were the right images. Like most marketers, I wanted to be sure that the images were achieving the desired effect. I wanted to make sure that the images were helping and not hindering the buying process.

But in truth, I never really liked any of those processes as a way to ensure that we were making the right decisions. That feeling of angst was intensified about 10 years ago when I discovered something called the Gestalt Principle. Simply put, the Gestalt Principle states that, for any set of black-and-white points configured into a single image, those points can simultaneously convey two separate and distinct meanings to a viewer of that image. Basically, in plain English, that means you and I can both look at the same picture and interpret it in two entirely different ways. For instance, take a look at Figure 12-1.

**Figure 12-1**   *Rabbit vs. duck Gestalt Principle*

Without overthinking it, answer this question: What did you see? Did you see a duck or did you see a rabbit?

The interesting thing about a Gestalt image is that, after you see the initial image (in this case, either a duck or a rabbit), you can make yourself see the alternative image. So if at first you saw a duck, you can make yourself see the rabbit, and vice versa. Yet I didn't change a single point on the image; it's a single set of black-and-white points arranged in a predefined format that you interpreted as a duck or a rabbit. I don't know what it says about you if you first see the duck or the rabbit (that's probably fodder for a different book), but every time I've ever shown this image in a presentation where I discuss the Gestalt Principle, roughly half the audience purports seeing a duck while the other half answers that they saw a rabbit.

Now, the really interesting thing about the Gestalt Principle is that if you close your eyes right now and then open them and look back at Figure 12-1, you will see the same image you saw the first time you looked at it. Even though as you look at it you can force your mind to see the alterative image, *your brain defaults to seeing the first image you saw.* Thus, if you saw a rabbit, you can look at the image and, in your brain, force yourself to see the duck; alternatively, if you saw the duck, you can force yourself to see a rabbit. However, *every time you close your eyes and then reopen them, you will revert to seeing the default image you first saw.* This is an incredibly powerful insight to keep in mind as you develop photographic materials for your marketing.

Here's why. The Gestalt Principle tells us that the deconstruction of a visual message occurs at the point of reception. The decoding of an image's meaning happens during the buyer's decoding process versus your encoding process—where you decide that the image you're using is a duck versus a rabbit. Furthermore, this means that imagery decoding is hardwired into our DNA. Think about that for a moment. You can provide all the context, meaning, or environment for a photograph that you want. But at the end of the day, your buyer is going to decode the meaning of that photograph based on a biological response to the photograph.

The Gestalt Principle thus tells us that although you might think that the image on your landing page, collateral, or ad is a duck, quite possibly maybe as much as half your audience will see a rabbit. That would be great if you were selling rabbits, but it would surely depress sales if you were selling ducks. And if such a dramatic change of interpretation can occur with a simple black-and-white drawing, ask yourself what will happen when you use an actual photograph that contains multiple colors and images.

That's exactly what I was wondering back in 2003. So I decided to test the hypothesis. I want to spend a few moments on the results because both the results and the technique are important tools for creating more effective photos for your sales and marketing efforts.

At the time, I was working in the advertising agency environment. I owned my own brand development agency, and we were doing a lot of work around developing brands, campaigns, collateral kits, and packaging. I loathed focus grouping our creative work to determine the right solution almost as much as I loathed the idea of a bunch of us sitting around a conference room trying to determine whether we were looking at a rabbit or a duck. So I developed an experimental research process I called Visual Palettes. The idea behind Visual Palettes was to deconstruct the Gestalt Principle before we created marketing and advertising programs. Instead of waiting until after we selected images to learn how our audience was interpreting the images, we wanted to understand how to craft the ideal image for use in our marketing materials. Our theory was that, by deconstructing how respondents were interpreting photographs, we would be able to develop a visual code that we could apply to create an ideal photograph.

Let me walk you through the approach so it makes more sense. In Figure 12-2, you see an array of photos that a group of participants selected. Each participant in the research study was asked the same question: When you think of the word *escape*, what images are you drawn to from this table of images? In front of each respondent was a large table that was filled with hundreds of images that we had cut out of magazines, taken off the Internet, and pulled from other sources. Each respondent was given a few minutes to go through the images and gather the ones that best represented *escape* to him or her. The respondents then did a second sort, where they were asked to perform the same task but this time select photos they associated with *relaxation*. We took a picture of the resulting collage for use later during the analysis phase.

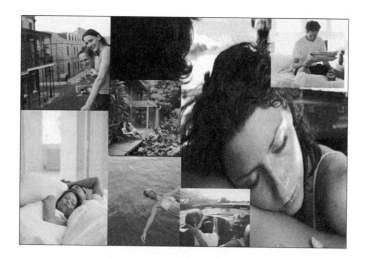

**Figure 12-2**   *Photos picked by married adults with children*

When all the respondents had completed the study, we began to look through their various piles of images to deconstruct common visual themes. It's important to note here that we used a convenience sample (a type of nonprobability sampling which involves the sample being drawn from that part of the population which is easy to access) that almost equally divided into married adults with children and married adults without children. That demographic distinction ended up to be quite important to the visual decoding you see in Figure 12-2.

When I ask audiences to tell me which word Figure 12-2 represents—*relaxation* or *escape*—the answer is usually *relaxation*. Unfortunately, that's the wrong answer. Figure 12-2 is actually a composite of *escape* photos selected by our adults who were married with children. This is a completely understandable mistake. All the photographs look very calm, tranquil, and serene. If someone showed you an ad or landing page design with those photos and told you the goal was to sell relaxation to married adults with children, it would make perfect sense, right? And that's why I'm spending the beginning of this chapter relating this research to you. It's the perfect example of the Gestalt Principle at work. You and I might see relaxation in those photos, but to these respondents, those images are an escape.

Now look at Figure 12-3. Here you see an *escape* photo composite generated by the married adults without children. This collage is much more in alignment with what most people would associate with an *escape* vacation. We see photos of groups having fun, people drinking, and people having a great time. But if you were selling escape vacations, you would need two completely different sets of banner ads, social campaigns, and landing pages to target these two groups of buyers. They simply don't visually interpret escape images the same way.

**Figure 12-3**   *Escape photos picked by married adults without children*

# The Modern Visual Palette Research

Recently, I decided to revisit this research. Pinterest, one of the fastest-growing social networks today, offers an interesting opportunity to replicate that same Visual Palette research, but on a far grander scale. Because you can attach (pin) any image to a Pinterest board (a dedicated space on a Pinterest profile where a person can "pin" images), respondents are no longer limited to the photographs that the researcher hand-selects. They can pin any photos they find on the Internet or, if they can't find anything suitable, upload their own images from a computer or mobile phone. This removes any bias by the researcher conducting the study that might inadvertently affect the outcome of the research. Additionally, because this format doesn't rely on a face-to-face meeting with respondents to perform the photo arrays, it allows anyone, anywhere with access to the Internet to participate. And with Pinterest a researcher can create a private board that only the participants of the research can see and thus invite those participants to participate privately. This makes the approach far more cost-effective than our hand-sorted photo arrays. Thus, I was interested to see if the results of an *escape* versus *relaxation* study conducted 10 years later via Pinterest would be different.

In spring 2013, that's exactly what we did. Forty-two adults agreed to replicate the Visual Palette research using Pinterest. We created two boards—one for *relaxation* and the other for *escape*. We encouraged each individual who participated to pin five images of their choice to each board. These images were selected from anywhere on the Internet or uploaded from the respondents' own computer to each board. The only thing we asked was that, in each case, the image should convey to them either *relaxation* or *escape*. By the end of the study, we had more than a hundred images on each board. A few very interesting visual themes emerged.

Overall escape images contained five key visual thematics: Visually, there was water, hard surfaces such as rocks, forests, a lack of people, and the presence of a path. Of these visual themes, the last theme (paths) was most interesting. You see, back in 2003 one of the common themes that came out of that research was that escape was about running away from something in your life. An escape vacation was all about running away from your responsibilities. And here in 2013, we were seeing imagery in which this concept of a path was a dominant visual thematic—as though the path represented the path to escape. Interestingly, although we hadn't asked for any verbal explanations, a number of respondents did include a rationale for their "pins" to the boards. Those path images often contained descriptions of "running away" or "escaping," echoing the themes we'd heard 10 years earlier.

Conversely, when we looked at the images of relaxation, we saw a very different set of visual themes. Like the escape visuals, the relaxation visuals contained water and lacked people. However, that's where the similarities ended. In a relaxation visual, the water was predominantly a beach or a pool, and there were strong elements of solitude. Easily the most interesting visual theme of the relaxation photo set was that any people or animals that appeared in the photographs were almost always lying down.

So here again, some 10 years after the original research, we were reminded of the Gestalt Principle. If one was to create a piece of marketing designed to convey a destination as an escape-based vacation, one would want to have an image without people that included a pathway—most likely through a forest, bounded by rocks, or including a stream. On the other hand, if one was trying to convey relaxation, one would want an image that was devoid of people, probably beachfront, that conveyed a sense of solitude and the idea that one could lie down. It might include a hammock, or if it included a person, that person would certainly be lying down.

And that is the power of strategically planning the photography in your marketing. A photograph is truly worth a thousand words. But it is imperative that you take steps to ensure the proper decoding of your visual messages, which is why this chapter introduced you to the Visual Palette approach first.

Now that you understand how to create more effective photography, let's spend the balance of this chapter learning how to create better photography.

# How to Shoot Better Photographs

In preparing to write this chapter, I interviewed two accomplished photographers: C.C. Chapman, a well-known content creator, blogger, and the co-author of *Content Rules*, and Sue Spaight, an award-winning photographer who spends her days as an account strategist in an ad agency. Both were kind enough to share their insider secrets. I found it interesting that, when I asked each of them to tell me how to take better photos, neither spoke about the technology and the tools. Just as Chris Yates and Brian Mattson focused on the need to be a better storyteller to create better video, Chapman and Spaight spoke of the power of a photograph to capture the sense of a moment in time.

Sue, who considers herself more of a documentary photographer, spoke in depth about the need to get close to your subject, to create a sense of intimacy between the viewer of a photo and the objects inside that photo. Much of her discussion about techniques, lighting, and even equipment centered on the central theme of finding ways to create greater intimacy. This idea of intimacy might seem artistic, but it has a lot of relevance when you think about the different types of photography you might need to produce as a part of your marketing efforts. You might include product shots, people shots, environmental shots, and shots of buyer outcomes—photographs of a customer who is using your product. In each of these cases, you can see where this idea of intimacy could elevate what might normally be a very bland, ineffective photo into one that really captures the eye of prospective buyers and draws them into your content.

Sue had three key recommendations to help you create more intimacy and more compelling photos. Her first recommendation was to get closer to your subject matter. Ideally, you need to get physically closer to the subject, whether that is a person, place, or thing. Now, in some cases, especially when you are trying to shoot people in an environment, you can create this closeness with a telephoto lens. By using a 300mm or 400mm telephoto lens, you can actually be very far away from a person and still capture high-quality close-ups that make it appear as though you are much closer to the subject. However, although Sue acknowledged that the zoom lens tactic works, she kept reinforcing that your first choice should always be to get physically closer so that you can use nontelephoto lenses. Her thinking is that those nontelephoto lenses give you more creative range in terms of things like depth of field, which we talk about shortly. And this range can elevate a photo to spectacular.

Her second suggestion was to move around your subject. Far too often, amateur photographers simply point a camera at a subject that is standing directly in front of them. The object of the photo appears in the center of the photo, and the picture tends to be shot with the camera on the same visual plane as the object or person. This creates a very bland and expected photograph. Instead, look for interesting angles that wouldn't occur naturally. Get above your subject, get below your subject, and look at your subject matter from all angles. Move closer or slightly farther away. What you do doesn't matter—what matters is that you try to find a visually unique point of view to present your subject matter to the prospective buyer.

Sue's last tip was the most eye-opening for me. As she pointed out, most of us think of a photograph as either a square or a rectangle. We see a photograph in two dimensions: height and width. But a professional photographer sees an added dimension: depth. Sue's last recommendation was that, as you're framing your photographs, think about what's in front of you in terms of a three-dimensional field. Look for ways to place things visually in front or behind the primary object that you're photographing. Look for visual lines that can enhance that feeling of depth to a viewer of your photograph. By doing this, you make the photograph more dynamic, more energetic, and, in the end, a more powerful and persuasive photograph.

C.C. went on to add an important point to take to heart. If you want to take better photographs, you have to become a student of the craft. As C.C. put it, "Too many people get a camera and never take it out of auto (the green setting). And while that is fine when you are starting out, it really helps to learn how to actually take photographs instead of simply pushing a button to generate a picture." He also pointed out that a simple but effective way to learn how to take better photographs is to study great photography. Look through magazines, websites, or photo books, and begin to deconstruct the techniques that reliably and consistently produce striking photography. Look at the photographs, and think about how the photographer set up the shot from a composition standpoint, from a lighting standpoint, and based on the angle at which the photograph was taken.

And let's conclude this discussion with one final point that I think both C.C. and Sue would embrace. If you want to shoot better pictures, you have to just get out and shoot more pictures. With today's digital cameras, there's actually no penalty for taking a bad shot or taking a lot of bad shots. Set aside some time in your day or on the weekend to just go out and take pictures. If a lot of your photography is going to be pictures of executives or employees of your company, then spend a couple of lunch hours gathering a few fellow employees and have an impromptu photo shoot. But don't just shoot a bunch of pictures—shoot those pictures with a purpose.

What I mean is that if your photography needs to be largely employees working at computers, then place one of your fellow employees in front of a computer and take that shot 10 times. Each and every time you take that shot, change a camera setting. Maybe change the shutter speed or the ISO setting or the f-stop, but systematically make changes so that you can see the effect those changes have on the resulting photography. Do the same thing with lighting, composition, and proximity of camera to your subject. And as with anything in life, by systematically breaking down the cause-and-effect relationship between camera settings and the resulting photograph, you will begin to learn how to take better pictures.

## Selecting Lenses

When you buy your camera, it comes with a standard lens, something like 35mm to 135mm zoom. This standard lens gives you a nice range to shoot things that are very close or zoom in on objects a little farther away. And in terms of starting to learn your camera and how to shoot better photographs, this is just fine. However, as you become more proficient and decide to expand your photographic skills in an effort to shoot pictures that make your buyer go "Wow!", you're going to want to invest in additional lenses.

The first lens you'll want to add to your camera bag is a 28mm or 55mm primary lens with a shallow depth of field, such as f/1.8 or f/2.8. The beauty of this little lens is that it's designed to have a really short depth of field. Depth of field determines which objects in a photo are in focus and out of focus. The larger your f-stop number, the greater the depth of field, resulting in more of the image in both the foreground and the background being in focus.

The beauty of the 28mm prime lens is that it's able to shoot at only a low f-stop, such as 1.8 or 2.8. Thus, every shot you take will have that nice "blurred background" effect in which the subject you're shooting is crisp and the rest of the background is blurred. So many people think they need to understand photography to create this effect, but the truth is, with the right lens, the lens and camera do all the work. And if your camera can shoot video, too, you can use this same lens when shooting video to create that very professional look and feel that I discussed in Chapter 11, "Creating Video." If you get this lens, I promise you, it will become one of your favorites.

Next, you might want to add wide-angle lens. Wide-angle lenses are especially useful when you're trying to create that intimacy Sue spoke about. They allow you to keep some of the visual context of your subject while simultaneously letting you get very close to your subject. Obviously, wide-angle lenses are also very good for anyone who needs to shoot landscapes, shoot interior building pictures, or room images. This lens might be ideal for real estate agents, remodelers, architects, and contractors. And if you're trying to create more dramatic and unusual headshots of your executives, a low f-stop, wide-angle lens might be just what you need.

The third lens that is ideal to have but that you're probably least likely to own is a high-end telephoto lens. You can buy a consumer-grade telephoto lens for a few hundred dollars. But if you really want a truly great piece of glass, as photographers call it, that will let you shoot close-ups from distances of 30 or 40 yards, you're probably going to spend upward of $1,000 to $2,000. The good news is that you don't actually have to buy these lenses. You can find numerous places on the Internet that rent lenses for a few days or even a week. Better yet, the cost is very reasonable. For instance, once or twice a year, I rent a 100mm to 400mm zoom lens to take my son's baseball tournaments. I use it to capture those really great close-up action shots of kids sliding into bases or catching balls in the outfield. The lens I rent easily retails for a couple thousand dollars, yet I'm able to rent it for three days at a cost of less than $100, including the shipping both ways. Personally, I like BorrowLenses.com for its pricing and service. But there are plenty of other sites on the Internet, so I highly encourage you to explore the rental option before you purchase an expensive telephoto lens.

Other lenses include a fisheye lens, which gives that cool rounded effect you sometimes see in photography. You'll also find a variety of prime lenses, high-end zoom lenses, and tilt-shift lenses, which creates a miniaturization effect that makes objects and people in the picture look like little toys in the lens instead of in post-production. As I said, when you need a really specialized lens, the solution often might be to simply rent the lens instead of buy it.

# Lighting

For most of your photography, you'll use one of three light sources: natural light, studio lights, or a flash mounted either on or off your camera. In my experience, and in talking with other photographers, natural light is always the preferred light source because it's the most natural. However, natural light can be really tricky and requires you to understand how to position your subject matter in relation to the light. Quite often, it also limits the times of day you can shoot.

The most common light source amateur photographers are accustomed to using is the flash on the camera. But if you need to use a flash, don't use the built-in flash. Instead, buy a separate Speedlite flash, which gives you a lot more flexibility and better quality. A Speedlite flash lets you defuse the flash by bouncing the light off the ceiling, the floor, a wall, or a reflector, which creates a more even lighting on your subject. Ideally, you want a flash that also turns left and right, to give you the added ability to bounce your light off a side wall, to create a pretty cool effect. But although Speedlite flashes are highly portable, they don't work outside or in large rooms, where walls and ceilings are too far away or high to bounce the light.

When a flash won't work, you'll want the option of studio lighting. Studio lighting can be flash based or constant. I focus on constant because constant light sets can also be used in video production, so this is a more cost-efficient solution. Here again, for a relatively low price point, you can invest in a simple, effective three-point light kit. I bought mine on the Internet for less than $200. It works great and is portable.

A three-point light kit consists of just that, three lights. You have a key light, a fill light, and a hair light. You can visit TheInvisibleSale.com to see how-to videos for various ways to set up a three-point light kit, but here's the most common setup. You set your key light to one side (approximately a 45° angle) from your subject and set the light to full strength. You'll notice that it creates shadows on the nose, eyes, and neck. To offset this, you set the fill light, at a 45° angle on the opposite side of the subject from the key light. The purpose of that light isn't actually to light the subject, but to simply to fill in the shadows created by the key light, thus creating a nice, even light source across the subject. Last, you set the hair light. The hair light is positioned above your subject matter and shoots down directly behind him or her, or maybe even slightly bouncing off the wall or screen behind the subject. The purpose of this light is to remove any shadow that might be cast by your frontal lights and also to create a distinct silhouette of your subject matter against the background. You'll use this simple lighting setup for the vast majority of headshots, group shots, and product shots.

Finally, we have natural light, the preferred light source of photographers everywhere. When using natural light indoors, place your subject matter near a window so that you can achieve a nice, soft light for shooting people, products, or even food. Always place your object perpendicular to the window or at an angle but never directly in front of the window as this will backlight the subject resulting in the subject appearing dark or shadowy.

If you're shooting outside, you'll have to plan accordingly. Either shoot early in the morning, if you want that nice, warm soft light, or wait until late afternoon, to get a warm, flattering light. You want to avoid shooting outside when the sun is high in the sky; the resulting light is harsh and tends to produce poor photos. When shooting subjects outside, always place the light behind you, allowing your subject to look at the sun. Otherwise, they will silhouette against a sunny background. Also if you are going to be doing a lot of outdoor photography, you might want to invest in a set of reflectors. Reflectors bounce natural light up into your subject matter, to remove any shadows caused by the sunlight. This can help you create more even lighting and, more important, eliminate any shadows caused by the natural light from the sun.

# Building the Ultimate Photography Kit

Honestly, if you have a good-quality DSLR such as a Nikon or a Canon and a solid tripod, you're in business. I also carry a monopod, which is a one-legged tripod. This can come in handy when you want the stability of a tripod or are shooting with a big telephoto lens and want to be able to quickly move the camera from one position to another.

When you're trying to decide on a camera, don't feel like you need to buy the top-of-the-line Nikons and Canons. These high-end cameras are certainly better, have upgraded features, and such, but they're not absolutely necessary to create great photos. For instance, I use a Canon 7D, which retails for about $1,600 just for the camera body. But honestly, I could have picked up a Canon T3i, which would have been just fine, for closer to $600. I chose my D7 for the fast shutter speed and full-sensor imaging, which results in really beautiful photos even when I'm shooting fast-moving objects.

To complete your ultimate photography kit, I recommend that you add a few items. First, buy an f/1.8 or f/2.8 primary lens. I have a 55mm, but if I had to do it over, I'd buy a 28mm because it lets you get closer to your subject matter. I find that sometimes my 55mm forces me to stand pretty far back to get group shots, and sometimes this causes problems when shooting in small areas. But be aware that a 28mm is about four times more expensive, on average. So think about the locations where you'll be predominantly shooting, and choose the lens that works best for you and your budget.

Next, pick up an adjustable Speedlite flash, which costs anywhere from a few hundred dollars to $500 or $600 for a really high-end version. I also recommend buying an inexpensive three-point light kit. Again, you can find these online for less than $200, and many of them are portable so that you can take them on location. The last piece of lighting equipment you'll want is a set of inexpensive reflectors, which you can find for as little as $30 online. You'll find tons of different versions and sizes, so just Google "photo reflectors." These reflectors are great for helping you direct natural light and can be a lifesaver when shooting video or photos under fluorescent ceiling lights by allowing you to bounce the light back up into the subject's face to create something a tad more flattering. You can peruse a number of helpful how-to videos on TheInvisibleSale.com that show other really imaginative ways to use Speedlites and reflectors to create incredible lighting for stunning portrait photographs.

When you finish with the lighting, purchase a portable two-sided background (white on one side and black on the other), which you can find online for less than $50. This gives you a nice range of options with backgrounds and lighting effects for both still photography and video. Also, if you're shooting pictures outside your company's headquarters where you can't control the backdrop, this tool gives you a consistent backdrop for all of your photos. In addition to black and white, you can get blue and, most important, green—you can then apply green screen techniques to replace the background with computer imagery.

Lastly, if you're going to be shooting products, you'll want to purchase a photo light box. You can find these online for between $50 and $100. The photo light box is a small fabric cube that you set your product inside. On the outside of the box, you place the lights; then you place your camera at the front of the open side of the box. This setup is how you shoot a product with no background, in which the product seems to be sitting on an infinite white background. Many photo boxes also come with alternative backgrounds, to create a high-contrast backdrop; this works well if your products are white. I've used these simple boxes in the past to shoot product images for e-commerce sites and have found the technique quite simple to master.

# Photo-Editing Software

Even the best photographers end up doing a bit of photo fixing "in post." This means that they fine-tune their photos using image-editing software. This is the point at which most people start to feel like the technology is beyond their ability. Let me assure you that nothing is further from the truth. I've been editing my own photos for years now, and I'm completely self-taught using YouTube, Google, and photography blogs. You just have to understand the level of editing you need to perform to help you pick the right software.

The primary question you need to ask yourself is what kind of editing you'll be performing. Specifically, are you going to need to enhance photos by adjusting highlights, shadows, colors, and simple cropping, or do you need to make things vanish? By *vanish*, I mean, are you going to want to be able to remove or, conversely, add objects to a picture? The answer to this question will help you determine whether you need a full-featured photography editing solution such as Photoshop or whether you just need a great photo-enhancement program such as Adobe Lightroom, which is what I use for my pictures.

If you need to truly edit your photos by doing things such as remove or add objects, you have two great options. If you want advanced editing capabilities, purchase a copy of Photoshop. This is Adobe's premier photo-editing software, and it is incredibly powerful. But on the negative side, at $500, it's not cheap, and all that power can make doing simple things seem really hard. I use the program and find that if I don't use it often, I quickly forget how to do things. Fortunately, if you don't need all that power but you still need a good photo-editing tool, Adobe makes Adobe Elements. Elements is the scaled-down version of Photoshop and offers all the photo-editing power most DIYers need. And at less than $100, Adobe Elements is much easier on your budget. I also recommend that, if you elect to purchase Elements, you purchase the Premier package, which combines both programs to create a really useful photo and video editing solution.

On the other hand, if you're primarily going to be fixing contrast, enhancing lighting, or applying interesting visual effects to your photos, I'd opt for Adobe's Lightroom. The feature I really like about Lightroom is the ability to create a photo effect, called a preset, and save that preset like a template. Then as you edit future photos, you can just apply the preset with a single click. This is incredibly useful when you want to give all the photos on your website, such as employee headshots or product shots, the same look and feel, even if they were shot at different times and by different photographers. Additionally, you'll find lots of predeveloped presets for purchase from various photographers. These presets can range from highlighting certain colors in the photo to applying lighting and shadow enhancement. Thus, with the click of a mouse, you can apply very advanced photo retouching without actually knowing how to do it.

## Mobile Photo Apps

No discussion of creating photography is complete without talking about the impact smartphones have made on photography. Most people are aware of apps such as Instagram, which lets you take a photograph and quickly apply a variety of predefined filters, but there are so many more out there. Here again, iPhones lead the way, thanks to a large and robust developer community. In fact, I could probably devote an entire chapter just to the discussion of photo apps. Instead, I've included my top 10 apps to get you started, and you can find more on the Photo Tools page of TheInvisibleSale.com.

**Photogene** works with both the iPhone and the iPad. This app works directly with the photos on your camera roll and thus doesn't require importing to begin. It features a very intuitive interface and lets you easily make adjustments and crops to your photos. The newest version even offers the capability to create photo collages.

**Photoshop Touch** is available for both the iOS and Android platforms. When you're ready for a full-featured version of Photoshop that gives you an enormous range of editing tools, this is the app for you. As with its desktop cousin, you work in layers and can perform sophisticated editing such as background removal using Photoshop's Refine tool to help you with difficult outline such as hairlines. This app is especially useful on tablets, where you have a big enough screen to really edit with ease.

**TiltShiftGen** is a favorite of mine. This app lets you create the ToyCamera effect that makes the objects in your picture appear to be miniaturized or toylike objects. It works best when you're shooting objects that are a bit of a distance away from you and when you're shooting from an angle above the object.

**Big Lens** is a great app if you want to add depth of field to your images. It gives you the most control over the f-stop setting, ranging from a very shallow f/1.8 to a more normal f/3.5. You can also select the type of blur, including an option to outline your object instead of simply applying a round, rectangle, or elliptical blur effect common in most photo apps. This is especially useful when you are shooting people and want the depth of field effect to seem more like the natural effect you get when shooting with a real camera. This one is a must, in my opinion.

Panoramic picture capability on both the iOS and Android platforms is one of the biggest advances in mobile photography since the advent of the smartphone. Both tools let you take beautiful panoramic photos by simply panning across the object or scene you want to photograph. The phone then does all the work to stitch the images together, to instantly create a single panoramic photo.

If you use an older version of iPhone, you have to settle for **AutoStitch**. This app lets you take multiple images and then stitch them together to create a single panoramic image that you can save as a JPEG. The resulting images are clear and can be custom-sized and cropped before exporting.

**Camera+** is another useful iPhone app to have on your phone. It also offers a host of editing and image effects, but the two features that really set this one apart from the others are image stabilization and rapid shutter. The rapid shutter feature is great if you are trying to take multiple pictures of moving objects or people, which is normally impossible with the built-in camera.

If you're planning to share a lot of your photographs on Facebook or other social networks, you might want to check out **GridLens**. The app lets you easily create preformatted or custom-formatted collages from existing images on your phone. Alternatively, you can actually create the collage in real time by simply clicking on the inside of the grid where you want your image to appear and then taking a picture. Then by simply moving to each of the grids, you can instantly create a great collage and upload directly to your social networks.

Another great tool for adding visual drama, especially if you want to create those artsy, moody black-and-white photos, is **Noir Photo**. Take any photo, import it to the app, and then convert to black-and-white or sepia tone. The app allows you to create lighting effects unlike any other app I've seen. You can actually place lighting on your subject as though you took the photo with studio lighting in place.

**ColorSplash** is another great app for creating high-impact black-and-white photos. But where Noir Photo allows the creation of lighting where none existed,

ColorSplash lets you selectively color black-and-white images. To do this, you simply import a color photo you've taken on your phone and then, with your finger, paint over the part of the image you want to keep in color. The rest of the photo converts to black and white, drawing the viewers' eyes to the color portion (highlight) of the photo. Here again, the resulting photo looks very difficult to create, but with this app, the software does all the work for you.

The beauty of mobile photography is its speed and simplicity. Carrying around a big camera is tiresome and often not a viable option. Furthermore, pointing a camera at people often makes your subjects camera shy. Nothing is better than a smartphone for capturing photography in the moment and then quickly workflowing that photo through your editing, approval, and posting process. I strongly encourage you to pick up a few of these apps and start playing with them to see what you can do to create more compelling photos for your lead-generation content.

# 13

# Creating Audio

You can use audio in your marketing in two ways. If you're just looking for an opportunity to change up your content type or give your readers a different way of experiencing your content, using streaming or downloadable audio can be an easy, inexpensive option. I've done this numerous times and plan to make greater use of this technique in the future.

But if you want to build an audience around your audio content, you're entering the world of podcasting. Podcasting is the regularly scheduled production and distribution of audio (or video) content. While not a necessity, podcasts are usually available via channels other than your website. These channels include destinations such as podcast directories, iTunes, and Stitcher, which buyers can use to find and listen to podcasts. Podcasts can be live or recorded, and you don't need an iPod to listen to them—they can play on any computer, MP3 player, or smartphone.

Podcasting also requires a commitment to producing higher-quality audio content. Although I show you how to create podcasts using nothing other than a smartphone, serious podcasters invest in audio equipment and software designed to produce a professional-level product. The good news is that even these professional-level products are within your budget and your ability to understand how to use them.

Before we turn our attention to creating audio content and podcasts, let's examine why I recommend that everyone consider adding podcasting to their marketing toolbox.

## Marketing at the Speed of Sound

According to a 2012 *Edison Research Study on the Podcast Listener*[1] awareness of podcasting has grown 105% since 2006, from 22% in 2006 to 45% in 2012. Likewise, the percentage of people indicating they have listened to an audio podcast has grown 163%, from 11% in 2006 to 29% in 2012.

So although almost half of adults over age 12 are aware of podcasting, just less than a third have actually listened to one. Of those who have listened to one, less than 1 in 5 have listened to one in the last month. And if we stopped there, we might say that the data suggests that we can all afford to set aside podcasting and that you can skip this chapter.

But if you chart the growth of podcast listeners on a graph (see Figure 13-1), as Pew does in the *State of the News Media 2012 Report*,[2] you see that, although the volume is small, the growth curve is fairly steady from 2006 through 2011. And look at the growth of listeners from 2007 to 2009. That's a pretty solid growth right?

Now mentally plot the 2012 percentage of people who have listened to a podcast (29%) on the chart and visualize the angle of the resulting line. It starts to look strikingly similar to the growth from 2007 to 2008 right? Remember, 2007–2008 was the beginning of the first significant rise in podcast listeners. Now we see a similar growth from 2011 to 2012. The question is, will the growth continue or plateau like it did in 2010?

1. www.edisonresearch.com/home/archives/2012/05/the-podcast-consumer-2012.php

2. http://stateofthemedia.org/overview-2012/

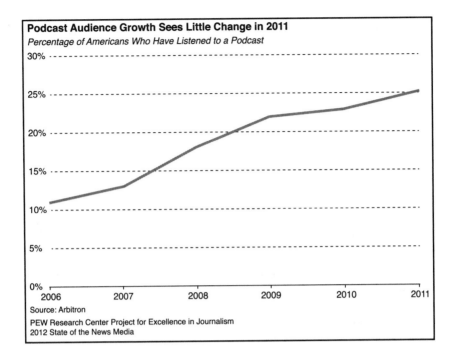

**Figure 13-1**   *Podcast Listenership Growth*

I think we will see continued growth in podcast listenership due to increased listenership via smartphones. Figure 13-2 shows the growth of people listening to online radio in their cars *via a cellphone* from 2010 to 2011. It's almost 100% growth in just that one year. And this number comes before Apple launched its iOS6 operating system for iPhones. This operating system is the first one to include Apple's Podcasts app preloaded on the phone's home screen. So now more than 300 million devices[3] just became one click away from discovering or consuming podcasts. This is a huge development because, in polling podcasters and asking why podcast growth flatlined in 2009–2010, they all pointed to the difficulty in finding and listening to podcasts. With smartphones, tablets, iTunes, and mobile podcast player apps such as Stitcher and Apple's Podcasts making it easy to download and stream podcasts at broadband speeds, those technology hurdles have disappeared. And with carmakers beginning to further integrate our smartphones into our cars with Bluetooth connectivity, we are looking at a perfect storm of usability and accessibility that will power the second coming of podcasting. For this reason, I think you need to pay special attention to this channel and consider how you might incorporate it into your marketing efforts.

---

3. www.apple.com/pr/library/2013/01/28Apple-Updates-iOS-to-6-1.html

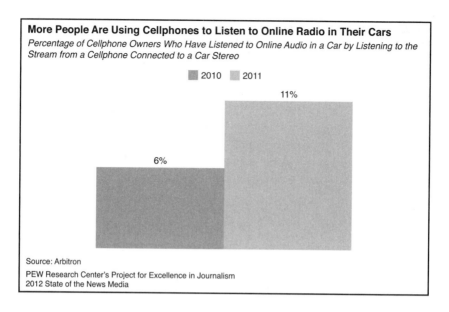

**Figure 13-2**  *Online radio listenership in cars via cellphones*

# The Benefits of Podcasting

Podcasting offers a number of benefits over text- and video-based content. Be sure to consider these six key benefits:

- **Podcasts last longer than blog posts.** In today's Internet ADD world, online readers are skimming more and reading less. This forces bloggers (both corporate and personal) to write shorter posts. Shorter posts lead prospects to spend less time with your brand. Because each session with your brand is short, creating a sense of attachment between your prospect and your brand takes longer. But with the average podcast lasting anywhere from five minutes to an hour, the prospect is making a bigger commitment to your brand and your content. Thus, it's easier to create that sense of attachment and drive top-of-mind preference.

- **Podcasts make information personal.** Forming a relationship with text is really hard. You can be a huge fan of a person's writing and maybe even form some kind of emotional attachment to him or her, but that's more the exception than the rule. Podcasting, on the other hand, lets the listener hear your voice, which means they can hear your passion, concern, and enthusiasm. In short, they can hear a bit of personality and then begin to form an emotional bond to you. Just as radio listeners form a bond with talk radio personalities, your listeners can develop a sense of attachment to you and your personality.

- **Podcasts are convenient to consume.** Your buyers are increasingly grappling with managing their most precious resource: time. One of the greatest benefits of a podcast is your buyers' ability to consume it while doing something else. People are listening to podcasts while driving to and from work, while working out, or during the work day. Thus, unlike text- and even video-based content, which requires your buyers' undivided attention, buyers can consume podcasts in the background.

- **Podcasts are easy to create.** If you want to create a truly world-class podcast, you're going to have to work at it, invest in tools, and learn techniques. But that isn't absolutely necessary. Podcasts, both live and recorded, can be created with any computer, with tablets, and even with a mobile phone. And if your format is interview based, you minimize even your prep time. Thus, for the time-strapped marketer, podcasts can serve as a fairly easy and time-efficient content-creation platform.

- **Podcasts are great twofer content.** As I show you in Chapter 14, "Creating Text-Based Content," converting audio content into text-based content is really easy. Thus, a podcast interview can serve double duty: It can work as a piece of audio content, and you can then transcribe the interview into text and use that text in blog posts, white papers, and e-books.

- **Podcasts can expose new audiences to your brand.** Because podcasts are indexed and offered on platforms such as iTunes, podcasts are sometimes more discoverable than text-based content. Buyers aren't scanning for new text content. The only way they will find your text content is via a search engine or referral on social media networks. However, with platforms such as iTunes and Stitcher, channel surfing for new podcasts is easy. Thus, podcasting gives your brand the chance to be discovered by buyers who wouldn't otherwise seek you out or consume your content.

# Different Types of Podcasts

I have always defined podcasts in very traditional terms. Podcasters create content in hopes of developing an audience that will tune in to *their* podcast, much like a radio station creates a talk show program to attract listeners to their station. However, Bob Knorpp, a well-known podcaster and the creator of The BeanCast™, opened my eyes to a second type of podcast, which I call the syndicated podcast. With a syndicated podcast, the podcaster isn't trying to create an audience that is tuning into *her* show; instead, she syndicates her podcast to other podcasters. In this syndicated model, the podcaster focuses on creating great content and then convincing other podcasters to include that content in their shows. Hence, the syndicated podcaster doesn't have to focus on audience creation—that part is provided by the established podcasters to whom she syndicates. Let's delve into these two forms and explore the pros and cons of each.

## Syndicated Podcasts

If you choose to follow the syndicated model, you really need to focus on creating short, easily digestible episodes. It's one thing for a podcaster to give you a minute or two of the show in exchange for great content, but ask them to give you more than that, and I think you'll see their willingness dwindle. To create compelling short content, focus your podcast on a narrow niche that your prospects care about. And remember, because you'll be offering your content to other podcasters, your content must be helpful or educational. Other podcasters need to feel like they are helping their viewers by broadcasting your content in their podcast. If it feels like an ad, it's an ad and you'll lose your right to syndicate through their podcast.

You can emulate a good model in traditional news broadcasts: the video news release. A lot of public relations agencies use these to promote their clients' products and services. With a video news release, the PR agency fully records a complete news segment. It then offers the segment to television stations to run in their newscast instead of sending a reporter to cover the story themselves. It's an effective tool for PR agencies and is a similar model to syndicated podcasting. The one significant difference is that these video news releases are one-offs, whereas your syndicated podcast will be an ongoing commitment.

To ensure that you'll meet this ongoing commitment, you need to establish a content calendar where you preplan the content of your shows many weeks (or even months) in advance. You might even want to invite input from the podcasters who agree to publish your podcast in theirs. This ensures a consistent flow of good, high-quality topics. In fact, I think it's even more important for syndicated podcasters to deliver their content on schedule than traditional podcasters. If a traditional podcaster misses an episode, he only risks alienating his fans. But a syndicated podcaster who misses a publishing date risks alienating the entire network.

Syndicated podcasts have their place, but companies that want to create a podcast designed to build an audience of prospects as a lead-generation tool almost always choose the traditional format.

# Traditional Podcasts

Traditional podcasts can range anywhere from five minutes to as much as an hour in length. There is no average or standard length. It's really up to the podcaster to choose, so be sure to think about the length of the podcast you're planning.

Think realistically about how much time your audience has to give to each episode. Consider factors such as the most likely consumption experience. Will your prospects most likely consume your podcast at the office, in the car driving to and from work, or while they're working out, or would they actually sit down in a dedicated listening environment just to listen to your podcast? This is vitally important to think about because you want to match your podcast length to the most common consumption experience. I think this is an oft-overlooked aspect of podcast planning. Podcasters just elect to go with a standard length, such as an hour or a half-hour, without considering the consumption experience.

When you decide on your podcast length, turn your attention to your publishing schedule. Just as in blogging, podcasting requires a commitment to a schedule and an audience. After you announce your publishing schedule, you need to stick to that schedule. Your audience is going to tune in or at least be looking for your new show based on that schedule. If you want the audience to commit to listening to you, you have to commit to being there on that regular schedule so they can download new podcasts and listen in. Furthermore, your audience is busy. And when you publish erratically, it becomes easy for the audience to forget that they haven't seen a new episode from you. Thus, you need that regularly scheduled episode so that your audience realizes they've missed your episodes.

But there's a second type of commitment marketers often miss: a commitment to your audience versus a commitment to yourself and the promotion of your company and your products and services. If you're just going to make this an infomercial, it's not going to be very successful. Instead, you have to make the commitment that your podcast is going to be about your audience first and foremost. You have to commit to providing them with meaningful, helpful, or educational content that makes them better at what they do because they listen to your show. Probably the easiest way to do that is to focus your podcast on solving or helping the listener solve problems.

Jump back to my friend Bob Knorpp, whose show The BeanCast is a great example of solving a problem and building an audience. When Bob set out to create The BeanCast, he felt that there was a big problem in the advertising and marketing community. The advertising and marketing world was moving so fast that it really became almost impossible for ad and marketing executives to remain current with the important marketing news of the day. As a business driven by culture and technology, failure to stay abreast of the latest news and trends was troublesome. Bob's solution was The BeanCast. The BeanCast in a one-hour topical newscast that not only makes the audience aware of the topic, but also presents multiple points of view from marketing industry leaders. Each Sunday night, Bob records the podcast. He hosts three or four members of the advertising and marketing community for a roundtable discussion of the previous week's news and major items. During the hour Bob routinely weighs in with his point of view and challenges his guests to offer their opinions as well. In doing so, Bob is creating really great pieces of helpful content. In the space of an hour, while commuting or working out, a busy marketing executive can catch up on the latest happenings shaping the world of marketing and gain enough knowledge to speak intelligently about the topic at work the next day.

So whether you decide to create a traditional or syndicated podcast, keep two points in mind. First, you have to commit to delivering great, helpful content. Second, you need to faithfully deliver that content on a regular schedule. If you can just deliver on those two key commitments, you're more than halfway to a successful podcast.

## The Secrets of Podcasting Success

When I look around the podcasting universe to find podcasts that are achieving a certain level of success, I regularly see three themes. I see people who are committed to their audience, who are solving audience problems, and who are really good at developing a personal relationship with the audience. We've already talked about those first two, so let's spend a few moments diving into the last one.

You really need to give a lot of thought and care to selecting a host for your podcast. Don't just assign this role to the product manager, the marketing director, or someone else based on their product or service knowledge. Just as Brian Matson pointed out that onscreen talent makes or breaks your video marketing, selecting your podcasting on-air talent drives the success of your show. The host not only must have a great voice that's easy to listen to, but more important, the host needs to have the ability to reach through the microphone and connect with the audience. If the person can't do that, it doesn't matter how much knowledge he or she possesses—no one will be listening.

The most successful podcasters are just like successful talk show hosts. They build a rapport with their audience. What you see is a fine balance between delivering helpful, professional content while interweaving their personal story. They open themselves up to the audience, warts and all. This opening up creates opportunities for the audience to develop a personal relationship with the on-air talent.

# Prospecting with Podcasts

Interview-based podcasts are great networking and prospecting tools. By interviewing guests on your show, you create the opportunity to invite prospects, vendors, partners, and customers onto the show to have discussions about whatever your podcast covers. And this creates a real opportunity for you. It allows you to shine a light on great vendors, strategic partners, and satisfied customers. By shining this light, you're creating a greater sense of attachment between those parties and your company.

Even better, you can use your podcast as a platform to invite people you'd like to meet. This can include prospects as well as people with whom you want to network but who might never be a prospect for what you sell. These folks might be in companies that you don't work with or organizations for which your product or service isn't relevant, but they know people you would like to know.

By inviting these people into your podcast, you create an opportunity to have a really great first and second experience with them. Here's how that works. Because many of your guests will never have participated in a podcast before, you offer to have a prepodcast call with them so that you can make sure they understand the technology and the format, and answer any show or technology questions. So now instead of having to cold-call people to meet them, you get to have a nice, warm, enjoyable first experience with them.

That leads to the great second experience, the actual podcast session. Here you spend 20–30 minutes with someone, having a discussion that makes the other person the hero. People always tell you that the best conversationalists are those who say the least and ask the most. Think about the format of an interview podcast. That's what you're doing. You're saying very little and asking a lot of questions, which makes your guest the focus of the conversation. And that's why so many people enjoy being on podcasts and why it's such a great experience for them.

But wait, it gets better. When your guest completes the podcast and has just had this wonderful experience, you have an opportunity to network further. You can then pop the question: "I'd really like to have somebody from Company A come on the show—do you know anyone there?" Well, of course you know that they know people there because you've already researched this fact. But instead of asking for an introduction in a prospecting way, you get to couch your intentions behind creating more great content for the show.

Interview-based podcasts are also a great new client prospecting tool. Nobody wants to try to call a prospect and say, "Hi, I'm Tom Martin, and I'd like to sell you something today." But who among us would shy away from making this call? "Hi, it's Tom Martin. I have this great little podcast that I think you would be perfect for. Would you mind being a part of my show?" That's not a tough call to make. If the person doesn't accept, you at least open a door that you can walk through at a later date with a more direct prospecting call. If the person does accept, you get at least two opportunities to build a relationship in a completely nonthreatening way.

Here again, if the person hasn't previously participated in a podcast, he's going to want to have, or you should suggest, a pre-call to review what you'll discuss, go over the show format, and test the technology.

Then, of course, there's the podcast itself. Again, you're going to make the prospect the highlight of the show. Not only do you want to entertain and inform your audience, but if you structure your questions correctly, you'll actually be educating yourself in a way that could help you more effectively sell to the prospect.

The third touch is the thank-you. Now that this person has participated in your show, you have a perfect opportunity to do a follow-up call to say thank you for participating. You get to tell the person he was great, say that you received awesome audience feedback, and gush about how you would love to have him on the show again at some point in the future. And now you have the beginnings of a relationship. You have contact information. You have the prospect's email address. Most important, you have permission to use all of that as you nurture the relationship through email, phone, or social media.

The networking and prospecting opportunity that podcasting affords you is the single most important reason everyone should consider adding audio and podcasting to their marketing toolkit. But if you approach this strictly in the selfish prospecting and networking mindset, I can assure you that your effort will fail. You won't develop an audience, which will make it difficult to convince prospects to come on the show—and that makes it hard to use podcasting as a prospecting tool. So keep in mind that core commitment to your audience. Produce a show that helps the audience. Produce a show that you're proud to claim. And if you do these things, the prospecting and networking will take care of themselves.

# Getting Started: Equipment and Software

I asked professional podcaster Todd Schnick of *Intrepid Radio* for his advice on equipment and software to get you started in podcasting. I asked him to design good, better, and best options for interviewing guests face to face as well as via Skype, which a number of podcasters use to record calls with guests. Here are his recommendations. As with everything you read in this chapter, you can find links to all the equipment and software at TheInvisibleSale.com/AudioTools.

**Good:**

This option is the bare-bones minimum to get started with audio as a marketing tool.

- You need a smartphone or tablet computer to record audio and/or video. You can use the built-in microphone or add an inexpensive microphone (discussed later in this chapter) to enhance sound quality.
- Create a SoundCloud account, and download the SoundCloud application to your phone and/or tablet computer.
- Create a YouTube account if you plan to create video podcasts such as AdoramaTV.
- Download any of the simple video-editing applications I list in Chapter 11, "Creating Video."
- Create a blog. Popular platforms include WordPress, Typepad, and Blogger. (I prefer WordPress.) You also need to register a website domain (www.youwebsite.com) and set up a web hosting account. This is where you will publish your shows as blog posts.

**Better:**

You can create and distribute a high-quality podcast with these tools. Your podcast won't look or sound like a professionally produced podcast, but you won't embarrass yourself or your company using this solution.

- Purchase a Blue Yeti USB microphone.
- Register with Skype and purchase the Call Recorder add-on. Note that this is a Mac-only add-on that allows you to record a Skype call, a common way to interview podcast guests (both audio and video) for use as podcasts. PC users can purchase Evaer Skype Recorder.
- Obtain a copy of Audacity (free open source program) or GarageBand (Mac only) to edit and polish your audio content. You can also use these to capture non-interview-based audio podcasts.
- Register for Blubrry (www.blubrry.com) or LibSyn (www.libsyn.com) to host your audio files.
- Create a self-hosted WordPress blog with the PowerPress plug-in to publish your content on your blog and syndicate it to iTunes.

**Best:**

When you're ready to step into the big leagues, you'll need a studio and professional-level components. Here's Todd's shopping list.

- Designate a room in your office or home for use as a studio. Apply sound-dampening foam to the walls to mitigate voice echo.

- Purchase professional-grade microphones. Todd recommends Sennheiser C835 table-top microphones with AKG K44 headsets. This way, guests can hear a high-quality, real-time feed of the podcast as you record it.

- Purchase a headset volume and audio control system that connects headsets to the soundboard mixer. Todd recommends the Behringer Powerplay Pro-8 Model HA8000.

- Purchase a soundboard mixer such as the Zed14 (which Todd uses). You plug all your audio inputs into the mixer. The soundboard mixer lets you level the volume of all guests (in case one speaks louder than another, for instance) so that the volume level on the broadcast remains consistent.

- Obtain Audacity, GarageBand, or WavePad for recording and editing your podcast.

- Create a self-hosted WordPress blog with the PowerPress plug-in to publish your content on your blog and syndicate it to iTunes. You also need an online podcast-hosting service such as Blubrry or LibSyn to host and stream your podcast files.

As you review the equipment list on TheInvisibleSale.com, you will surely notice the range of costs between the Good and Best options. Again, don't feel the need to jump into the deep end here. Start with the Good and Better options, both of which are within even the most modest marketing budget. Then after you've achieved success, built an audience, and begun to generate convertible leads, slowly begin to upgrade your equipment (starting with the studio) to the Best-level tools.

# Creating a Mobile Recording Studio

Mobile devices really make podcasting easy and efficient. You can create both live and recorded podcasts using inexpensive apps on your iPhone, Android phone, or tablet. The quality won't be as good as a podcast produced using your computer, using high-quality microphones, sound-mixing equipment, and software, but the increased mobility and capability to record, edit, and upload from anywhere can make this an ideal solution in certain cases.

You can create a live podcast using your mobile phone in two ways. The first way works on any mobile phone—and with any landline phone as well. The platform is called BlogTalkRadio (BTR). The thing I like about BTR is its simplicity and price—it's free. Both you and your guest simply dial in from any phone, and the BTR platform does the rest. They provide a free embeddable streaming audio widget, which you can place in your blog or website, and the shows are automatically recorded and archived for your listeners. Finally, BTR lets you have up to five guests on one show and simultaneously host a live chat with your listeners. If you want additional features, BTR offers several different levels of paid accounts that are designed to convert your podcast into something that more closely resembles a radio call-in show, with the host taking listener calls live on air.

The other option, which is truly a mobile phone option, is iPadio. But don't let the *i* fool you: This app is available for both iPhone and Android platforms. The goal of iPadio is to make podcasting drop-dead simple. The app gives you two publishing options. You can record your podcast and publish it later, or you can create a live phonecast (their name for a live podcast). If you choose the live phonecast option, the app dials an iPadio phone number, asks you for your authorization PIN (displayed in the app), and then begins to live-stream your podcast. As with BTR, the live podcast is automatically recorded and made available for download almost immediately. Finally, when you create your iPadio account, you can elect to have iPadio create an iTunes Podcast account for you. Then each time you do a phonecast or upload a recorded podcast to your iPadio account, the platform automatically publishes the podcast to iTunes. This last feature alone makes iPadio an interesting option for low-tech podcasters.

The drawback of both of these options is a lack of control over quality, editing, and the final product that is your podcast. For that, you need to create a mobile podcasting studio. You need three pieces of equipment: an iPad, a Snowball USB microphone, and the Apple Camera Connection Kit. You'll also want to purchase the iPad version of GarageBand and create a SoundCloud account. I talk more about GarageBand and SoundCloud shortly.

To create your mobile recording studio, you need to connect your Snowball to your iPad using the Apple Camera Connection Kit. After you activate GarageBand, the software will recognize the Snowball microphone. From here, you just need to adjust your Snowball microphone based on the type of podcast you're going to create. If you're recording just yourself, leave the microphone setting on the number 1 setting. However, if you're going to do an interview with another person, move the setting selector to the number 3 setting. This activates the directional recording settings of the microphone. Hence, if you position the microphone between you and your guest, you will obtain good audio from both of you with minimal background noise.

That's what I like best about this setup: It doesn't require you to be in a completely silent room to get a decent interview-based podcast. In fact, I've tested the setup in relatively noisy environments and found that the resulting recording is quite clear, even though it does have some background noise. What this means for you is that you have a small, lightweight, and easily transportable podcasting setup. This can make capturing podcasts at conferences, trade shows, or other events incredibly easy and convenient. Also, because you can easily edit on the iPad, you can delete any "ums" and "ahs," goofs, or pauses to produce a high-quality podcast.

Finally, because you're capturing, editing, and storing your podcast all on the iPad, you're one click away from publishing your podcast to the Internet. If you use a platform such as SoundCloud, you can then upload directly to your SoundCloud account from inside GarageBand. This makes the workflow around capturing, editing, and then publishing your podcasts quite simple. Additionally, after the file is loaded into SoundCloud, you can embed that file on your own website. And if you've connected your SoundCloud to an iTunes podcast account or other podcast services, SoundCloud alerts each service that a new episode is available.

This chapter is by no means a complete tutorial on podcasting. Entire books have been written about podcasting, and for good reason. I find it far more technologically challenging than blogging and even video. But you now have a good basic grasp on the intangibles of podcasting and the knowledge to create a basic podcasting studio to get started with podcasting. Now go interview someone.

# 14

# Creating Text-Based Content

*Video, audio, and even webinars are infinitely sexier and more fun to create and consume, but the Internet and the invisible sale are still powered predominantly by text-based content. And until Google's spiders (also known as a Googlebots—the tool that Google uses to discover new and updated web pages that it adds to the Google index) can watch a video or hear an audio file, text will remain the dominant content for winning the Google search box. Unfortunately, text is often harder and takes longer to create than those other forms of content.*

*You might be asking yourself, how is he going to spend an entire chapter talking about creating text? How much can he really type about typing? Well, hold that thought, Grasshopper, because there are tools, tips, and short-cuts that you don't know about. But once you've been exposed, you're not only going to get excited—you're going to instantly start creating more text-based content with less effort and in less time than ever before.*

If you want to create more text-based content, you really need to understand and focus on three key areas. First, stop typing and start talking. I show you how to use an inexpensive piece of software and your mobile phone or tablet to turn downtime into writing time. I also talk about an inexpensive tool to convert interviews into great text content. Second, I tackle the discipline of writing because most people's biggest challenge is that they just don't approach their writing with a plan. Thus, they waste both time and effort. Finally, I talk about the various types of content and how you can use them to win the Invisible Sale.

## Talking Versus Typing

I've written sections of this chapter while driving in my car, waiting in the carpool line, and walking on my treadmill while watching a Texas Rangers game. I can do this because I'm talking, not typing. I'm turning what is normally considered downtime into uptime because I'm multitasking. And all you need to join me is a software program, a computer, an app, and a smartphone or tablet.

If you're older than 50 and you worked in the executive ranks, you might remember dictation machines. In the old days, corporate executives didn't type their own letters, memos, or documents. They dictated them, and a secretary transcribed and typed them. I don't know about you, but I haven't had a secretary in many, many years, and so transcription has never really been an option for me. I create text content the old-fashioned way: I type it. But the technology has finally caught up and now gives us the opportunity to use voice-to-text transcription to create more text than we could ever type.

I use Dragon Dictate for Mac. There's also a PC version, and Nuance (the maker of the software) offers both an Android and an iPhone app that functions as a portable digital recorder. Or if you like, you can use a standard digital recorder to capture your missives. Although the ability to dictate directly onto my Mac is truly helpful, the real leverage point here is the smartphone app.

Depending on traffic, my daily commute is somewhere between 10 and 15 minutes long. I used to use that time to listen to music or maybe make phone calls. But more often these days, I use that time to write. By simply opening the Dragon app and recording my thoughts, I can usually craft about 1,000 words of content. If you're not accustomed to equating word count with content length, 1,000 words is about two pages in a Microsoft Word document. In the online world, the average blog post runs between 500 and 1,000 words. So at a minimum, I can easily write a position memo, point-of-view document, or blog post on my daily commute to or from the office.

The app captures not only all your words, but also your punctuation. Of course, you have to remember to speak that punctuation, but the app is incredibly accurate when you remember to do so. Additionally, its transcription is exceptionally accurate. By using the headset that came with my iPhone, turning off the radio, and setting the air-conditioner to low, I can usually achieve 90% accuracy in the transcribed text, versus about 95% to 98% accuracy when I use the desktop program with the supplied headset.

But I've discovered a nice trick that improves mobile app accuracy to almost the same level as desktop accuracy, even in noise environments. Instead of using my iPhone, I use my iPad with the Dragon-supplied USB headset. To do this, you need Apple's iPad Camera Connection Kit. It's a simple little adapter that you can find online, at an Apple store, or at RadioShack for about $30. With this adapter, the iPad recognizes the Dragon USB headset, which is specifically designed to enhance spoken words and diminish background noise, resulting in a cleaner audio track that transcribes with a far higher degree of accuracy. This setup has proven to be so much more accurate that I've begun using the iPad/headset setup in the car instead of using my iPhone with the Apple headset

The entire process is pretty simple. As I said, you record whatever you intend to write. The app even lets you start and stop by simply clicking the big button in the middle of the app screen. When you're finished, you save the file on your device for transfer to your computer; you can even give the file a custom name. The app claims to allow you to transfer the file over WiFi, but I've never been able to get it to work. Truth be told, I haven't tried that hard because Dragon makes it easy to simply transfer the file via iTunes. I simply connect my iPhone or iPad to my laptop, open iTunes, and click my device in the menu on the left. That opens the device sync options. From there, you select the Apps tab and scroll down to the bottom, where you see a list of any apps that have the right to transfer files to your computer via the sync cable. You then select the Dragon app and can see all your voice recordings. Simply click the ones you want to transfer, pick a file folder on your computer, and click the Save As button. In a few seconds, those files are on your computer and ready for transcription.

Next, open the Dragon Dictation application and, under Tools, select Transcription. This opens a dialog box. From there, select the audio file you want to transcribe. When you start the transcription process, you'll see your words appear on a Notepad window, and the program indicates its progress. A 20-minute file takes 3 to 5 minutes to transcribe, and then you're ready to work with the text. Just copy and paste it into Word, and you're ready to correct any transcription errors, add formatting, and prep the text for use in a final document.

The biggest challenge I find in dictation versus typing is that dictation requires a bit more planning. My writing process used to be fairly undisciplined. I sat down to the computer and just typed a stream of consciousness onto the page, with little planning. Then I copied and pasted the various sections, to make everything flow logically and keep the document easy to understand. However if you approach voice-to-text writing the same way, you will wind up with files that meander and go off on tangents. Because of this, the resulting editing process will take so long that you will erase any benefit you receive from turning that downtime into writing time by using voice to text.

To counter this, you'll want to invest a few minutes into planning your dictated pieces. This can be as simple as using a 3x5 notecard to outline your piece. Remember, you can realistically expect to create 1,000 words for every 20 minutes of dictation. You don't need to outline *War and Peace*—just stick with the basics. State the main ideas of your piece, list three key support points and then summarize and close the section. By simply giving yourself this simple outline, you'll be able to focus your thoughts. This will result in more "finished" files that require a lot less editing after transcription. It might feel like you're wasting time or being unproductive as you do this planning, but the extra 5 or 10 minutes of effort will result in a much better finished piece.

# Write Your Content 1,000 Words at a Time

Could you build an entire car? I'm guessing you can't. Building a car seems like a very complex process that requires a lot of skills that you and I don't possess. But although we can't build that car, we could complete a single piece of the process as a worker on an assembly line. After all, that's why car manufacturers use assembly lines. They realize that it's not only difficult for a single person to build an entire car, it's also inefficient. Instead, automakers break the car-building process down to its discrete and individual steps that you and I can do. String enough of these steps together, and you build a car. When you think about creating larger text content, you need to apply that same assembly line mentality.

Writing larger pieces, such as white papers, eBooks, and actual books, is a daunting endeavor. The sheer size of these pieces can make them feel impossible to create. The secret to creating these longer forms of content is that assembly line process. Outline the major content buckets you need to create. Define the major themes or sections. Then define the subsections of those sections. Again, what main points and ideas do you need to highlight or reinforce? Keep breaking down the content until you arrive at discrete sections that you expect to need about 1,000 words to complete. By approaching the creation of longer content as sections, you'll be able to generate these larger pieces without killing yourself. Additionally, if you can train yourself to approach your text content creation in this manner, you'll immediately create more content in two key areas.

The first area is blogging. Read any of the current thinking on blogging or best practices in blogging, and you'll find that it's pretty much universally agreed that you should blog at least two times a week, if not more. Lots of well-respected inbound marketing outfits such as HubSpot strongly encourage you to blog daily, to increase web traffic and leads. However, anyone who's ever tried to do that will tell you that it can become very, very difficult. But by breaking down your bigger pieces into smaller pieces and using a voice-to-text application such as Dragon Dictation, you make daily blogging more attainable.

A disciplined process also can impact your ability to generate text content in the area of Cornerstone Content. Cornerstone Content includes things like white papers, eBooks, or, in my case, an actual book. In Chapter 16, "Cornerstones and Cobblestones: The Content Creation Framework," I talk about creating Cornerstone Content. For now, you just need to understand that well-designed Cornerstone Content is little more than a well-planned combination of smaller pieces of content that are designed to stand on their own as individual content pieces and that can also combine to create a piece of Cornerstone Content. Here again, you're creating content that is usable at multiple levels (blog and Cornerstone), resulting in a more effective use of your limited time.

# Using Interviews to Create Text

While we're on the topic of voice-to-text solutions, let's talk about another great text-creation trick. One of the easiest ways to create interesting, compelling, and informative text content is to transcribe interviews. These interviews might be with customers, clients, vendors, or thought leaders in your industry. It might be an interview that you conduct over the phone, via Skype or even face to face. The common theme here is translating that interview audio into text-based content for use as blog posts, in white papers, and in eBooks. However, this is the one place where programs such as Dragon Dictation simply don't work because they're trained to dictate your voice, not that of your interviewee. So you need to find a different solution.

Luckily, some great services out there are very inexpensive. In some cases, you'll even have the choice between a verbatim transcript and a formatted transcription that removes all the extra *ahs*, *ums*, and other filler words.

One service that I like and use is SpeechPad. SpeechPad offers transcription for as little as a dollar per minute, with a one-week turn-around. If you need the transcription sooner, they offer $1.50 per minute (48 hours turn-around) and $2.50 per minute (24 hour turn-around). With an average interview ranging anywhere from 30 to 45 minutes, this is a very cost-effective way to very quickly turn audio content into text-based content. I also like it because you can record the interview live using the Record-a-Call feature.

Transcribing audio feeds from interviews or videos is also useful for your website and blog. When you post audio or video content, you can add a transcript of the file to make the post more search engine friendly. But that isn't the only way to use this technique.

For instance, in addition to doing a series of audio interviews at a trade show for your podcast, you can use a service such as SpeechPad to convert that podcast to create quotes for use in an eBook. Instead of going back through to listen and transcribe the interviews yourself, you can send the files to a service such as SpeechPad and, for a few dollars, receive a text document that you can easily cut and paste to create that eBook. This is yet another example of how the easiest way to create more text-based content, which is the workhorse of the content marketing world, is to quit typing it and just start saying it.

As you've probably figured out, I've become a huge fan of audio-to-text as a content-creation tool. But audio-to-text isn't a silver bullet. It certainly makes it easier to create more text, but the key to writing more is to write smarter. And writing smarter is all about having a writing process. As I noted earlier, I don't really have a system. Better stated, I didn't used to have a system. In writing this book, I've discovered that the only way to create huge volumes of high-quality text content is to develop a disciplined writing process. So let's talk about my process and how you can adopt or evolve my process to help you create more high-quality content.

# A Disciplined Writing Process

The first step in your writing process has to be planning. It's not enough to just sit down at the computer and start typing. That approach can work, but it will lead to inefficient usage of time and the creation of suboptimal content. Push aside the desire to "just start writing." Instead, dedicate yourself to planning your content. If you do this, you'll enjoy the three hidden benefits that come with proper planning.

First, planning helps you see the entire spectrum of your topic. So often, when you just write based off "an idea for a post," you end up leaving out valuable content. This happens either because you force yourself into a predetermined length of content or you don't think through the entirety of the topic. However, by spending some time really thinking through the topic—not just the immediate content need—you will find a number of additional points, angles, and key points that you can include. Most often this leads you to create not a post, but a series of posts. Thus, you end up creating a lot more content in less time than if you just sat down and started writing.

Second, your writing will be more succinct and focused. Remember, online content readers are consuming your posts quickly. They're in a hurry because they're in search of information to make a decision. Therefore, they prefer content that's simple, to the point, and easy to read. Thus, you need to ensure that your content doesn't suffer from fuzzy logic or extraneous verbiage. By planning the content at an outline level and then filling in the blanks, you produce focused, helpful, and easy-to-consume content.

Third, you'll write more engaging and unique content. Rarely is your first take on a subject matter the best. As with any art, writing gets better with time and perspective. If you're disciplined and you outline and think through your content before you start writing, you give yourself time for this perspective to emerge. Often this perspective illuminates a unique angle or point-of-view that elevates your content from mundane to shareable—the ultimate compliment and the goal of great content.

For shorter pieces such as blog posts, use a simple 3×5 notecard to outline your blog post. Lead with a strong introduction paragraph that immediately grabs the reader's attention. Imagine that this is the only paragraph the reader might read, and plan to write it accordingly. The purpose of this paragraph is to make the reader want to consume the rest of the post. Then outline the main points and finish with a strong call to action in the final paragraph.

For longer pieces such as white papers, eBooks, and books, you need to outline the content and then sleep on it. Because these Cornerstone pieces are so much bigger and more complex, it's important to really focus on the outline step. Don't rush it. Outline the entire piece of content, and then set it down for a day. Revisit it and either edit to improve the content and flow or begin writing.

Next, don't try to write the entire document in one sitting. Obviously, this isn't possible with a book or even an eBook; but even with white papers, choose not to do so. Instead, write a few pages. For instance, in writing this book, my process was to write half of a chapter in a single sitting. Whether that took an hour, three hours, or most of a night, I would write only half of a chapter at a time. Then the next night, I'd write the rest of the chapter.

After you've written a chapter or, in the case of a white paper, a major section, set aside the document and go about your life. Wait at least a day to revisit the document. Then read over the document for grammar, style, consistency, and, most important, storyline. If you can't follow the storyline, you need to rewrite the document to make that possible. If the document is part of a larger body of work, such as a book or eBook, review a few chapters or sections at a time. Every few weeks, gather all the sections or chapters and read them sequentially from beginning to end. This makes sure that your storyline and logic flow through the entire document.

Lastly, read the entire document backward. That's right, read it backward word-by-word. We used to have a saying in the advertising business: The biggest typos are always in the headline. **Your mind can make you see what you meant to write versus what is actually on the paper.** However, by reading your document backward, you force your brain to consume each word as an independent concept instead of part of a larger sentence. Thus, you'll catch those spelling errors. When you've completed that edit, read the piece normally to ensure that the flow of the document is the very best it can be before you release the document for use in the sales and marketing program.

# Using Content Templates

Let's revisit the assembly line analogy again. What makes the assembly line work isn't just breaking down the complex into the simple—it's making it easy to teach anyone that simple, repeatable task. This same philosophy also applies to content. Wherever possible, you want to make it easy for anyone in your organization to create highly repeatable content with minimal training and effort.

To do this, think through the various content needs that you have in your prospecting and sales process. This might include how-tos, frequently asked questions, opinion pieces, product comparisons, or client success stories. This varies by industry, but every industry has common types of content that are repeatedly produced in support of digital sales and prospecting efforts.

In my business, one of the most common templates that we use is a point-of-view (POV). It is also a fabulous blog post template for creating *thought leader* posts or posts designed to persuade your buyer to select your product or service. A POV is produced when a client wants the agency's official thoughts about a marketing opportunity, a new platform, or some other marketing issue. In my career, I've written thousands of these POVs. In my early days, writing one used to take me a long time, not because I lacked the knowledge and expertise that I have today, but because I started from scratch every time I wrote a POV. I was wasting most of my time trying to figure out how to format my thoughts or how to put all the information into a document that made sense to the reader. Then I developed a template.

Figure 14-1 is my template for a POV. I want to share it with you for two reasons. First, for some of you, this document template might be one you want to use. Second, by seeing the template, you can see how I break down the larger issue of writing a POV into its subcomponents to create a highly repeatable, simple format that I've given to hundreds of executives over the last 20 years. Even now, two decades into my career, I still fall back on this simple template to focus my thinking and rapidly create persuasive POVs and blog posts. And that's the power of a template.

CONVERSEDIGITAL

| TO: | Client Name |
|---|---|
| FROM: | Converse Digital Employee |
| DATE: | Date |
| RE: | **Converse Digital POV** |

- **Summarize situation** or what we've been asked to comment on – digital strategy, online platform, etc. Don't assume the client remembers the context or that the client that requested the POV is the only audience for this document. Write accordingly.

- **State idea or response** you recommend. Clearly and concisely convey your opinion or recommendation.

- **Explain how it works or analysis that was undertaken**. If you are proposing an idea or strategy, explain how the idea will deliver the business goal. If you're providing an opinion to a question posed, explain the research or analysis undertaken to arrive at the recommendation stated above.

- **Reinforce key benefits**. Pick the THREE most persuasive support points or benefits the client will realize if they act on your idea. If you're writing a POV, give the three most persuasive support points for your recommendation.

- **Suggest easy next steps**. Tell the client what they need to do to act on your POV. This can be something as simple as, "To authorize the activation of this idea, please send an email with 'Your POV of [date of POV] regarding [title of POV] is approved.'" The goal here is to make the next step fast and simple.

**Figure 14-1**   *Converse digital point-of-view template (© Tom Martin)*

Before you go any further in this chapter, stop for a moment and ask yourself about the templates you could create. Are there certain documents that are consistently part of the sales process? Are you repeatedly required to provide clarity on frequently asked questions or areas of confusion about your product or service? Do you create product reviews, or are you required to submit written proposals for services? Can you create "Top X Reasons to Purchase Y Product" posts for your website? All these are candidates for templates that you can create. Look for opportunities to craft a template that make it easy for anyone from the least experienced to the most experienced member of your team to quickly and easily create sales and marketing content. Not only will this make everyone more efficient, but it will also facilitate the process of spreading the content-creation duties across your team.

# Pushing Through Writer's Block

All the templates in the world can't solve the classic writing challenge: writer's block. We've all had days when we look at a blank sheet of paper or a blank screen, and nothing comes to us. It's classic writer's block, and it usually strikes when you can least afford it. Luckily, some great techniques can help you break through and quickly get back into the content creation rhythm.

First, remember that it's a lot easier to write long than it is to write short. So even if your task is to create a 450-word post for your company blog, ramble on and get as many words down on paper or screen as possible. Allow yourself to go off on tangents. Don't even worry about making any logical sense. Just start writing or dictating. You'll find, especially if you're dictating, that, at some point, you'll start to find a theme or notice that you have a few points that you can string together to create a useful piece of content.

Second, read something that interests you but isn't on the topic you're trying to write about. Quite often as you're reading something completely disassociated with what you're trying to write, you'll actually make an interesting connection. You'll see a story that you can use as an analogy, or you'll see an angle that you hadn't seen before. Regardless, something about stimulating your brain with nonessential content triggers your ability to begin writing.

Third, ask a few colleagues or friends for their opinion on the subject. Quite often their point of view will stimulate your thinking. In fact, if you're lucky, you might even get into a really good explorative conversation with them about your topic. That conversation might just end up being the text you need to write your post, so try and record those conversations! Even if you don't get that lucky, your colleagues and friends might approach the problem from an alternative angle or see it through a different lens. Exposing yourself to stimuli often can push you through the block.

These are just a few techniques that I've found work well for me. You can find a lot more by doing a Google search or visiting TheInvisibleSale.com. As you read through the examples and options in this book, you'll see a common theme recommended: Stop thinking about what you need to write. The key to breaking writer's block seems to revolve around freeing your mind to create new associations. These associations lead to the ideas that fuel your writing. So when you feel the block, just stop and do something else. Chances are, that will do the trick.

# Text Content Options and Tips

In your content marketing, you want to provide your perspective buyer with different-sized pieces of content. This ranges from a short, simple answer, to a frequently asked question, to a longer-form eBook of 50 to 80 pages. The reason for this is that, at different points in the buying cycle, your prospects want more or less information. At the beginning of the cycle, they might be looking for top-level answers to basic questions so that they can whittle down the universe to a manageable short list of options. As they move through the buying process, they will want more specific information, often at a deeper level. That's when you'll want to provide things like position papers, product detail pages, white papers, or in-depth how-to manuals.

One of the things you need to think about when creating text is consumption platform. As my friend Tim Hayden likes to say, "Man was not meant to type." Reading content on a computer is an unnatural position, and one that I think is largely responsible for what is commonly referred to as the Internet attention deficit disorder. For a long time, we have attributed the fact that people won't read long content on a laptop or desktop to lack of attention or a short attention span. However, I submit that it isn't Internet ADD that drives this phenomenon, but the fact that reading long documents on a computer isn't comfortable.

But the long-form content savior has arrived in the form of tablets. Tablets really reopen the world of long-form content. The tablet makes it easy to download a position paper, how-to manual, or product comparison research study in a format that is very comfortable to read in the office, at home, or on the train. In fact, in spring 2013, Kindle launched the Send to Kindle button. With the Send to Kindle button, companies and bloggers can let a reader or prospective buyer send an entire blog post or web page to the Kindle for reading. This truly reopens the opportunity for long-form content and represents an opportunity for brands to create deeper, more engaging content.

# eBooks

eBooks are truly becoming a workhorse for the content marketing world as companies trade free eBooks for prospect leads. This "download our free eBook" approach to lead generation is an effective and relatively inexpensive approach to generating qualified leads. If you decide to include eBooks in your content marketing, you'll need to understand your options.

Two predominant eBook formats exist. You can choose to publish your eBooks as PDF files, which are easy to create using Microsoft Word, PowerPoint, or Apple's Keynote program. After they're created, they're easy to share via your website, with marketing emails, and in social media. Not only are PDFs easy to create, but they can be read on computers, tablets, and smartphones. Creating PDF-formatted eBooks is the quickest way to begin using eBooks in your sales and marketing efforts.

Your other option is to create an EPUB-style eBook that is formatted for Kindle, Nook, or iBook readers. EPUB books are more advanced file formats and require a bit more work on your part. But don't let that deter you; numerous platforms allow you to convert your raw text document into a Kindle-, Nook-, or iBook-friendly format. And although it does take a bit more effort, the advantage of this format is that the reader can enlarge or change text and render it correctly on all devices, regardless of type size selected or orientation of device during reading.

## White Papers

Although eBooks are great, they're also a ton of work. You'll likely produce them far less frequently than other forms of text content. For those times in the sales cycle when your buyer needs more information than you can provide in a blog post but probably doesn't need or want to read a book on the subject, you can produce white papers. White papers have long been a staple in the technology and telecom industries. Given the educational requirements required to make many of the purchases in these industries, white papers make perfect sense. They allow companies to reach interested buyers early in the buying cycle and set the stage for lead-nurturing programs, primarily powered by email.

You can create white papers for pretty much any product or service. A white paper is not a certain *type* of document as much as it is a certain *length* of document. The average white paper is 7 to 15 pages long. Furthermore, white papers are not designed to complete the sale. They usually give a good deal of information but stop short of allowing a buyer to completely self-educate. Ultimately, the role of a white paper is to give invisible buyers the opportunity to reveal themselves to you by exchanging an email address for the white paper.

## Blog Posts

Finally, we have blog posts. Blog posts are the offensive line of content marketing. Day after day, blog posts are driving traffic to your site, aiding your search engine optimization and generating leads for your company. But this familiarity leads companies to often treat blog posts as to-do items instead of true content-creation opportunities. Far too often, companies are "mailing it in" on their blog posts. In an effort to produce more content than their staffs are equipped to generate, these companies begin to skimp on quality in favor of quantity. Don't do that.

Although an eBook or a white paper might drive more leads than any single blog post, total blog post leads will likely outshine any single eBook or white paper. Just as four singles equal a home run in baseball, a string of well-crafted blog posts can generate just as much return on investment as any white paper or eBook. So why then do companies allow less-than-perfect blog posts on their websites? They allow it because they get behind, suffer from writer's block, or, more often, run out of ideas. I can't necessarily help you with falling behind, and we've already addressed writers block so let's finish with a few starter ideas to help you ensure an endless stream of blog posts.

First, pay attention to your blog post format. A certain format has been proven to work and actually makes writing a blog post easier. Think in terms of scannable content. Make liberal use of subheads and bolded copy, to let the reader get the gist of the post by simply reading the bolded text. Keep your paragraphs short, and use lots of white space. Web readers need to think that they can read the content quickly, so use white space to give the allusion of brevity.

Next, write like a reporter, not a college student. Your first paragraph should convey the essence of your post. Don't build your arguments through the post and finish with a big conclusion. Your college professor might give you an A, but the common web reader will click on to the next article. Instead, just state your point or key message and then use the rest of the post to support your main point. Use images to quickly convey points or maintain reader attention. Lastly, use links to let the reader dive deeper into your content, but don't overwhelm the reader with a hyperlink in every other line of copy.

Now that you understand how to create a good blog post, let's talk about a few of the different posts you might want to create. This is by no means a complete list of blog post types, but it will get you started. If you're interested, you can find more post types on TheInvisibleSale.com under Text Tools, or just subscribe to the *Painless Prospecting* newsletter:

- **FAQ posts:** Buyers tend to have the same set of core questions about a product or service. Companies commonly put the answers to these frequently asked questions on a page of their website but often neglect to use them as blog posts. Don't make that mistake. Poll your sales teams and find every question that a customer has ever asked. Then write a 300- to 500-word answer and publish the answer as a post.

- **Round-up posts:** Think about what kinds of information your buyers need to do their job better. This information might have nothing to do with your product or service, but it helps your buyers become more valuable to their companies. For instance, if you sell advertising space to ad agencies and client marketers, you could create blog posts about the latest technological developments in the marketing and advertising industry. Each day, week, or month, create a post that lists a handful of these important pieces of content; then add a bit of context from you and post the blog on your website.

- **Resource posts:** Another form of post that is designed to simply be helpful is the resource post. If you're an interior designer, you might want to create posts that list reputable contractors, landscape architects, lawn maintenance companies, and other resources a homeowner might need. Although this doesn't have anything directly to do with interior design, it does make your blog more valuable to homeowners.

- **How-to posts:** These are pretty self-explanatory. If you sell a product, your customer and prospect base has questions about how to use your product. Use your blog posts to provide directions, video tutorials, step-by-step instructions, or tips and tricks. Your customers will love you for it. The search engines will reward you for it, and your prospects will reward you with new sales.

- **New feature or news posts:** Most important, these are timely. By definition, "new" is a timely concept. Although these posts are extremely effective at building an audience, they require your team to be ready to comment on breaking news, industry trends, or product updates.

- **Versus posts:** These are an often-overlooked tactic in the larger marketing communication world. Each year, billions are spent on advertising by products or services claiming to be better than a competitor. Yet a simple Google search most often fails to return brand-sponsored content comparing the product to the competitor. This lack of verifiable evidence of superiority ultimately degrades the effectiveness of that ad spend and opens the door for your competitor or a random person to own that Google search term.

Text-based content has been and likely will be in the near future the vast majority of the content you create and share online. But don't be afraid. Applying the tools, techniques, and tips contained in this chapter prepares you to create all the text-based content you'll ever need.

# 15

# Creating Live and Recorded Webinars and Product Tutorials

*I'm a huge fan of online product demos and webinars—both live and recorded—because they let me easily educate myself about a product or service I'm considering. As a business, you should love these tools as well because they help prospects self-select into your sales process. If you think that all prospects are leads, you'll probably disagree with what I'm about to say.*

*The single best reason to invest in product demos is to help your prospects realize that you're not the right solution for their need. This might sound counterproductive to traditionally minded sales teams, but consider this point before you decide. A salesperson can handle only so many sales calls, live demonstrations, and other customer interactions in any given day. Additionally, your product or service is never going to be the right solution for 100% of the prospects who visit your website. Thus, you have two choices.*

You can let unsuitable prospects figure that out on their own without wasting your sales team's time, or you can let your salesperson help them discover that fact during a live demo or during the sales process. The choice is yours, but I'd submit that your sales teams will be happier, more productive, and maybe even smaller and less expensive by letting your prospects self-select themselves out of your sales funnel. By having your salespeople follow up on only qualified leads, you might even be able to reduce the size of your sales team because your staff will be making fewer but more qualified sales calls.

For companies that sell services, recorded webinars can serve the same purpose as the product demo. They give your prospects an opportunity to sample your service and determine whether your company should make a short list of contenders. From here, you can move them along to a live webinar or a sales call. Not only will they have to reveal themselves by providing a valid email address, but you'll also be able to begin to learn a bit about their needs through marketing automation software that tracks their content consumption on your site after they've provided that email address.

Given that online product demos are fairly straightforward, I focus most of this chapter on the tools and strategies for creating live and recorded webinars. At the end of the chapter, I spend a bit of time on product demo videos and thoughts about how to gain maximum advantage through demos on your website. For now, let's talk about webinars.

# Five Keys to Successful Webinars

The biggest mistake marketers make with webinars is assuming that they can just fire up their PowerPoint and their webinar or screen recording software and then start presenting that sales deck they created for Customer A last month. Nothing could be further from the truth. Successful webinars must be practiced and delivered to both inform and persuade. You need to have a communications and sales strategy for every webinar you create. Think about what you want the attendees to do next. What action do you want them to take? What feeling do you want to leave them with? *Hint:* More often than not, the action isn't "buy now" and the feeling isn't "The folks who presented this webinar are super smart."

You have to use your webinars strategically. For instance, as I noted, recorded webinars are a great way to allow prospects to self-select into your sales funnel. Thus, you need to decide whether you want to allow some or all of your recorded webinars to be viewed without requiring prospects to provide an email address. This question is hotly debated in business-to-business (B2B) circles. One side firmly believes that gaining that email address must be the primary directive of any online webinar. On the other side, the qualified lead group believes you shouldn't collect an email address or even begin tracking prospects until you know they are truly leads.

Both sides of this issue present strong arguments. Before you begin using webinars, you should think through these arguments and determine where your company is going to fall on the continuum. Regardless of your position, you still need to plan and execute great webinars. To help you achieve that goal, consider the five key steps you need to execute with every webinar you produce, whether live or recorded:

1. **Write a great title and description.** If your webinar title is dull, broad, and businesslike, it's not going to generate a lot of interest. I'm not saying you have to write super-creative titles and descriptions (although that helps), but you do have to create anticipation. For instance, one of my most successful recorded webinars is "28 Tips & Tricks to Creating Awesome Content on an iPhone," a recorded version of a presentation I delivered at the BlogWorld & New Media Expo Conference. At the writing of this chapter, the webinar has been viewed 17,314 times.

   That's not a very creative or sexy title. But remember, the goal of the title is to entice people to register or watch for your webinar in the first place. The title should make them stop and think, "Yes, I *have* to have this information. This will be a good use of my time. I'm registering!" If you're interested in using your iPhone to create online content, that title quickly conveys that my webinar is for you.

2. **Focus on creating deep versus wide webinars.** I remember actually feeling bad when I created the "28 Tips & Tricks" presentation. It was so basic, so simple, and I felt like I was "mailing it in" versus delivering something truly powerful to my audience. Boy, was I wrong. That presentation taught me that prospective buyers would rather see you drill deep into a very small, vertical topic than have you deliver a 30,000-foot summary presentation.

   This is a powerful point. I watch a lot of webinars online, and I see companies repeatedly making this mistake. They're trying to make their webinars all things to all prospects. Don't do that. Take the opportunity to segment your information and create a series of deep, helpful webinars.

3. **Keep it short.** If you follow the previous rule, this will be easy to accomplish. For some unknown reason, 1 hour seems to be the standard length of time for a webinar (recorded or live) online. I think this is a holdover from offline conferences, where sessions are commonly 45 minutes of presentation with 15 minutes of Q&A. And although

that works great in a live, offline presentation, an hour of webinar is tough to sit through and even tougher to deliver. Instead, focus on creating shorter webinars. Start with 30-minute versions, and try to cut those down to 15 minutes. By getting shorter, you increase the chances that prospects will attend. Who doesn't have 15 minutes to spare in their day to access a bit of truly helpful information that they are excited to hear? Additionally, because these webinars are shorter, you can offer them multiple times throughout the day, which helps you accommodate different time zones. This particular point is key for companies whose prospect base is national or global.

4. **Keep it moving.** Here again, presenters forget that the dynamics of online webinars are completely different from those of offline presentations. In a face-to-face presentation, the audience and presenter feed off one another. A compelling stage presence allows the speaker to remain on a single slide for many minutes without the audience noticing. The same is not true in webinars. Unless you have an incredibly good storyteller delivering the webinar, you need to make sure your slides are advancing every 30 seconds to 1 minute. That visual movement on the screen keeps the audience engaged. Remember, the audience is looking at the same computer screen that houses their email, social networks, and other work. It's incredibly easy for them to just click over to these other applications and multitask instead of giving you their undivided attention.

5. **Give good sound.** Just as Chris Yates pointed out in Chapter 11, "Creating Video," bad audio kills good video—and the same rule applies to webinars. The only stimuli you have in a webinar are your slides and your voice. Nothing ruins the effectiveness of a webinar faster than not being able to hear the speaker because of background noise, room echo, or a bad microphone. And remember, as I noted in rule 4, sometimes attendees are exposed to *only* your voice, so it is imperative that they can clearly hear you.

If you're going to get serious about using webinars for your lead-generation campaigns, invest in a good USB microphone such as the ones I discussed in Chapter 13, "Creating Audio," and list on TheInvisibleSale.com/AudioTools. You'll also want to purchase or create a tabletop audio recording booth. This simple tool reduces or, in some cases, removes the sound bounce that causes that echo effect in which the speaker sounds like he or she is sitting alone in the middle of large room. I give you a few suggestions on the Audio Tools page.

# How to Record Your Webinar

There are two ways to record webinars. In some cases, you'll create a presentation that is specifically designed as a recorded webinar. In other situations, you'll want to record a live conference presentation, product demo, or sales presentation to use as a downloadable webinar. Let's go through the options you have for recording each type of webinar.

First, if you or any members of your company are actively presenting at conferences or trade shows, or even directly to clients, you'll want to record those presentations for use as recorded webinars. If you're giving those presentations in front of a live audience, you'll need a screen capture program. As the name suggests, screen capture programs record everything you see on your screen in an editable video file. These programs capture any image on your computer, any sound created by your computer, and, if you choose, both external audio and video streams. All of this is combined into one, editable digital file.

Although you can record external video and audio, you'll usually just want to record the external audio. To do this, you need to attach a wireless microphone such as the ones I talked about in Chapter 13 to your computer's microphone jack. After you've tested the audio to ensure that your signal is working, you're ready to begin. First, start the screen capture and activate the presentation view of your Keynote or PowerPoint file. After a 3-second onscreen countdown, which you'll see on your screen, you're recording everything. When you're finished, just stop the screen capture; you're placed in the Camtasia or ScreenFlow edit screen. At this point, you can save the file for editing later. The big benefit of using this approach instead of using the mobile phone approach we talk about later in this chapter is that this technique records any videos or audio files you play during the presentation. Thus, if you use a lot of multimedia in your presentations, this technique enables you to keep all that in the recorded webinar version, too.

In some cases, your presentation can be delivered online as a live online webinar, which gives you an additional recording option. You certainly can use screen capture software to record your live webinars, but you also have another option. If you're using GoToMeeting or GoToWebinar as your online webinar hosting solution, you can simply click the Record button before you start your presentation. When you're finished, click the button again to stop the recording. At this point, you're prompted to "convert the file"; then you'll have a fully recorded digital file ready for uploading to your website or YouTube. Alternatively, if you want to edit the file to remove pauses, the Q&A, or other items, you can simply import the file into any video-editing program, make your desired changes, and recompile as a finished video product ready for uploading.

The process of creating recorded webinars is exactly the same as the process of recording your live offline presentations. The only difference is that you don't need a wireless lavaliere microphone, but you will want to use a good USB microphone. Just as you did for the live recording, you'll want to activate the screen capture software first, place your Keynote or PowerPoint in presentation mode, and wait for the countdown to complete before you begin presenting. When you finish, turn off the screen capture; then you're ready to either begin editing or save the file for future editing.

# How to Record Webinar Audio Using a Smartphone

As noted earlier, webinar recordings are ideally made using a high-quality microphone attached to your computer. When you're recording a live presentation to use as a recorded webinar, you want to use a lavaliere (lav) microphone to maximize sound quality. But occasionally, you are required to present your presentation using someone else's computer. In those cases, you can fall back on a nifty trick I picked up the hard way. You can use your mobile phone to record the audio and then use Camtasia, ScreenFlow, or SlideShare to create a recorded webinar. Here are three ways you can record your webinar audio using your iPhone or Android phone.

## Option 1

Grab the headset that you use to make phone calls, and fish the end you connect to your phone down the inside of your shirt (to make yourself look good). The microphone is located about six to eight inches from one of your earbuds. To properly place the microphone to obtain the best recording quality, loop the microphone through your top button or maybe through a buttonhole, if you're wearing a pullover Polo-style shirt. Then tuck the earpiece inside your shirt. Finally, fish the headset connector out through the bottom of your shirt and connect it to your phone, which you can place in your pocket. This way, your audience won't see the microphone wire, which looks more professional. More important, the microphone will be placed in the optimum position to pick up your voice and not the room noise.

Next, activate the voice recorder app on your phone. For iPhone users, just use the Voice Memos app. For Android users, I've been told Dragon Dictation and the Evernote app are both solid choices. Then deliver your talk as you normally would. When you're done (and before you start Q&A), pull your phone back out and stop recording. Save the file on your phone.

# Option 2

The standard headset will work in a pinch, but the recorded audio quality is certainly substandard and shouldn't be your first choice as a recording option. I really offer it up here only as a fallback position. I myself have used it to record audio that is later embedded in my own webinars, and although the audio wasn't the worst thing I'd ever heard, it certainly was not ideal.

Thus, I recommend suggest an alternative option, using the *exact* same setup noted in Option I, with one little change. Instead of using the supplied phone headset, use a wired lavaliere microphone. I'm a fan of the Audio-Technica mics. As with most things in the audio world, there's a huge range in price and quality. The basic mic, which retails for around $30, is just fine. However, if you want really good sound and low or no background noise, you might want to invest in one of the higher-quality mics. *Note:* If you want to use *any* external microphone with your iPhone, you'll need to invest $30 in the special KV Connector cable I talked about in Chapter 13. Without it, you're stuck using the headset for all recordings.

# Option 3

If you really want to have the most flexibility, or if you're a female and you're wearing a dress that doesn't allow you to place your iPhone in a pocket, you might want to step up to a wireless lav system. A wireless lavaliere system has two parts. First, a transmitter unit is attached to the lavaliere microphone and second, a base station, which you attach to the headphone jack of your phone. Again, if you want to plug the base station into your iPhone, you'll need that KV Connector cable. Then just attach the transmitter station to your belt or skirt, and wire yourself up as you do with the wired lavaliere microphones.

The big benefit of this option is that the wireless base station has an audio out plug. That means you can have someone in the audience, such as a coworker, listen to your live audio feed via a headset as you're recording that feed to your phone. This can be a *huge* advantage, especially if your listener notices any hiccups in the audio. This actually happened to me once when the lavaliere transmitter's batteries died and my listener suddenly lost my audio signal. He was able to immediately alert me so that I could fix it on the spot instead of having to rerecord the audio and splice the missing audio into the master audio file during editing.

Now, this option is surely the most expensive. A decent wireless lavaliere system costs about $300, but if you're going to do a lot of presentations that you want to convert to webinars, it's a great investment.

# How to Convert Your Recordings to MP3

If you're using an Android smartphone, you can skip this part of the chapter because your recorded file is already in MP3 format, a universal recording standard for digital audio files. However, iPhone users need to take one additional step to prepare the audio file for use in a recorded version of their presentation. This is because the iPhone records in Apple's proprietary ACC format. Luckily, Apple gives you an easy tool in iTunes to quickly convert ACC-formatted files into the universal MP3 format.

When you get back to your computer, use iTunes to sync the file into your iTunes Music Library. Then find the file and select it. Click the Advanced file menu and select the Create MP3 Version option (see Figure 15-1).

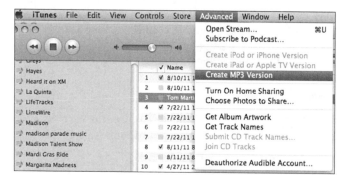

**Figure 15-1**   *Using iTunes to convert an ACC file to MP3*

iTunes converts the file in a few seconds, and then you'll have a duplicate file in the MP3 format. Because iTunes duplicates the track name, I recommend that you immediately rename the copied file with the name of your talk or webinar. This makes it easier to locate the file on your computer during the editing process.

# How to Synchronize the Audio and Slides for Your Webinar

Now that the hard part is over—yes, the audio capture is actually the hard part here—it's time to start the final process of creating your recorded webinar. Again, you have two options: Either create a Slidecast on SlideShare.net, or synchronize the audio to your slide deck using Camtasia or ScreenFlow. Let's talk about the SlideShare option first.

The first step of the SlideShare process is to log onto SlideShare.net. SlideShare is often referred to as the YouTube of PowerPoints and is a wonderful resource for presentations on any topic you can imagine. As such, it's a great place to upload your presentations and webinar decks. More important, SlideShare has a simple tool to convert regular PowerPoint files into streaming webinars that can be viewed on SlideShare.net or embedded in any website with a simple embed code.

After you've logged in or created your account, find your presentation file on your computer and upload it to SlideShare. Although SlideShare can accept PowerPoint and Keynote, I find that it's best to simply convert your presentation to PDF format (especially for Keynotes) and then upload that file. Then you'll want to tag it and give it a title, to optimize the file for search and improve the chances that your file will show up when a prospect searches for presentations about your topic on SlideShare.

Inside your SlideShare account, click My Uploads, located in the main file navigation menu of SlideShare. Navigate to the MP3 file of your presentation audio on your computer and upload it. *Tip:* Use your computer's search function to search for the custom name you gave the MP3 file. After you upload it, you're greeted with the Webinar Synchronization Tool (see Figure 15-2)—or, as SlideShare calls it, the Slidecast Maker.

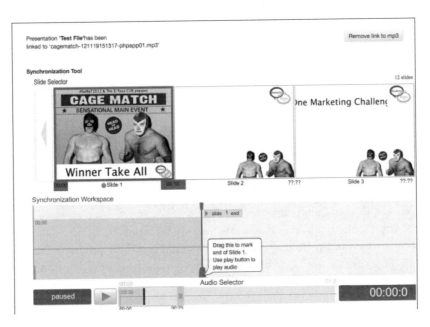

**Figure 15-2**  *Slidecast Maker screen on SlideShare.net*

SlideShare truly is a super simple and easy-to-use synchronization tool. But just in case, I've created a how-to tutorial video on my website. You can access it at http://goo.gl/zTCNC or search for "How to Make a Recorded Webinar with Your iPhone" on Google; click the Converse Digital post.

When you've completed the Slidecast, click the Publish button. You're greeted with a finished webinar that streams perfectly. To embed this webinar in your own website, just click the Embed link at the top of the webinar viewer window. From there, you embed it just like a YouTube video by pasting the embed code into your website or blog's HTML.

I really like the SlideShare option and have used it numerous times, but it does have one drawback: Viewers can't download the file to view offline. This causes two issues. First, prospects can't view the webinar if they're on an airplane or somewhere without Wi-Fi access. Second, you can't use the file as a lead-generation tool for which you provide access to the file in exchange for a prospect's contact information. But don't fret: You have another simple option for synching your smartphone audio to your presentation file to create a downloadable and streamable version of your presentation.

To do this, you need to manually create the file in Camtasia or ScreenFlow, and you have two options to choose from. The first option, and the easiest, is to simply play the PowerPoint or Keynote file as though you were giving the presentation. Start a Camtasia or ScreenFlow recording session, and turn off Record External Audio. Then activate the Present option in PowerPoint or Keynote just as you would if you were presenting the deck at an actual conference or client presentation. Finally, start the playback of the audio file you recorded. Then as you're listening to your audio file, advance the slides at the appropriate times. When you're finished, stop the presentation and the screen capture. Now you have a complete recording of your presentation that is ready to synchronize with your audio file.

To begin the synchronization step, insert the audio file of your presentation into the screen capture file you just created. Because you advanced the slides manually through the recording of the presentation, the timing of the audio and slide advancement should match up perfectly. From here, just export the screen capture as you normally would, and you're finished.

Of course, this isn't something *you* have to do. If you're good at placing audio cues in your presentations to clearly indicate that you've switched to a new slide, pretty much anyone can listen along and advance the slides at the appropriate times. Even if the slides are off a tad here and there, your audience probably won't realize it or even mind.

Your other option is to open your PowerPoint or Keynote file and export the entire presentation as JPEGs. Then open a blank presentation in ScreenFlow or Camtasia. Next, insert the audio file of your presentation. Then you can import those JPEGs of your presentation file into ScreenFlow or Camtasia and then insert the individual slides one at a time into the blank presentation. Here again, you or someone on your team will need to listen along to the audio to know when to insert the next slide image so that the slides synchronize with the audio.

Of the two options, I prefer the first option. It takes a little longer because you can't fast-forward through the audio to find the next slide transition as you can with the second option. But it's a lot easier and can be executed by anyone on staff, whereas the second option requires a bit more knowledge about the various software programs (Camtasia, ScreenFlow, PowerPoint, and Keynote). Then again, if someone you know is familiar with both the presentation pacing and the programs, the second option can be completed more quickly.

Now that we've covered webinar creation in detail, let's talk about creating those product videos.

# Creating Great Product Demonstration Videos

You can create two kinds of product demonstration videos for use online. If your product is digital, you can use screen capture programs such as Camtasia and ScreenFlow to record product demos to feature on your website. These programs capture everything you see on your screen, along with any audio the computer produces. You can add your voiceover via your computer's microphone, and you can choose to either create that voiceover as you're recording the demo or do it "in post production" after you've imported the screen recording session into Camtasia or ScreenFlow.

Both programs have built-in editing functionality, too. Thus, after you finish recording a product demo, you can edit out mistakes, "ums," "ahs," or anything else that you don't want in the final video. Additionally, you can create zoom effects, to magnify sections of your screen so that viewers can more easily see exactly what you're clicking or activating, which is especially useful when you're accessing program menus. Finally, you can enhance the audio or add other audio tracks, such as background music, to complete the video.

The other type of product demo video is for real-world products. You can record this demo with any digital camera and then edit it in a desktop editing program. When shooting these demos, you need to decide whether you want an onscreen talent to demonstrate the product or you want to shoot without any audio and record the voiceover separately. The key to making a great product demo video is to shoot from a variety of angles and vary your shot from wide (where you see the entire product) to close-ups (where you're demonstrating a key feature or function). This makes the video more useful and interesting to watch. For this reason, you might want to record your voiceover separately; the blending of multiple camera shots is easier with a separate voiceover because you don't have to worry about sync-sound—where you synchronize the audio track with the video from the various cameras or camera angles.

Product demonstration videos give your prospects the chance to test-drive your product before purchasing it. This creates a sense of trust and comfort in the purchase decision that moves prospects farther down the purchase funnel before they reveal themselves to your sales team. This creates a win-win for both parties: Your prospects are allowed to self-educate, and your sales team receives far higher-qualified leads to close.

# Planning Product Demos

As I mentioned earlier, you can't just pick up a camera or fire up the computer and hope to create compelling and effective product demo videos. You need to approach these pieces of content in the same way an advertising agency thinks about a commercial or a film director approaches a movie. You need to storyboard your ideas. With a storyboard, you plan both the visual frames of the video and the associated audio. This preplanning helps you craft a more compelling video and ensures that you maintain visual interest throughout the video.

You have three options for storyboard planning and creation, ranging from doing it by hand to using software specifically designed for storyboard creation. If you decide you want to draw your storyboard by hand, I recommend ordering Storyboard notepads from Levenger.com. These formatted sheets have three storyboard windows apiece, along with a place for you to write dialogue copy or notes. I use these a lot because I'm not storyboarding my videos down to the second. Instead, I'm using them to help myself think through the general flow of a video, to ensure that I hit the important points and skip over the less important aspects. These sheets make the process super simple and fast.

If you want to keep everything digital or just save a few dollars, use PowerPoint or Keynote to create your storyboards. This is better for doing storyboards for product demos when you are using photography of your product or can generate screen grabs of software. Then place your audio script in the Presenter Notes. Use the Slide Sorter or Light Table (Keynote) view to visually check that your video will flow well. When you are ready to print your storyboard, print it as a handout with three slides per page, and make sure you click the Include Notes option. This generates a "three scene with script" view that makes a perfect storyboard.

Finally, if you want something a bit more polished, you can purchase special software, such as StoryBoard Quick, for a few hundred dollars. The benefit of this software is its built-in graphic elements, such as people, props, and scenes. With these tools, you can draw scenes that you need to shoot even if you have no artistic capability. The software also gives you plenty of professional-looking output options.

Regardless of which tool you use to create your storyboards, do force yourself to go through the process. Take it from someone who has failed to enforce this discipline on himself in the past: If you don't think through your videos with a plan, you will inevitably end up rerecording sections or scrapping entire videos, resulting in a huge waste of time and effort.

# 16

# Cornerstones and Cobblestones: The Content Creation Framework

*The fuel that powers your Painless Prospecting system is content. As we discussed earlier, the single biggest challenge to developing and maintaining an effective Painless Prospecting system is your ability to consistently produce and distribute high-value content throughout your entire digital footprint.*

*The reason we all have so much trouble producing the necessary content is that, fundamentally, we're producing content at the wrong level. When you talk to content marketers about their content-creation activities, they speak in terms of individualized content. They talk in terms of blog posts, YouTube videos, podcasts, and any other individualized pieces of content. But what they won't talk to you about is how they are creating an ecosystem of content. They won't talk to you about how they're planning one blog post that is designed to be an anchor piece, which they will link to and from various blog posts appearing on open or closed platforms where they maintain publishing rights.*

The power of the Cornerstone and Cobblestone (C&C) approach is how it evolves your content marketing. More than a process, C&C is a philosophy you apply to every piece of content you create. No more creating content at the individual unit (blog post/podcast or other single content unit) level. Instead, you approach publishing your content like a mini campaign. Whether deconstructing a major piece of content such as a white paper or writing a single blog post, always look for additional opportunities to repurpose your content and create additional propinquity points.

## Cornerstones and Cobblestones Explained

By forcing you to think about your content as an ecosystem, the C&C framework reduces the work required to produce the vast amounts of content Painless Prospecting platforms require. Although the system is designed primarily around the concept of deconstructing bigger cornerstone content into its smaller cobblestones, I encourage you to apply the C&C approach to every piece of content you create. We talk more about that later—for now, let me define what I mean when I refer to cornerstone content and cobblestone content.

Cornerstone content refers to large, educational pieces of content, including but not limited to white papers, e-books, research reports, and comparative buying guides. These bigger, meatier pieces of content are simply too large for most companies to produce with great frequency. Additionally, these larger pieces aren't consumed by prospects at the same rate as smaller individual pieces of content, such as blog posts. Thus, cornerstone content is designed for consumption by more serious buyers versus casual self-educators.

Cobblestone content refers to smaller pieces of content, such as blog posts, conference presentations, magazine articles, guest posts, email marketing executions, podcasts, and webinars, to name but a few. Cobblestones are the most commonly produced types of content. These are the day-to-day building blocks that create the propinquity necessary to create top-of-mind preference.

Traditionally, companies produce cornerstone content and then attempt to break it down into discrete individual pieces that they can then use as cobblestone content. This approach has two challenges. First, the deconstruction process is very time-consuming because it requires the deconstructor to be intimately familiar with both the cornerstone content and the editorial preferences of each propinquity point where the company wishes to seed the resulting cobblestone content. Second, the deconstructor must possess above-average writing skills to effectively resynthesize the various portions of the cornerstone content into these new cobblestones.

The C&C framework eliminates these two challenges by reversing the cornerstone content-creation process. Instead of starting with the cornerstone, start with the cobblestones. Look first at your propinquity points and what kind of content those propinquity points favor. Next, devise outlines for your cobblestone content based on the propinquity points you target. Finally, using the cobblestone content outlines as a framework, reverse-engineer the cornerstone content.

Seldom do cobblestones simply roll up into a nice, easily organized cornerstone. This is where creative writing skills play an important role. Often you need to add sections to the cornerstone to provide the necessary context and information flow required to create a finished piece of cornerstone content. As you create this additional content, evaluate it for other uses within your content ecosystem.

After you've crafted the final cornerstone and published it online, it's time to begin the deconstruction and seeding process of publishing cobblestones at each propinquity point.

Because cornerstone content is predesigned to easily deconstruct into cobblestone content, the deconstructor doesn't need advanced analytical or writing skills. Instead, the deconstructor extracts each predefined cobblestone and applies the proper level of formatting, wordsmithing, or other simple editing to create appropriate cobblestones for each propinquity point. And this is the hidden power of the framework. Because the cornerstone content was designed to be deconstructed in this manner, and for these particular propinquity points, this process is simple and easy, and it can be performed by less experienced team members or outside resources.

# Repurposing Content

As you probably figured out, the key to the C&C framework is repurposing your content. But by "repurposing," I'm not simply speaking of repurposing the message within a single medium (copy and paste)—more importantly, I'm talking about repurposing the message across multiple media. And most importantly, the need to plan that reuse *before* you ever create the original piece of content.

Let me give you two examples to make this clearer. The first involves the creation of a conference presentation. This is a common content type marketing and sales executives use in a vast array of industries. In a repurposing mindset, a conference presentation becomes, at a minimum, four separate pieces of content.

First is the presentation itself, delivered either virtually or in person at the conference. However, with minimal additional work, that same conference presentation can also exist as a podcast or some other audio file; a video of the entire presentation, with the audio synced and then shared on YouTube (the second-biggest search engine in the world); and a blog post where you've transcribed the audio to a text script. You would also link to the YouTube video and podcast from the blog post. Thus, with a minimal amount of additional expense and effort, that one presentation now lives in four separate channels consumable in four (live, text, video, and audio) different formats. Three of these formats are shareable via social networking and are indexed by Google.

Another great example is what Chris Brogan, CEO of Human Business Works, does with his weekly email newsletter. Chris understands that not everybody wants or has time to read a newsletter. He's also aware that plenty of people prefer to listen to text (audiobooks) instead of reading it. Therefore, each Sunday, before he sends his email newsletter, he records himself reading the entire newsletter and publishes it as a podcast. He even references the podcast in the newsletter, suggesting that if you'd rather listen versus read, you can click the handy link to be transported to the podcast. This is a brilliantly simple idea that allows Chris to apply just a little more effort to double the amount of content he creates that day.

Make it your goal to never create any piece of content only once. I realize that you won't always be able to live up to that goal—none of us will. That's okay. But understand that if you continue to create content at the individual unit level, you'll never produce the necessary volumes of content required to create propinquity against your prospects and maintain some semblance of work/life balance. You must begin to approach your content creation from a systems perspective. Every piece of content you create on your Home Base (your website or blog) must live in another format, in another digital location, with links back to the original content on your Home Base. And the best time to create those additional content units is when you're creating the initial piece of content.

# The Cornerstone and Cobblestone Framework

The C&C Framework has three levels of content creation and dissemination:

- **Content published on channels that you own.** This includes your home base, a podcast that you distribute, and blogs that you manage.
- **Content published on open networks.** Recall from Chapter 8, "Creating Your Painless Prospecting Platform," that open networks are platforms such as YouTube, SlideShare, Pinterest, and so on, where membership gives you the right to publish your own content anytime you choose.
- **Content published on closed networks.** Again, remember from Chapter 8 that closed networks are publishing platforms that another individual or company owns that grant you permission to publish on that platform, pending review and approval by their editorial staff. This includes guest posts on blogs or articles written for other online communities or media properties.

Figure 16-1 shows a prototypical C&C framework. Let me take you through the pieces and parts that you see so that you can understand how a C&C framework might look for your company.

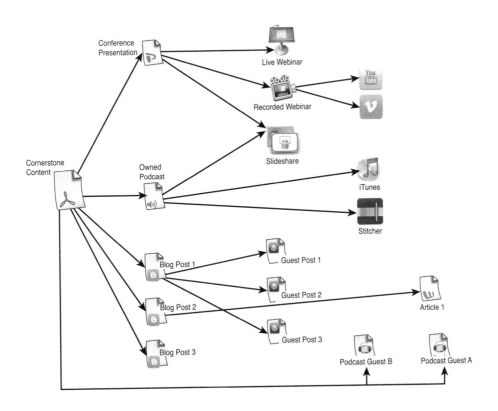

**Figure 16-1** *Cornerstone and cobblestone framework map*

On the far left of Figure 16-1, you find the single piece of cornerstone content. As I mentioned earlier, cornerstone content varies by industry or category. As long as the content is significant, provides a great a depth of information, and is designed for consumption primarily by highly qualified prospective buyers, it qualifies as cornerstone content.

The first step in the deconstruction process is simply reformatting the cornerstone content into other formats. Thus, if the cornerstone is a white paper, reformat it into a conference presentation. Start by turning each subsection of the white paper into a single slide. When a single slide can't house all the key subsection message points, add slides. Finish the presentation by adding cover and end slides.

Second, turn the cornerstone into as many *owned* cobblestones as possible (your own blog posts and podcasts). At a minimum, each subsection can live as a blog post. If any subsection is too long for a single blog post, create a series of posts. Because the original cornerstone was reverse-engineered to create these cobblestones, this step is easy. If you produce a podcast, interview the author of the white paper about the key content or themes it discusses. Record someone delivering the conference presentation to create a recorded webinar.

Third, create guest posts to appear on closed networks your prospects favor. But don't just copy and paste your own posts and submit them as guest posts; the owners of those closed networks won't appreciate your leftovers, and Google penalizes duplicated content.

Instead, apply ecosystem thinking. Your home base audience remains fairly consistent. Thus, writing about the same subject matter from various angles is difficult because your readers will recognize and resent the similarity between pieces. Your readers want a consistent flow of *new* material, not summer reruns with a few different words and a new title. However, it is possible to reframe the content of a single blog post to form various guest posts for use on closed platforms. Sure, you've strategically picked your propinquity points for their overlap against your prospect, but that doesn't mean you can't repurpose content across those closed platforms without offending your prospects or the owners of those platforms.

# Repurposing Content: The Importance of Ecosystem Thinking

Let me show you an example of how this might work, using Chapter 14, "Creating Text-Based Content," as my cornerstone content. Chapter 14 easily deconstructs into multiple individual blog posts. One blog post idea for publishing on my own website is an overview post such as "How to Use Voice-to-Text Transcription Software to Create More Blog Content." The post summarizes a few key points from Chapter 14 without going too deep into any one of the points. For instance, the post can include the following sections:

- Defining voice-to-text software options
- Using mobile voice-to-text apps to turn downtime into writing time
- Using voice-to-text software to overcome writer's block

This is a simple, helpful blog post. Most content creators would stop there—but that's a mistake. By focusing on the mobile angle, I can repurpose this post into three distinct but similar guest posts for publication on owned platforms where I have publishing rights and my prospects look to for content creation insight.

Figure 16-2 shows how I can repurpose this post by simply expanding on the mobile voice-to-text application theme and show how a blog content creator can utilize the mobile app to create more blog content.

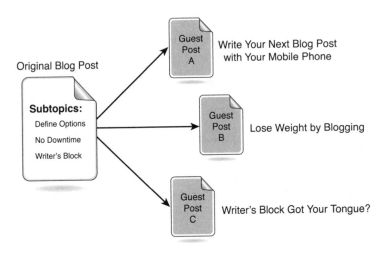

**Figure 16-2**   *Content ecosystem planning*

First, I create Guest Post A that defines the mobile voice-to-text option, describes the mobile app, and then explains how the blogger uses the mobile app to write a blog post. Notice that all this information is in my original post—I'm just reorganizing it and presenting it through a different lens. Whereas the original post discussed *all* voice-to-text options, for this guest post, I limit the discussion to the mobile app.

Second, I reframe the content for Guest Post B. Instead of just explaining how to write a blog post with audio-to-text apps, I present that capability in the context of multitasking. Specifically, I can write Guest Post B to solve two common complaints business content creators voice: lack of time to write and exercise. This post contains a lot of the same information, but it's presented through an exercising lens and in a less serious tone.

Third, I present the same information again (Guest Post C), but as a solution to another common business content creators' challenge: writer's block. This post focuses on the idea of breaking through writer's block by using the voice-to-text mobile app and just recording stream-of-consciousness thoughts. The core information in the post is similar to the content in Guest Post A and Guest Post B, but again, I change the lens to create a different post.

If I created these three posts on my own blog, my readers would figure out that I'm just repurposing the same post through three different angles and would likely abandon my blog. But because these three posts appear on three different media outlets, my true prospects are less likely to make the connection. Even if they do, they won't penalize me for repurposing content—they'll understand that I'm writing content for various audiences, and that makes it okay to produce similar posts for different platforms.

*This point is really important:* Your ability to create propinquity and brand awareness is powered by publishing content on closed networks that have their own readership. It is an absolute must if you are going to be successful. *Guest posting is simply advertising in different clothes.* You're buying access to eyeballs, just like you do with advertising. But there are three key differences.

First, you pay for your access with content instead of money. Second, your prospects invite your message into their world; you don't interrupt them with it. Third, your content educates rather than sells. And while your prospects will willingly invite greater amounts of your helpful content into their world, you need them to do this because your selling message is softer and might take longer to create the sale.

Thus, the only way to economically produce the necessary volume of content to accomplish your selling goals is to follow the process that I outlined for you in Figure 16-2 for each and every cornerstone and cobblestone you create. You have to think in terms of an ecosystem. With a little thought, planning, and imagination, you can easily turn a single blog post into multiple guest posts, a podcast, and even a video tutorial. But if you don't plan to do it, it won't happen. This is how you use Cornerstones and Cobblestones to amplify your message and create that all-important propinquity against your target prospect.

## The Art and Science of Guest Posting

Guest posting is at the heart of C&C approach. If you're going to achieve the goal of never producing anything to use just once, you need to create a significant network of blogs and websites where you can post your content. You need a big one because each platform limits the total number of posts you can submit, to allow room for their other authors. Thus, if the goal is to never publish any post just once, and you blog once a week, you need a network of at least 10–15 sites where you can post a repurposed version of each blog post.

Finding guest posting opportunities is easier than most people think. First, scan your propinquity points to see if any of them utilize guest posts. In some cases, you'll find an open call for guest posts, such as this one on SocialFresh.com: http://socialfresh.com/contribute/. In other instances, especially for popular personal blogs, you won't find a solicitation for guest posts, but the blogs will accept them. To find these opportunities, you need to go back through the historical posts to determine whether any of them are authored by people other than the blogger. If you find a significant number of posts not authored by the blogger, then find the blogger's contact information and add it to your outreach list. Finally, you can use a few Google Search tricks to help you locate blogs and websites within your target industry that accept guest posts.

Figure 16-3 shows a number of really useful search strings (words users enter into a search engine to locate needed information) from Kaila Strong and Brynna Baldauf's incredible link-building presentation, *Powerful and Effective Link Strategies with Advanced Search Commands*. (Visit http://youtu.be/PUgszZfVoJI to see the entire presentation.) Just type these search strings (exactly as you see them in Figure 16-3) into the Google search box to find websites that accept guest posts. If you want to narrow the list of sites Google returns, just add keywords associated with your industry at the end of the search string.

---

### EXAMPLES OF EFFECTIVE SEARCH COMMANDS

*Keyword* inurl:tag

(intitle:guest post) (intext:"this is a guest post by") blog

(inurl:guest-post) (intitle:guest post guideline)

(inurl:write-for-us) (intitle:guest post OR guest blog OR guest writer)

"write OR blog OR guest * for us" OR "submit OR add OR suggest OR contribute a guest post OR blog"

www.verticalmeasures.com                              @cliquekaila
                                                       @little_bry

---

**Figure 16-3**   *Google guest post opportunities search strings*

After you've created a list of websites and blogs that accept guest posts, you need to rate each guest posting opportunity. Just because a site accepts guest posts doesn't mean that crafting a guest post for it is a good use of your time. As with defining propinquity points, attempt to quantify the site's audience size and composition. Ideally, you want to guest post only on sites that have both significant website traffic and high target prospect composition. But that isn't always achievable. However, don't immediately delete a prospective guest posting opportunity from your list just because the site isn't predominantly trafficked by your target prospect.

For example, say there's a highly trafficked website called AllThingsIphone.com. It's the most-visited iPhone content website in the world. The site accepts guest posts that focus on iPhones, iPhone apps, and content creation with iPhones. It doesn't have a lot of sales and marketing director readers (my target audience), but it has a strong PageRank[1] (the algorithm Google uses to assign importance to web pages, which affects how the page ranks in Google search). Pages with a high PageRank pass along some of their value to websites that are referenced or linked to from within the high PageRank site. Thus, if I submit a "5 Awesome iPhoto Apps" guest post to AllThingsIPhone.com, it will likely be accepted. If the post contains keyword-rich anchor links such as *mobile content marketing* that link back to my blog, those links transfer some of AllThingsIphone.com's PageRank value to my website. So although I might not directly obtain any quality traffic from the post, my guest post bolsters my website's PageRank against key terms such as *mobile content marketing*, which my prospect searches for in Google and around which I create a lot of content on my site. I thus improve my SERP (Search Engine Results Page ranking) and indirectly aid my Painless Prospecting efforts. Thus, guest posting to AllThingsIPhone.com is a good use of my time.

Follow these four easy steps to qualify guest posting opportunities:

1.  Check the website's traffic by searching for the URL on Compete.com and QuantCast.com. These two websites provide projected traffic for websites. The sites don't track every website, so don't disregard a guest post opportunity just because you don't find traffic data.

2.  Determine the website's PageRank. You can use a variety of Internet sites, such as PRchecker (http://bit.ly/12fItBa), or you can install a plug-in on most Internet browsers that automatically reports the PageRank for every website you visit.

---

1. http://en.wikipedia.org/wiki/Google_PageRank

3. Review the current guest posts on the website. Randomly select 50 posts over the last 12 months (or as many as you can find). Create a spreadsheet, and tally the number of comments and unique commenters for each post. You're trying to understand whether the site has an active readership or whether the site owner's mom, dad, and three brothers are the only people reading and commenting on posts.

4. Looking back through the same posts on your spreadsheet, tally the number of social shares via Twitter, LinkedIn, Facebook, Google+, and other websites. This is easy because any website worth guest posting to will include social sharing buttons on every post (see Figure 16-4).

**Figure 16-4**  *Social sharing buttons*

Although I cannot prove this, I strongly believe that readers elect to share a blog post to a *single* social network. Thus, the blog post shown in Figure 16-4 was shared more than 1,300 times, which I believe represents more than 1,300 individuals who are interested in scientific explanations of influence. Thus, if a review of guest posts from this site revealed a similar pattern across all posts, I would classify this website as a good guest posting opportunity.

After you've created your short list of websites and blogs to apply to as a guest author, begin reaching out to each site. This is where social networking can really help you. Before officially requesting guest posting credentials, find and follow the site owner(s) on social networks. Twitter is ideal for this because you can follow anyone. Take the opportunity to get to know that person and, more important, to help him or her get to know you. This gives you a real edge in the guest author application process. Remember, you're likely not the only person to determine that a website or blog is a good guest posting opportunity. Thus, creating some level of relationship with a site owner before you suggest or request guest author status could be the difference between acceptance and rejection of your offer.

For sites with formal "write for us" pages, just fill out the form and submit it. If you've taken the time to form a relationship with the site owner, send him or her a personal note after you submit the form. If a site doesn't have a "write for us" page, and for personal blogs, send an email to the owner of the site, explaining how your content will help the audience. This step trips up the vast majority of companies trying to gain guest author credentials. You need the site more than the site needs you. Remember that, and craft your solicitation accordingly. Again, if you plan to approach a number of high-value personal blogs and web communities, you really should establish a personal relationship with the site owner or key content players *before* you suggest that they allow you to guest post.

In either case, your job isn't done after you're granted guest posting privileges. Make sure your first post is absolutely awesome. Don't just copy and paste something from your cornerstone. Take the time to write a compelling piece that the site's audience will appreciate, comment on, and share. The site's owner will notice and appreciate your effort. This will ensure that when you want to post in the future, the site will always have a slot for your content.

## The IVS Case Study

Now that we've covered the framework and a few key suggestions, let me demonstrate the approach using a real-life example: *The Invisible Sale*. That's right, the book you are holding in your hands is the single biggest piece of cornerstone content I've ever created. Before writing a single word of this book, I went through the very steps I just explained to you. If you look back through this book, you notice that each section can exist as a stand-alone cornerstone. Within each section, each chapter makes complete sense without having to read any of the other chapters. And within each chapter, the individual sections easily convert to blog posts and guest posts. This is all by careful design so that, as I've written the book, I've deconstructed pieces of it into cobblestones published on my blog and other blogs. I've created conference presentations, recorded webinars, and leveraged the content to secure guest appearances on relevant podcasts. I've captured a small slice of these cobblestones in Figure 16-5 to help you understand how all these cobblestones fit together to help me win the invisible sale.

Before the book was even completed, I combined a number of key concepts, such as propinquity, funnel-optimized websites, and painless prospecting, to create my *Painlessly Prospecting for Clients* SoloPR Conference presentation, which I attended at no cost to my firm.

Using ScreenFlow, I recorded the entire presentation and offered conference attendees an opportunity to receive an emailed copy in exchange for their business card. Each of these attendees were also added (with their permission) to a private

email list that I maintain for periodically sharing the best research and marketing thinking I find on the Internet. I also edited the entire presentation down
to a 2-minute trailer (think movie trailer) of the presentation that I uploaded to
YouTube (http://youtu.be/7tciDDwJICA). I embedded clickable links in the video
so that viewers can request a copy of the entire presentation. Periodically, I share
that video on my various social networks to gain new leads.

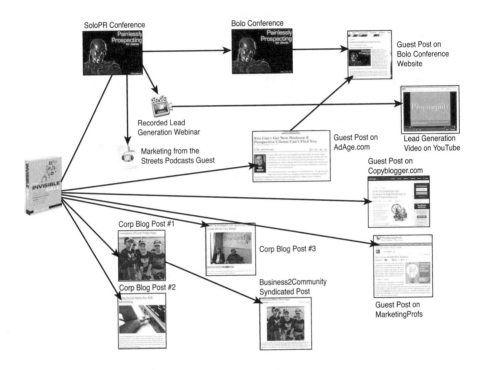

**Figure 16-5**   Invisible Sale *cornerstone and cobblestone posts*

Every SoloPR presenter was offered an opportunity to appear on Todd Schnick's
*Marketing from the Streets* podcast. I secured my slot and recorded an episode
(http://bit.ly/12PEyS3). When he published the podcast, I shared it on my social
networks. Then I repurposed his podcast and combined it with a few paragraphs
of text explaining the key themes from the SoloPR presentation to quickly create a
blog post for my firm's blog (http://bit.ly/12eF0Tx).

The SoloPR audience reaction confirmed that ad agencies and PR agencies were
hungry for my Painless Prospecting system. I began to look around for other ad
agency–focused conferences. I had spoken previously at the Bolo Conference (an
ad agency business-development conference), so I contacted them and suggested
that their audience might value the *Painless Prospecting for Clients* presentation.

They booked me to speak at the conference and asked me to guest post on their blog (http://bit.ly/12PFuph). I did so by combining pieces of the presentation with pieces of a post I wrote for Ad Age's Small Agency Diary. I crafted the Ad Age piece by repurposing various sections of the book into a cohesive narrative that would appeal to ad agency business development professionals and agency owners (http://bit.ly/12PFFAY).

I have also leveraged the book content to quickly create numerous posts on the Converse Digital blog. I lifted parts of Chapter 12, "Creating Photography," to create "5 Awesome iPhone Photo Apps" (http://bit.ly/12eG4GY), which was automatically syndicated to the Business2Community website, where I'm a registered blogger. The site automatically pulls my new blog posts and republishes them on their site (http://bit.ly/12PGDNR). This syndication greatly expands my reach in terms of both the site's readership and, just as important, the site's readers who share the posts on social networks.

In some cases, I repurpose content very directly, as with the iPhone photo apps post. In other cases, I take pieces and parts of different chapters to create entirely new posts on the Converse Digital blog. An excellent example of this is "Using Social Media for B2B Networking" (http://bit.ly/12eGux6)—I combined content from multiple chapters to create that post.

Finally, I've used content to create numerous guest posts that appear on key propinquity points in my Painless Prospecting platform. I leveraged the propinquity content in Chapter 7, "Propinquity," to craft a popular "How to Leverage the Science of Relationships to Gain True Influence" post for Copyblogger.com (http://bit.ly/148GCBd). The next day, my first post on MarketingProfs.com, "How to Lose Weight While Blogging" (http://bit.ly/148GMs4) posted. All the content for that post comes from Chapter 14.

As you can see, this is a significant amount of content—all produced while simultaneously writing a book and running a company, and without pulling the invisible dad/husband routine. More important, this is just a small slice of the cobblestones that I'm creating and will create from a single piece of cornerstone content. I've written but not published additional posts on the Converse Digital blog, I've produced guest posts that are still awaiting their day in the sun, and I'll deliver some of my webinars and conference presentations later this year. All of these would be impossible to create if I treated each as a new, unique piece of content. Only through the strategic planning of cobblestones am I able to deconstruct the cornerstone into this much content. And you can, too, if you adopt the techniques I've shared here.

# Section 4

# Closing the Deal

As I noted in Chapter 3, "The Self-Educating Buyer," research shows that customers are 57% of the way through their purchase decision before they first make contact with your sales team. These digital-savvy buyers are sophisticated and silent. They're doing recon work on your brands and your company, searching for product reviews and tapping into social networks for recommendations and first-hand experiences. These invisible buyers are slipping past your sales team, stepping out of the shadows only after they've decided that your company is in the running for their dollars.

To close the deal with these invisible buyers, your selling process needs to change. But more important, your closing process has to change. Your sales teams need to fundamentally reprogram their approach to this new self-educated buyer. Whereas your sales team used to have the knowledge advantage, the Internet has narrowed the knowledge gap between buyer and seller. Closing the self-educated buyer is a more elegant process, in my opinion. It requires technique, patience, and a more sophisticated approach. But when it's done well, it leads to increased conversion rates and shortened sales cycles.

In this final section, I give you the missing piece of the inbound marketing and selling puzzle that you won't find elsewhere. We've spent 16 chapters talking about how to find, market, and sell to a self-educating prospect. But now I want to spend this last section helping you understand how to close that prospect. In my opinion, this is the most overlooked piece of the puzzle. Yet in many ways, it's the most important piece. You can develop the most powerful Painless Prospecting system in the world—a system that routinely fills your sales funnel with plenty of highly qualified leads—but if you can't convert those leads to customers, it's all wasted effort and money.

So let's talk about what your sales team is going to change to be sure to close those invisible sales prospects each and every time they make themselves visible.

# 17

# Closing the Deal

*Invisible closes come in three flavors. First, there's the strictly online close, where you engage and close a prospect using social media, links to your own content, and email communications. This is the least likely close, but it does happen from time to time. The second type is a strictly offline close via phone or, more likely, face to face. This is the second mostly likely scenario for high-involvement purchases or complex B2B sales. Finally, the third and most likely scenario for all products and services is a blended close, in which you use social media and email communications to arrange a phone, video conference, or face-to-face meeting to win the deal or sell the product. The common underlying theme to each of these options is data. In each scenario, you leverage the insights gleaned from your data tracking to create a better sales closing strategy and win the sale.*

But data is a double-edged sword. Used correctly, it gives you an almost unbeatable edge to capture more sales. But used incorrectly, it turns off prospects and likely costs you sales both today and in the future.

# How to Blow the Invisible Close

Because you've invested in creating a Painless Prospecting platform and a data-based sales and marketing program, you have enormous insight into your prospect's buying motivations. But don't make the biggest mistake I see salespeople make every day: Don't let your prospects know you have all this information. Don't tell them you've been tracking them—that's just creepy and will kill your sale faster than anything else. And yes, I have actually seen salespeople do this.

For instance, I once watched a salesperson tell a prospect (I'm paraphrasing here): "Hi Chris, I see that you received our email about product A and you read the product description and the case study for your industry. What more can I tell you about the product so that we can get your company on the program?"

Chris responded, "No, I think you have the wrong person—I've never received an email from your company, much less read one."

Tracking software doesn't lie, but people do. Because this salesperson freaked out Chris by making it clear that the company had been tracking his activity, Chris ended the call—and likely ended the sales opportunity for the salesperson.

Don't show your cards, but *do* use the information to ask smart questions. This is the power of the invisible close. Like a lawyer in a courtroom, you ask only questions for which you already know the answer. You know the answer is favorable to your argument, so thus your strategy is to keep prompting for answers that favor your product. Then you string together all those answers to form a strong argument for buying your product or service.

# The Invisible Process Versus the Traditional Sales Process

Let me show you how this works using a hypothetical sales example from the hotel industry. Hotel salespeople are responsible for convincing groups to hold their events at the hotel. This includes corporate sales events and association meeting events. For many of these events, the meeting planners prefer to move the host city/property each year, to keep attendees interested in returning the next year. This is especially true of association meetings where member attendance isn't mandatory. Let's look at two hypothetical sales approaches to see how two hypothetical salesmen, Lonnie and Tristan, might approach trying to convince Nicole, the meeting planner for the Ultimate Tailgater Association Annual Conference (UTAAC), to come to their hotel property next year.

# TRADITIONAL SALES APPROACH EXAMPLE: TRISTAN

Tristan deploys a traditional outbound effort to acquire the UTAAC contract. He sends an introductory letter to Nicole, follows up with a meeting planner kit, and places Nicole in his prospecting database. As such, Tristan regularly calls and emails Nicole, telling her how much his hotel would love to have the UTAAC next year. He goes on to explain all the great features of the hotel and even sends additional direct mailings designed to highlight the hotels' high-tech offerings, its proximity to the convention center, and a great "first-time conference" pricing discount he can offer the UTAAC. He continues this program of calls and emails, hoping to eventually receive a call back.

But because Nicole never calls Tristan back, he's unable to properly qualify her or discover her key selling points.

# PAINLESS PROSPECTING EXAMPLE: LONNIE

Lonnie has spent more than a year building a powerful Painless Prospecting program. He has filled his hotel's website with keyword-rich, helpful content designed for meeting planners doing online research. Like Tristan, Lonnie really wants to win the UTAAC contract. He, too, introduces himself to Nicole, but he sends a personal email with single (trackable) link back to his hotel's website and indicates that if he doesn't hear from Nicole within a few weeks, he'll follow up with a call.

Nicole doesn't call Tristan or Lonnie, but she does click the link in Lonnie's email. This takes her to a web page that Lonnie has created just for her, with a simple, personalized message inviting her to learn more about his hotel. Impressed by the personalized approach, Nicole begins to look around the website. She clicks links for meeting room specs, accommodations, and nearby attractions (where she reads about the aquarium, river walk, and putt-putt course). She ends her session but returns a few days later to read more. This time she focuses on a number of articles about ways to make a conference family-friendly, how to create fun days for attendees' families, and a suggested packing list for attendees who bring their families to conferences or meetings held at the hotel.

Lonnie's Painless Prospecting system alerts him that Nicole's online behavior indicates that she is a "hot" prospect and presents him with a dossier of her activity. At this point, Lonnie calls Nicole and leaves a voicemail reminding her of his previous email and his hotel's continued interest in hosting next year's UTAAC. He asks for a chance to see if the hotel is a good fit for next year's event. Nicole emails him back, acknowledges receipt of his voicemail, and offers Lonnie a few minutes of her time the next day to learn more about his hotel.

Lonnie calls at the prearranged time and begins asking questions based on her behaviors on his website. He asks if she's looking for a location that is within walking distance to area attractions. He then asks whether attendees tend to come alone or bring their families. Nicole indicates that more than 80% of attendees bring their families and make a summer vacation out of the conference; thus, having family-friendly activities nearby is a plus. Lonnie was already pretty sure this would be her answer because Nicole spent so much time reading family-friendly content on his website.

Lonnie asks if Nicole was aware of all the family-friendly activities located within walking distance of his hotel. She says she remembers reading about that on his website. He then asks if she got a chance to read about the hotel's Dinner and a Movie night, where conference attendee parents can explore the city with their spouse and other conference attendees while the hotel hosts a dinner and drive-in night for kids. Nicole says she didn't, and Lonnie immediately sends her a link to that page on his website.

I can go on further with this example, but you see the point. Whereas Tristan is just throwing key benefits at Nicole and hoping one will open the door, *Lonnie is leveraging his data to craft the perfect sales call*. He's immediately able to present his hotel as a relevant option for Nicole, establish a relationship, and gain permission to send additional information via email. With helpful website information and one phone call, Lonnie has placed himself well ahead of Tristan in the battle to win the UTAAC contract.

# The Online-Only Close

The online-only invisible close is certainly the least common of the three invisible closes. However, if you're selling software, educational content, or even hotel rooms (remember back to Chapter 10, "Social Selling," and The Drake Hotel example) and other products that are easily researched online, there's certainly a chance that you'll win a few invisible sales without ever talking to your buyer by phone or face to face. However, you need to have a lot of patience and keep your sales instincts in check. The biggest mistake I see people making online every day is trying to close the sale far too quickly.

Nowhere do you see this more than on LinkedIn. I think it is because LinkedIn is often considered the *business social network*. Thus, it's the network that most salespeople turn to as a prospecting and networking platform. Unfortunately, these same salespeople bring their bad sales habits to their online networking, with disastrous effects. You especially never want to make two particular mistakes.

The first is what I call the *discussion sale*. If you've spent much time in LinkedIn groups, you've likely seen the discussion sale. Within LinkedIn groups, people start discussions, usually pertaining to an article or question. For instance, someone might post an article about the effectiveness of email marketing as a lead-generation tool. Group members begin posting comments and questions. Eventually, as the discussion grows, they post replies and answers to each other's questions and comments. Sometimes one or more group members indicate that they're experiencing challenges with email marketing. And that's when it happens.

A group member, who often hasn't even been active in the discussion, swoops in and leaves a discussion sale comment. These comments appear in two forms. The commenter either just outright tries to sell an email solution or writes an incredibly long dissertation on email marketing that doesn't really address anyone's comments or questions in particular and essentially reads like a really bad ad. It's a shame, really—if these salespeople would have a bit of patience, they might create a sales opportunity. But because they don't take the time to build relationships, their transactional, opportunistic attitude turns off the other members and results in a lost opportunity.

The second mistake is the *connection sale*. As in other social networks, LinkedIn makes connecting with others pretty easy, especially if you're in the same LinkedIn group with another person. Normally, you have to be a second- or third-degree connection with someone to send that person a request to connect on LinkedIn. If you're not, you have to buy InMails, and you pay for the right to send an invitation to connect to a total stranger. One exception exists, though: If you and the person you want to connect with are in the same LinkedIn group, you can send that person a connection invitation, regardless of the current degree of separation.

Thus, a lot of people participate in groups as a way to find and connect with new prospects. But too many people are doing it wrong. The correct manner is to send an invitation to connect to the people you converse with in your LinkedIn groups. Thus, if during the course of a LinkedIn discussion you begin commenting back and forth with a particular member of the group, or maybe over several discussions you find that you and this person often interact, you then invite him or her to connect on LinkedIn directly. From there, you can trade emails, get to know one another, and network outside of the group discussions.

Unfortunately, too many people abuse this great LinkedIn feature. Let me share a personal example to make it a bit clearer. As I've said, I'm pretty active in LinkedIn groups. During one group discussion, I commented on a fellow member's comment. He commented back, and then I received a note from him noting our group discussion and asking if it would be okay to connect. Having enjoyed our discussion, I agreed. He sent a connection request. But he couldn't help himself—he immediately revealed his true colors by including his sales pitch in the invitation!

I captured the conversation in Figure 17-1. Two things to keep in mind as you read through it. First, read the conversation from the bottom of the figure (where it starts) to the top (where it finishes—the offending connection sale). Second, the person in question does not speak English as a first language, and thus, his first message (bottom of the figure) may seem grammatically incorrect, but that's not uncommon, in my experience, when conversing online with non-English speakers.

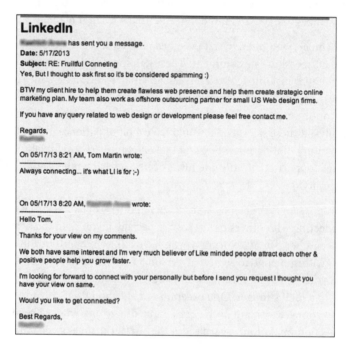

**Figure 17-1**   *LinkedIn connection sale example*

Beyond the fact this sender's connection purporting to create flawless web presence is strewn with grammatical and spelling errors (even factoring his non-English as a first language status), **what makes this particular example so appropriate is his comment about not wanting to seem like he was spamming me**. In his mind, because he had my permission to send me a sales pitch disguised as a connection request, he was "doing it right." Nothing could be farther from the truth. Thankfully, he and I are no longer connections on LinkedIn. The invisible close, especially the online-only version, is like fly-fishing. You have to combine skill and patience to craft just the right bait and present it perfectly to entice your prospect to bite.

The goal of the online-only close is to constantly be helping your prospect make the right buying choice. Just be a source of helpful information and try to stay as unbiased as you can. Obviously, you aren't unbiased, but that's okay. Your prospects know this, and as long as you're trying to keep the discussion balanced, they will see you as a trustful resource. When you push or recommend your product or service, do so with a knowing nod to your bias. Whether it's adding a wink ";-)" at the end of a tweet or using obvious text like "shameless plug," your prospect will appreciate the honesty, which helps you achieve the TOMP (top-of-mind preference) necessary to win an online-only close.

# The Offline Close

The biggest difference between the online and offline close is lack of access to your historical data on a buyer. Most often, the prospect enters one of your physical locations and deals with a member of your sales team. That salesperson isn't privy to all the tracking data on the prospect. This makes the offline close much trickier and requires different tactics and training. The key to making the offline close work is to immediately perform prospect triage to determine whether the prospect is self-educated. If not, your salesperson can proceed as they normally would. But if the triage reveals a self-educated buyer, your salesperson must deploy Aikido sales tactics. Because Aikido sales tactics apply to the online and blended close, too, I address that shortly. For now, let's focus on the prospect triage process.

Prospect triage is a four-step process to quickly determine whether the prospect is self-educated and then determine the depth of that education.

**Step 1** is simple: Ask if the prospect has done any research yet. Sure, prospects might lie and claim that they haven't, but in my experience, self-educated buyers jump at the chance to tell you they've done their research. If the prospect claims not to have researched the purchase, probe for further clues. Ask if the prospect has read much about the product or category. Ask if he or she has talked with any friends or family who have recently purchased your product or the competitor's. If all answers continue to be no, the salesperson can proceed with confidence that this is a noneducated buyer. However, if during the course of this conversation either the buyer admits to self-educating or the subsequent probing questions suggest that the prospect has done some level of education, the salesperson needs to move to the next step.

**Step 2** uncovers the depth and breadth of the prospect's knowledge base. Probe to understand how the prospect conducted research. Determine which online websites or social networks were consulted. And if prospects indicate that they conducted online research via a search engine, determine which one(s) and probe for key search terms used. This is important for two reasons.

First, by documenting the prospect's search terms, your salesperson is helping the marketing team better understand what search terms *your* customers use so that the marketing team doesn't have to rely on general search trends to guide the content marketing strategy. Second, by monitoring what information makes page one or two for specific search terms, your marketing team can prepare your sales team for complications. For instance, if a key search term for your product returns a set of results with a particularly unflattering review of your product on a review site, chances are good that self-educated buyers will see and read that review. This might create issues during the selling process. But if your salesperson knows about this bad review and your sales and marketing team has already formulated a response, your salesperson is now armed to handle any objection with a well-planned response versus something "off the cuff."

In **Step 3,** your salesperson defines the prospect's biggest unanswered questions, needs, and hurdles to purchase. This should feel quite comfortable for any seasoned sales professional because it's a standard part of any selling process. Here, though, your salesperson is looking to do more than just uncover key pain points or objections. *The salesperson is looking for areas where the self-educating prospect's research might have fallen short.* Again, don't just ask the questions—also document the answers. Over time, the answers will reveal content marketing opportunities for your own Painless Prospecting platform. Additionally, your marketing teams can create lists of favorable existing web content that salespeople can use to complete the prospect's education process in a manner that favors your product or service.

In **Step 4,** your salesperson tries to identify the competition. Here again, the goal isn't just to define the competitive set—it's also to define what research the prospects conducted and what knowledge they gained. It's not enough to sell against the competition—your salesperson needs to *sell against the competition's content.* After completing triage, it's time to move into selling mode and begin the Aikido selling process, which I'll discuss shortly.

# The Blended Close

The third and most common close is the blended close, in which you use social networking, web content, and email communications to achieve TOMP. However, before prospects will convert, they need to talk to someone in your organization face to face or by phone. They may want to ask additional questions, try to negotiate better sales terms, or feel that they need to "meet" you before trusting you enough to give you their business.

For salespeople, the blended close feels most like traditional networking because it *is* traditional networking—but using different tools. Instead of attending networking events, getting a prospect's card, and then working the sale through emails, phone calls, and the occasional lunch or round of golf, you conduct follow-up through small chats and online touches. The power of the blended close is scalability. As we discussed in previous chapters, traditional networking approaches don't scale well because one person can talk to or meet with only so many prospects per day. But with online tools, you can touch hundreds of prospects a day without ever leaving your desk.

The key to the blended close is establishing multiple propinquity points with each prospect. By connecting to your prospects on different platforms, you give yourself additional opportunities to touch them. Additionally, people use their various social networks differently. They might be professional on LinkedIn, act more open on Twitter, and save the personal stuff for Facebook. By connecting with them in these various places, you can customize your touches to match the platform.

For instance, Facebook tends to be the place where people share more of their personal lives. This opens up a host of opportunities for you to find nonbusiness touchpoints if you can get a prospect to "friend you" on Facebook. You might discover that a prospect loves wine or is a foodie. If you share this passion, you can engage that person in conversations about these topics. Or you might find out that a prospect is planning to attend an event or visit a city where you have connections. For instance, one of my prospects posted on Facebook that he was coming to New Orleans for the Sugar Bowl. It was his college alma mater's first trip to the Sugar Bowl, and he was excited to make the trip. I have friends on the Sugar Bowl committee, so I asked one of them if she could get my prospect on the field before the game. She agreed, so I sent my prospect a message on Facebook with an offer to put it together. Just like that, I had one very happy prospect.

Through each of these touches, you are building trust and credibility with the prospect. You are building a relationship today that sets the stage for a sale tomorrow. Sounds a lot like traditional networking, doesn't it? But it goes further online. Let's look at how you can combine Twitter and Facebook to set the stage for a phone conversation and a blended close.

Twitter is very promotion friendly. If you look at the network, you see lots of people sharing lots of information. They share blog posts, pictures, articles, location updates, and promotional information. Imagine for a moment that you are a lawyer practicing contract law. As part of your Painless Prospecting program, you regularly post tips for creating better contracts on your blog. Each time you post, you share that post on Twitter. This gets you noticed by conference organizers, who book you to conduct contract law workshops for small businesses. You announce each of these workshops on Twitter, too.

One of the small business groups maintains a private Facebook group, and eventually, after one of the workshops, the administrator of the group invites you to join. You do and find that the group is full of prospective clients, many of whom are also on Twitter and LinkedIn. You begin to connect with many of them on these other networks, but mostly you focus on being a helpful member of the Facebook group, offering advice and opinions wherever it seems appropriate.

At one point, a member of the group starts a discussion thread around a contractual issue in which you are especially well versed. This particular Facebook group member is also active on Twitter, and you've regularly tweeted with him and developed a nice relationship. Seeing the post, you provide a short, helpful comment. But then you go one step further. You private-message him (Facebook offers a private message function akin to email or chat) with a message that clearly offers your services to help. The conversation continues back and forth over a few days.

In the meantime, you and the prospect both participate in a Tweet Chat, and a similar contractual issue is discussed. At this point, you note to your prospect, "This reminds me of our FB discussion last week." The prospect sends you a private note that he hadn't made that connection, but now that you mention it, he is intrigued.

From here, you send an email with links to numerous blog posts that help frame the original and this new contractual issue, workshops you've conducted on the issue, and maybe even a testimonial from past clients. The prospect doesn't respond to the email, but he does message you on Facebook with a few more questions. Eventually, all this multiplatform communication results in a request for a videoconference so that you and the prospect can "meet" and talk through how you might help him.

See how that worked? How the sales conversation was fluid and jumped from one platform to the other? Did you see how all the Twitter activity positioned you, the lawyer, as a thought leader on the subject, while your helpful Facebook activity made you likeable and maybe even trustworthy to the prospect? This is how the blended sale works in reality. You leverage the relationships you've established on each platform to discover opportunities to strengthen relationships, uncover sales opportunities, and discover knowledge gaps that you can leverage to turn a prospect into a client. But in all three cases, the key is patience. You have to let the sale come to you versus you going to the sale. Master that, and you'll close more business.

# Aikido Selling

Aikido selling leverages the buyers' self-education to more quickly close the sale. I patterned the approach after the Japanese martial art of the same name developed by Morihei Ueshiba. Wikipedia defines *aikido* as a "way of combining forces":

The term *aiki* refers to the martial arts principle or tactic of blending with an attacker's movements for the purpose of controlling their actions with minimal effort. One applies aiki by understanding the rhythm and intent of the attacker to find the optimal position and timing to apply a counter-technique.[1]

Do you see how this applies perfectly to closing a self-educated buyer? If not, let me show you.

Instead of blending with an attacker's movements, you blend with the buyer's education. Instead of understanding an attacker's rhythm and intent, you seek to understand a self-educated buyer's knowledge and goal for using that knowledge in the evaluation and negotiation of the purchase. And instead of applying a counter-technique, you surface counterarguments that target a self-educated buyer's knowledge gaps. Instead of trying to stand toe to toe with buyers and outsell them, you direct their action by redirecting their knowledge to serve your best interests.

Self-educated buyers are empowered buyers—or so they think. They believe they've done their homework. They believe they know what they need to know to have a balanced discussion with a salesperson in which the buyer can't be "sold" by the salesperson. But self-educated buyers have one huge blind spot. The Aikido approach exploits that weakness to rebalance the selling process in favor of the seller.

Put simply, *self-educated buyers don't know what they don't know.* Because they're not immersed in the product or service they're buying, they don't always know every question to ask or every scenario to consider. This creates a unique opportunity for the salesperson to create awareness of this knowledge deficiency. And where there is a knowledge deficiency, there is the opportunity to create doubt in the mind of the self-educated buyer. Doubt is a salesperson's best friend because it shifts the selling process balance of power back to the salesperson.

By starting with the knowledge or questions a prospect didn't know to ask or search for, the salesperson regains the position of authority without disrespecting the self-educated buyer and his or her efforts. From this point, the Aikido sale is designed to exploit the buyer's knowledge gaps and create the opportunity for the salesperson to complete the buyer's self-education process. The salesperson's goal is to teach the buyer what he or she couldn't learn independently and, in doing so, establish trust, credibility, and TOMP that translates into closing the deal.

The Aikido technique takes months of practice and study to properly master. However, every Aikido sale involves a few key steps that you should understand and utilize in your own efforts to close the invisible sale.

---

1. http://en.wikipedia.org/wiki/Aikido

First, understand that self-educated buyers have done their homework. They likely will be well versed in the strengths and weaknesses of your offering. Thus, cede points that you can't win. If the competitor's product does something better than yours, say so. This simple step establishes credibility with the self-educated buyer, which is paramount to developing a sense of trust and respect. You'll need that trust to discover the buyer's knowledge gaps. This is an example of blending with the buyer's education.

Second, self-educated buyers often find mistaken or outdated information during their research. Take the opportunity to correct mistaken information before you begin sharing new information. Self-educated buyers are proud of their efforts and believe that they possess correct information. Thus, approach the correction of inaccurate info carefully. This is an example of surfacing counter arguments.

One big mistake salespeople often make is that they are so desperate to show buyers that they themselves are the true bastion of knowledge that they attack the misinformation in a manner that appears argumentative. This is the antithesis of Aikido selling because it aligns the salesperson and the buyer as opposing forces. The salesperson then has difficulty blending with the buyer's knowledge and successfully redirecting that knowledge to close the sale.

Third, after you've established what buyers do and do not know, begin to complete their education. But don't sell. Instead, teach. The goal of the Aikido sale is to let buyers sell themselves by simply completing their research in a manner that favors your product or service. They *want* to sell themselves. Understand that psychological underpinning, and then leverage it to close the deal and win the invisible sale.

# In Closing

*Winning the invisible sale requires a complete revamping of your entire sales and marketing approach. From how you create awareness of your product or service, to the sales prospecting process and, finally, the closing process. You are dealing with a fundamentally different buyer.*

*But this doesn't mean you need to abandon your existing processes. Those processes likely are working for you at some level. Instead, aim to first augment those processes and expand your ability to win more sales. Over time, you might determine that your Painless Prospecting program is more efficient and effective. If you do, then begin to phase out your traditional program. If, however, you find that both programs continue to drive sales, albeit different kinds of sales, then allow the two to peacefully coexist.*

The goal of writing this book wasn't to convert you to a new way of thinking. It was to expose you to a new way of thinking and empower you to take the necessary steps to adopt it if you decide to do so. I want to continue to help you take those steps. To do this, I've made additional information available at TheInvisibleSale.com, including all the Power Points from Sections 1 and 2. You can unlock everything by joining the IVS community with a valid email address and the password *IVSreader*. I've also created a Painless Prospecting newsletter that you can subscribe to for new tips and tricks, to help make your quest to win the invisible sale more effective.

You can also experience the invisible sale *live* by booking me to speak at your conference or scheduling a private workshop. Each presentation is customized and designed to help you understand how you can apply the principles, tips, and tricks in *The Invisible Sale* to your businesses.

Or if you want to start Painlessly Prospecting for new customers, email me at TomMartin@ConverseDigital.com. I'd love to help you adopt the principles of the Invisible Sale to increase the efficiency of your sales prospecting programs.

Finally, you can win a *free* Invisible Sale Workshop! If you liked this book, please tell a friend—or a few hundred friends—and include the hashtag #TheInvisibleSale. If you share that information on Facebook, please make the post public so that I can find it and thank you personally for helping to spread the message about *The Invisible Sale*. If you see the book at a bookstore, take a picture and share it with the #TheInvisibleSale hashtag. And if you're so inclined, I'd love to hear your thoughts, good or bad, via a review on Amazon or Barnes & Noble.

But don't just do this for me—do it for yourself. We'll catalog all the mentions of #TheInvisibleSale, and on November 11, 2014, I'll select one lucky person to win a *free* Invisible Sale Workshop. Visit TheInvisibleSale.com for complete details.

Most of all, thank you for buying *The Invisible Sale*. I hope you feel like you got your money's worth.

# Index

increasing content exposure, 72-73

knowing wants versus needs, 65-66

in service sector, 71-72

trust in experts, 69-71

Hoey, Gavin, 47

home base (in digital footprint), 94
creating, 95
funnel-optimized website design, 96-100
in propinquity maps, 109-111

hosts
for effective videos, 153
for podcasts, 186

how-to blog posts, 206

# I

images. See photography creation

iMovie, 157, 161

inbound marketing
AdoramaTV case study, 43-44
*funnel-optimized website design, 51-55*
*podcasts, 46-47*
*progression to Adorama Learning Center, 45-46*
*purpose of AdoramaTV, 44-45*
*scaling, 47-49*
*success metrics, 55-57*
*tips for success, 57-58*
*traditional advertising, 51*
*vendor relationship development, 49-50*
defined, 10
outbound marketing versus, 18
personal selling versus, 15-16

increasing online content exposure, 72-73

industry/occupational propinquity, 84

inefficiency of database selling, 19-20

information architecture, 96-98

Instagram, 176

Internet access
broadband access, 33
utilization patterns, 34

interviews
on podcasts, 187-188
timing tips, 154-155
transcribing, 197-198
video-framing techniques, 153-154

intimacy, creating in photos, 169-170

invisible sales opportunities, defined, 13-14

Invisible Sale Workshop, free, 248

iPad, Camera Connection Kit for, 195

iPadio, 191

iPhone
DIY video blog case study, 158-159
video-editing software, 160-161

IVS (The Invisible Sale) case study, 230-232

# J

*Jerry McGuire* (film), 63

Jobs, Steve, 86

joining LinkedIn groups, 140

# K

Keyword Generator Tool, 102

Knorpp, Bob, 184-186

# L

Lapse It, 160

length of webinars, 209-210

lenses
depth of field, 151
selecting, 171-172, 174

lighting
for effective photographs, 172-174
for effective videos, 155, 159-160
selecting equipment, 174

LinkedIn. *See also* social selling
creating sense of attachment, 137-139
as embassy (in digital footprint), 108-109
joining groups, 140
online-only closes, 238-241

links
embedding in YouTube videos, 52
looking for, 99

listening statistics for podcasts, 180-181

listening to customers
Caterpillar example, 130
geographic social listening, 99-104
importance of, 57-58
social listening, 101-99

Live Blogging, 140

Live Tweeting, 140

live webinars. See webinars

long documents, reading on tablets, 203

# M

marketing
collaboration with sales teams, 38-39
inbound marketing
*AdoramaTV case study. See AdoramaTV case study*

# Y

# Z

# THE INVISIBLE SALE

How to build a digitally powered **marketing and sales system** to better prospect, qualify and close leads.

TOM MARTIN

# FREE
# Online Edition

**Safari**
Books Online

Your purchase of *The Invisible Sale* includes access to a free online edition for 45 days through the **Safari Books Online** subscription service. Nearly every Que book is available online through **Safari Books Online**, along with thousands of books and videos from publishers such as Addison-Wesley Professional, Cisco Press, Exam Cram, IBM Press, O'Reilly Media, Prentice Hall, and Sams.

**Safari Books Online** is a digital library providing searchable, on-demand access to thousands of technology, digital media, and professional development books and videos from leading publishers. With one monthly or yearly subscription price, you get unlimited access to learning tools and information on topics including mobile app and software development, tips and tricks on using your favorite gadgets, networking, project management, graphic design, and much more.

## Activate your FREE Online Edition at
## informit.com/safarifree

**STEP 1:**  Enter the coupon code: BZYZKCB.

**STEP 2:**  New Safari users, complete the brief registration form.
Safari subscribers, just log in.

If you have difficulty registering on Safari or accessing the online edition,
please e-mail customer-service@safaribooksonline.com